Untying the Knot of War

Untying the Knot of War

A Bargaining Theory of International Crises

T. Clifton Morgan

Ann Arbor

THE UNIVERSITY OF MICHIGAN PRESS

Copyright © by the University of Michigan 1994
All rights reserved
Published in the United States of America by
The University of Michigan Press
Manufactured in the United States of America
♾ Printed on acid-free paper

1997   1996   1995   1994   4   3   2   1

A CIP catalogue record for this book is available from the British Library.

Library of Congress Cataloging-in-Publication Data

Morgan, T. Clifton, 1956–
    Untying the knot of war : a bargaining theory of international
crises / T. Clifton Morgan.
        p.   cm.
    Includes bibliographical references and index.
    ISBN 0-472-10277-X (alk. paper)
    1. Crisis management—Mathematical models.   2. Negotiation—
Mathematical models.   3. International relations—Mathematical
models.   I. Title.
JX4471.M625   1994
327.1—dc20   94-12341
                                                                  CIP

To Mom and Dad

Contents

Preface

In spite of the cold war's end and frequent proclamations that a new world order has emerged, international conflict remains a pervasive phenomenon. Militarized disputes within and between states persist, and the threat of war continues. Although the threat of a cataclysmic war between superpowers has abated, lesser wars can still result in the deaths of tens or even hundreds of thousands of people, as the 1991 Gulf War shows. Furthermore, we must recognize that the future may bring more superpowers and more superpower confrontations that could potentially destroy much of the planet.

Efforts to avoid and end wars are even more numerous than the events these efforts seek to control. As I write, major diplomatic initiatives seeking to achieve peaceful resolutions to conflicts in Eastern Europe, the Middle East, and Africa are underway. A characteristic common to all these efforts is that each is hindered by being based on a less-than-perfect understanding of why wars occur. We do not yet have an adequate theoretical or empirical basis from which to prescribe peace-seeking policies. We simply do not know which potentially manipulable variables determine which conflicts lead to war. Our hopes to avoid, or at least minimize, wars must therefore rest either on luck or on our ability to develop an understanding of the causes of wars. If peacemakers do not know which levers to pull and how to pull them, the success, or failure, of their efforts is left largely to chance. It is possible that our luck may run better in the future than it has in the past, but I believe that we are better off casting our lot with understanding.

My purpose in this book is to contribute to the development of such an understanding. It has been argued that while some crises do not end in war, all wars are preceded by crises; thus, our ability to explain war rests with our ability to explain crisis outcomes. I accept this argument and focus my efforts on trying to determine how certain variables characterizing crisis situations affect whether war occurs. My approach is deductive. I develop a formal model incorporating these variables and derive hypotheses associating them with crisis outcomes. While I do not, in this book, subject the theoretical expectations to a systematic empirical test, I do show how these expectations are consistent with empirical work found in the literature, and I do show how the model provides a useful way of analyzing several specific cases.

I must acknowledge that the arguments presented here do not fully explain war. Many pieces of the theoretical puzzle remain, and much empirical work should be done before we can be confident that we understand why wars occur. I believe the theory developed in this book moves us in the right direction, however. It answers some questions, and more important, it provides a way of thinking about the problem that is potentially quite useful. It focuses our attention on the issues over which disputes occur, and while we must accept that some determinants of crisis outcomes may not be susceptible to manipulation, it provides an indication of what some policies aimed at avoiding war might look like. In short, my aim is to take a first step in developing a general, theoretical understanding of international crises that can also provide an intellectual basis for those working toward peaceful resolutions of specific conflicts. I believe that my arguments do, at least, constitute such a first step.

The ideas presented in this book began to be developed years ago. The genesis of the project was a term paper I wrote for Mel Hinich's class on the spatial model of voting. It struck me that the basic model we were using to study voting behavior could be adapted to the study of international conflicts, and I sought to demonstrate that the model could provide a useful representation of crisis situations. That paper became an article, and I subsequently expanded that article into my dissertation. I continued to (and still do) use the model to address different questions and have published a number of articles and book chapters based on it. This book represents an effort to tie some of this work together into a more complete analysis of international crises. Much of the material in this book is new, and some of the arguments are presented more fully than they have been previously, but most of the ideas and some of the presentation of these ideas have been taken from my earlier work. I gratefully acknowledge permission to reprint portions of my earlier articles: "A Spatial Model of Crisis Bargaining," *International Studies Quarterly* 28 (December 1984): 407–26; "Power, Resolve and Bargaining in International Crises: A Spatial Theory," *International Interactions* 15 (1990): 279–302; "Issue Linkages in International Crisis Bargaining," *American Journal of Political Science* 34 (May 1990): 311–33; "Mediators, Allies, and Opportunists: Third Parties in International Crises," in *Politics and Rationality,* William James Booth, Patrick James, and Hudson Meadwell, eds., Cambridge University Press, New York (1993): 266–80.

As with any book, the author must accept responsibility for all shortcomings that remain. However, I am indebted to a number of people whose time and efforts have helped remove many flaws. Bruce Bueno de Mesquita, Pat James, Mike McGinnis, Jim Morrow, Peter Ordeshook, Jim Ray, Val Schwebach, Ric Stoll, Harrison Wagner, Rick Wilson, Frank Zagare, and several anonymous reviewers provided comments on parts or all of the manuscript. Though I imagine some found me to be singularly unreceptive to criticism, I appreciate all of their efforts, and even if it does not always show, I have learned a great deal from our interactions. Thank you all.

Jack Levy and Mel Hinich have had an especially great impact on my development as a scholar in general and on the development of this project in particular. This book would simply not have been written without them. I owe more to each of you for your teaching, cajoling, criticism, and friendship than I can express or repay.

This book has taken many hours that could have been spent playing, and it has often made me a grouch, so I would also like to thank my wife, Kay, and my children, Tom and Emily, for their patience, understanding, and support. I love you all.

Finally, I would like to remember, with gratitude, Mel Blanc, whose voice characterizations have brought the world such pleasure.

Figures

CHAPTER 1

Introduction

If you have not lost your self-control and sensibly conceive what this might lead to, then, Mr. President, we and you ought not to pull on the ends of the rope in which you have tied the knot of war, because the more the two of us pull, the tighter the knot will be tied.

—Nikita Khrushchev to John F. Kennedy at the height of the Cuban Missile Crisis

Over the centuries, a great deal of intellectual effort has been devoted to determining why interstate wars occur. Philosophers, historians, social scientists, and others have all sought to understand how state leaders have been able to devote material wealth and the lives of their citizens to such an enterprise. The high level of interest in the topic is not surprising if one considers only the frequency of war. For example, in just the thirty-five years from 1945 through 1980, a period deemed by many to have been particularly peaceful, there were 125 nation-years of interstate war (Small and Singer 1982, 92–95). Although most states were at peace most of the time, an average of about four nation-states were engaged in war on any given day. Even if improving our knowledge about the world in which we live was our only concern, understanding a phenomenon as pervasive as war would be worthwhile.

It is also the case, however, that wars have a dramatic impact on the people who participate, the states involved, and the international system. Obviously, lives are lost or deeply affected by the experience, but .1e repercussions of war can reach far beyond those directly involved. Governments have been overthrown (Russia in World War I) and states have been dismembered (Austria-Hungary in World War I) or even eliminated (Palestine) as a result of war. In fact, the very structure of the international system can be fundamentally altered because of war (e.g., after World War II). Thus, even if one believes that wars have been (or will become) rare events, the magnitude of their impact provides ample reason to study the causes of war. It is necessary to understand why wars occur if we are to have any hope of preventing or controlling their outbreak, and developing this capacity may have become crucial in the present age when the destructive potential of modern weaponry is so great.

In spite of all the speculation and theorizing that have been devoted toward explaining war, our record of achievement is unimpressive at best. We have yet to devise an explanation for war that has been accepted by even a sizeable minority of the scholarly community as logically consistent and empirically supported. The purpose of this book is to present yet another attempt at explaining why states sometimes fight. A thorough understanding of any phenomenon can only be achieved through a well-integrated, empirically supported, explanatory theory. While my aim in this study is more limited than reaching a complete understanding of the causes of war, I hope to move in this direction by presenting a model on which such a theory could be based and by using this model to derive some of the theoretical pieces of the puzzle. This exercise should provide some insight into the occurrence of wars in that I have attempted to conceptualize the problem in an interesting and useful manner and in that the variables I have included are among those commonly believed to be the most important determinants of war. Admittedly, the ultimate goal, a full understanding of why wars occur, must await further theoretical developments as well as empirical confirmation of the theory. I hope that since the model I propose is extremely flexible, in that additional variables can be easily incorporated, this study can provide a foundation for future work.

The majority of the book will be devoted to the presentation and development of the model; however, a number of preliminary points must be made. In this chapter I provide the basis for the subsequent analysis by presenting and justifying my conceptualization of the problem at hand, by defining the key terms, and by discussing the basic nature of the analysis to be used.

Crisis and War

The first step in any investigation is to identify that which is to be explained, that is, the dependent variable. In one respect, paying a great deal of attention to conceptualizing *war* seems unnecessary—after all, most of us know a war when we see one. However, a major shortcoming with many attempts to explain war rests with the failure to conceptualize, clearly and precisely, the dependent variable. Many of the earlier traditional studies, for example, focused on one particular war (or perhaps a few wars) and sought to determine the historical conditions that could be associated with its outbreak. Clearly, such research cannot produce a general explanation. The conditions associated with the outbreak of one war might be absent when other wars occur. Furthermore, even the specific explanations for individual wars must be suspect because the coincident conditions might also be present when no war occurs. Simply stated, such research programs, though suggestive, provide flawed general explanations because they do not identify a dependent *variable*, and only variables can, or need, be explained.

Over the past half century or so scholars have become concerned with precisely defining *war*. This interest arose in tandem with the desire to conduct systematic analyses aimed at developing a general theory of the causes of war. Those working in the tradition of Wright (1965), Richardson (1960), and the Correlates of War Project (Singer and Small 1972) sought to examine systematically all instances of war in an effort to identify conditions associated with all, or most, cases. The desire to identify all occurrences of war in a given period required a precise definition of *war* that could delimit wars from all other events.

Many definitions of *war* have been suggested (see, e.g., Beer 1981, 6–7; Bernard 1944, 28; Malinowski 1968; Small and Singer 1982, 36–38; Wright 1965, 8), but for this study I will adopt that proposed by Levy, who defines war as "a substantial armed conflict between the organized military forces of independent political units" (1983b, 51). Levy's definition does identify, at an intuitive level, what we have typically understood war to mean. It does not unnecessarily exclude events that we would normally consider as wars (as does, for example, Wright's definition, which, by requiring a formal declaration of war, would exclude the Vietnam War), nor does it include events that we would not consider as wars (for example, the requirement that the conflict be "substantial" excludes small-scale border clashes). In short, this definition clearly accomplishes the task of delimiting the phenomenon of interest by specifying three conditions that are individually necessary and jointly sufficient to establish an event as a war.

Some of the research coming from this tradition has aimed at identifying the conditions present when wars occur. Such studies do permit generalizations beyond a single case of war, but it is still possible that the conditions associated with war are also present when peace reigns. Other studies have sought to identify necessary and sufficient conditions for war by examining both times of war and times of peace. Most and Starr (1982, 1983, 1984, and 1989) have convincingly argued that this research strategy is also logically doomed to fail. In brief, they argue that no such conditions could, in any case, be both necessary and sufficient for war, in part because "through time and across space, similar factors could plausibly be expected to trigger different foreign policy acts . . . [and] different processes could plausibly be expected to lead to similar results" (1984, 383).

The source of the problem is that previous research has not been guided by an adequate conceptualization of war. A definition such as Levy's does accomplish the first step of such a conceptualization (delimiting the phenomenon and identifying the population of cases to be studied), but more is needed.

It is also necessary to identify a variable, for which *war* is but one value (Morgan 1990). The variable implicit in most investigations seeking to identify necessary and sufficient conditions for war is something akin to a "state of the world" variable that can assume two values: *war* and *peace*. Since the *peace* value of this variable is not defined (other than as the absence of war), it is not clear that this is the best conceptualization on which to base our research. To explain when one value of the variable obtains, we must also explain when the other value(s) holds, yet how can we explain what we have not conceptually defined?

Some studies have used conceptual definitions such as Levy's as the basis for operational definitions that in turn specify some variable to be explained. The approach followed by those using this form of definition is usually to identify, in some sense, the amount of war occurring at the systemic or nation-state level (in terms of, for example, the frequency of wars in a given period or the severity or duration of the wars that occur) and then to attempt to identify the factors that best account for the variation in these variables (see, e.g., Levy 1983b; Small and Singer 1982). Presumably, the explanation for war rests in the discovery of the set of factors that determines whether the amount of war occurring is zero.

While this body of research has contributed a great deal of insight and understanding variations in the amount of war is certainly important, a compelling criticism of this research strategy can be made. Note particularly that the "zero war" point is treated as just another level. That is especially true because most quantitative studies have used statistical methods that incorporate the assumption of linearity in the data (e.g., linear regression, factor analysis). Thus, *zero* is treated the same as every other point on the scale; furthermore, the difference between 0 and $0 + e$ is viewed as being the same as the difference between N and $N + e$ $(N \neq 0)$. It would seem more useful to view the move from *no war* to *some war* as being fundamentally different from the move from *some war* to *a little more war*. This approach requires that we focus on explaining the onset of war, which, of course, necessitates the conceptualization of a variable that delimits *no war* as well as *war* values. The difficult question that this approach suggests is, how do we conceptualize what constitutes a *nonwar*? Until we can identify a set of occurrences that are not wars but that share enough in common with wars to permit meaningful comparisons with wars, we cannot devise an explanation of war.

Another approach, which is becoming increasingly popular, is to focus not solely on wars but on the situations that may turn into war. One example is the body of research that has grown out of the Correlates of War Project that focuses on Militarized Interstate Disputes, which are defined as a set of interactions between nation-states that involve the threat, display, or use of military force (see, e.g., Cusack and Eberwein 1982; Gochman and Maoz

1984; Maoz 1982; Siverson and Tennefoss 1984; Stoll 1982). The goal of this research is to identify the set of disputes in which a threat or display of force has been made and then to uncover the conditions and processes that determine which disputes escalate to war.

A similar orientation is that adopted by those who have focused their research on international crises (e.g., Brecher 1980; Brecher and Wilkenfeld 1982, 1989; Hermann 1972; James 1988; Lebow 1981; Snyder and Diesing 1977), which can be defined as "sequence[s] of interactions between the governments of two or more sovereign states in severe conflict, short of actual war, but involving the perception of a dangerously high probability of war" (Snyder and Diesing 1977, 6). These scholars have noted that all wars are preceded by crises but that all crises do not result in war; thus, they believe that the key to an explanation for war can be found in the patterns of crisis behavior. By discovering the conditions and behavioral dynamics that lead some crises to end in war while others are resolved peacefully, we can have a much better understanding of why wars occur than can be achieved by determining only what factors are present when wars occur.

This approach has a number of advantages. It does identify a *variable* (crisis outcome) that is to be explained, and it permits an examination of a relevant set of nonwar outcomes that can be compared to the set of wars. This approach affords a more complete conceptualization of the research problem than most other approaches provide. Furthermore, a focus on crises, and crisis decision making in particular, provides a means for integrating a great deal of existing research. One can examine how the structure of the international system and the nature of nation-states affect crisis behavior and outcomes as well as how more idiosyncratic aspects of crisis dynamics, such as misperceptions or particular strategic decisions, interact to determine process and outcome. That is, we can integrate background structural and situational factors into an explanatory framework that also includes more proximate, behavioral determinants of crisis outcomes.

In fact, a great deal of prior theoretical and empirical work into the causes of war can, with slight modification, be incorporated into our understanding of international crises. James (1988) has devoted the majority of his book to just such an effort. He considered several bodies of research into the causes of war, each of which had traditionally sought to identify the conditions at one level of analysis (systemic, nation-state, individual) associated with the occurrence of war. He showed that each could be reinterpreted to contribute to an explanation of crisis outcomes, that the resulting explanations were better supported empirically than were the original arguments, and that, by using the focus on crises as a common denominator, the arguments could be combined into a far better explanation.

I accept the argument that focusing our research efforts on international crises is the most fruitful approach toward an understanding of why wars occur and have adopted this perspective for this book. Although we know that war is one type of crisis outcome, we have not yet identified the other value(s) that our variable can assume. Our definition presupposes that a crisis involves some conflict of interests between the participants. Since this conflict must be resolved in some manner if war is to be avoided, it is reasonable to define the nonwar value(s) of the dependent variable as the alternative means of conflict resolution. Elsewhere, I have suggested that all conflicts must be resolved by adjudication, voting, bargaining, or force and that, in the context of international crises, war is an instance of force (Morgan 1990). We can safely say that adjudication and voting are infeasible as means of resolving crises, primarily because the international system contains no mechanism to enforce the outcome of such processes. Even attempts at using a method such as binding arbitration to resolve a crisis must rely on the mutual willingness of the parties to abide by the decision. Since crises involve perceived vital interests, few participants would subject themselves to such a procedure, and even fewer would abide by a decision deemed unfavorable. That, in effect, implies that a mutually bargained agreement is the only alternative to war. Thus, our dependent variable, crisis outcome, has two values: war and bargained agreement.

In sum, the research problem is conceptualized as involving the explanation of crisis outcomes. I assume that crises must end either in war or with a bargained settlement and that once we understand the background conditions and processes associated with particular outcomes, we will have made a significant advance toward explaining war. How best to achieve such an understanding is the next question to which I shall turn.

Method of Analysis

The aim of this study is to provide a theoretical foundation that can be used to explain and predict crisis outcomes. Although the usefulness of any theory ultimately depends on how well the hypotheses derived from it are supported empirically, I shall not perform any such tests at this time.[1] I shall restrict my efforts in this book to presenting a model that can serve as the basis for a theory of crisis behavior and to using this model to derive some hypotheses relating some variables of particular interest to crisis outcomes. Obviously, that will lead, in some sense, to an incomplete research project; but since the quality of the ultimate output of such a project depends on the theoretical foundation, it is justifiable to devote a great deal of effort to the initial theoretical development.

The empirical world will not be completely ignored, however. I shall attempt to show that the theory is consistent with some empirical evidence found in the literature, and I shall demonstrate that the theory provides a novel way of interpreting some results that were perplexing or, when taken together, contradictory. I shall also show how the model can be used to represent and interpret some historical cases. While these case studies are not intended as definitive tests of the theory, they should provide an empirical referent for and serve as illustrations of the theoretical arguments. Readers should remember that all the empirical references are meant only to be suggestive and are intended to illustrate and complement the development of the theory.

The theory developed here is based on a formal, mathematical model. My goal is to use this model to deduce logically hypotheses relating a number of variables to crisis outcomes. Although the level of abstraction in a mathematical representation of international crises will result in some loss of descriptive power, the increased precision allows for a much more rigorous analysis. The interactions among the variables can be precisely specified, and the derivation of the hypotheses can be made explicit. Since my concern is with general explanation, the loss of descriptive power is of less concern than the increase in analytical rigor. The specific model to be used is a synthesis of the spatial model of voting behavior (see, e.g., Enelow 1984; Enelow and Hinich 1981 and 1984; Hinich, Ledyard, and Ordeshook 1973; Hinich and Pollard 1981) and some aspects of traditional utility-based bargaining theory (especially Nash 1950 and 1953; Pen 1952; Zeuthen 1968). The remainder of the book is devoted to the development and application of the model, but a few comments justifying this approach are in order at this time.

Since the problem has been conceptualized such that the alternative crisis outcomes are war and bargained agreement, it is sensible to turn to bargaining theory for some of our insights. Bargaining theory has been developed to deal with situations in which two or more parties attempt to resolve some conflict of interest through mutual agreement. While the situation is most obviously characterized by conflict, it is generally assumed that a cooperative element exists as well. Specifically, the parties have a mutual interest in avoiding the alternative to a negotiated agreement. For example, when a seller and a buyer negotiate a sales price, they are in conflict over whether the price should be high or low; but each has some desire to avoid continuing the search for another buyer or seller with whom to deal. Clearly, deals are not always struck—sometimes both are better off with the alternative outcome, and sometimes mistakes are made. It is the goal of bargaining theory to determine when agreements will occur and what these agreements will be. Formal bargaining theory typically considers only highly abstract versions of bargaining situations. When one considers these abstractions, the parallels between buyers and sellers (or labor and management, or litigants) and crisis participants is striking. Crisis participants' preferences over the issues at stake diverge, but they share a common interest in avoiding war if possible.

Furthermore, a number of the questions that will concern us here have been addressed by bargaining theorists in one form or another. That is, the independent variables determining the parameters of most bargaining models are generally believed to be those variables most influencing crisis behavior. For example, the relative power and resolve of the parties involved are often considered to be vitally important in determining behavior in crises (Blechman and Kaplan 1978; Brecher and Wilkenfeld 1982; Snyder 1972), and these variables (in some form) are among those often believed to exert some influence on bargained outcomes (Rubin and Brown 1975, 36–38).

Thus, while bargaining models have generally been developed to address different questions (usually problems of economic exchange), minor modifications should make them applicable to the study of international crises, and we should be able to draw heavily from existing theory for insight into the determinants of crisis outcomes. That bargaining theory can be fruitfully applied to questions of this sort is indicated by the ability of Pillar (1983) to draw on bargaining theories for some of his insights into the processes by which some wars are terminated. Snyder and Diesing (1977) have also used bargaining theory, though of a different type than I use in this book, to analyze international crises. Their analysis has significantly added to our knowledge of crisis behavior, but as I will argue in the next chapter, I believe the model presented here provides a more fertile theoretical basis.

There exist a large number of bargaining models from which to draw, though none is completely adequate for addressing all the questions of interest here. Each focuses on slightly different variables and is based on a slightly different conceptualization of the bargaining problem. The model presented here draws from a number of these models and incorporates the various aspects of each that provide useful insights into the explanation of crisis outcomes.[2]

I must point out that the resultant model does not constitute a new development in bargaining theory; rather, it represents the explicit connection of a number of elements of bargaining theory that are useful in understanding how crises can end in war. The intention is for the synthesis of the spatial theory of voting and various aspects of several bargaining models to provide a novel and interesting means of studying international crises. It should also be noted at the outset that while the model developed in this book draws heavily from bargaining theory, it does not constitute a theory of bargaining per se. No theory of moves or concession rates is presented, and I do not consider the question of what particular bargaining offers should be made. Treating the source of offers as exogenous does, of course, lead to an incompletely specified model. One must always set boundaries for any investigation, however, and all studies must ignore some important questions. By ignoring questions regarding particular concessions and offers, I hope to focus more fully on questions regarding how the context of crises affects outcomes. The theory is sufficiently general with respect to bargaining offers that the conclusions I reach should hold however such offers are made and from wherever such offers arise. Thus, my results do not depend on any particular theory of moves and can be merged with (and perhaps guide) any such theory that is ultimately developed.

The chief concern of this study is to determine how the conflict situation constrains and affects crisis behavior and outcomes. One aspect of the situation that has usually been overlooked in studies of international crises are the issues at stake and the parties' attitudes toward these issues. The spatial model provides an extremely useful means of representing a conflict situation in terms of these factors. This permits the analysis of a number of questions regarding how the issues are addressed. We can, for example, determine whether the nature of the agenda should have any impact on crisis outcomes as well as what types of issues facilitate logrolls. The focus on the issues in dispute that is at the heart of the spatial model leads to insights unobtainable from other models. The adaptability of these models to international situations is demonstrated in the work of Morgan (1984); Bueno de Mesquita, Newman, and Rabushka (1985; see also Bueno de Mesquita 1990); and Morrow (1986), all of whom have used various versions of spatial theory to study international political phenomena.

The use of the spatial model to adapt traditional bargaining theory should produce an extremely fertile model of international crisis behavior. We can focus on many different questions within a single framework, and the model is sufficiently flexible that additional variables, not included in this study, can subsequently be added. While the focus in this book is on theoretical development, the goal is for the hypotheses derived to be testable. This provides another motivation for developing a rich theoretical basis that can address numerous aspects of the problem. Should future empirical tests support some of the hypotheses, we can increase our confidence in other, untested hypotheses derived from the same theoretical structure. The synthesis of the two theoretical traditions is thus intended to produce a rich, integrated theoretical framework on which future theoretical and empirical work can build.

Organization of the Study

Obviously, one could ask a great many questions about international crises and numerous variables could affect crisis outcomes. No single book could explore all possible avenues of inquiry, and that is not my purpose. While a large number of variables can be incorporated into the spatial bargaining model, the effort in this book is much more limited. I have tried to identify those factors many believe to be the most important determinants of crisis outcomes and restrict the analysis to these variables. This approach should provide the most mileage for the least effort and should provide a good foundation from which to build. The results produced should suggest which of the variables truly are important, which are less so, and what avenues of future research are likely to be most fruitful.

By the very nature of the formal, mathematical model on which the theory is based, the derivation of the hypotheses is technical in nature. I have tried to keep the exposition as accessible as possible for those without mathematical training. I have tried to explain the logic behind the derivations in straightforward language, and I have tried to rely heavily on simple hypothetical examples to illustrate the main points. It must be kept in mind, however, that ultimately, the logic behind the arguments is in the mathematical sections. The formal derivations are set apart, and one can get the gist of my argument without working through the math; but much of the richness and complexity of the arguments will be lost. For example, many of the conclusions suggest the existence of fairly complex relationships among the variables. Much of that is reflected in the mathematical exposition far better than it is in the English version.

I have also attempted to organize the book in a manner that will ease the reader through the development of the argument. I begin with an extremely simple representation of crises as symmetrical, two-party, zero-sum situations and build progressively on this construction. Each chapter relies on the previous chapter in that variables are added to the model and in that the model becomes increasingly general. In order, I drop the symmetry assumption, the zero-sum assumption, and finally the two-party assumption. As we shall see, the hypothesized relationships become more complex at each successive step.

Thus far I have discussed the problem this book addresses and presented in very general terms the type of model that is used in the analysis. In the following chapter I shall present a review of the literature dealing with bargaining models that are of interest for this study and assess the strengths and weaknesses of this body of work. The purposes of this review are to determine which aspects of which models are most useful for coming to grips with the problem at hand, to determine what modifications are necessary, and to identify those variables generally believed to have an impact on crisis behavior. The basic model used in this study is also described in chapter 2. In that chapter, I introduce and discuss the independent variables incorporated into the model. I also present and justify the specific assumptions that the model comprises, and I demonstrate how, in a very general way, the model can lead to predictions regarding crisis outcomes.

In chapters 3, 4, and 5, the model is used to derive a number of hypotheses regarding crisis outcomes. Chapter 3 contains the analysis of how the relationship of crisis participants, in terms of their relative power and resolve, affects outcomes. The variables considered in that chapter are those often believed to be the most important determinants of international crisis behavior, and the emphasis is on (1) determining how variations in these variables can be expected to affect the probability that crises will end in war and (2) how these variations can be expected to affect the nature of a negotiated agreement that may be reached. The examination focuses on the impact of the variables acting in combination as well as singly, which allows us to identify any interaction effects. Chapter 4 focuses on questions regarding how the treatment of the issues under dispute can affect outcomes. We determine whether the order in which the issues are addressed (or if they are considered simultaneously) has any impact, and we see how the characteristics of the issues affect the possibility that logrolls will occur. Chapter 5 is devoted to an analysis of the effect third parties have on international crises. I identify a number of motivations for third parties to become involved and show how these motivations affect the impact this involvement has on crisis outcomes. In the conclusion, I attempt to evaluate what I have accomplished. I point out some of the weaknesses of this approach and suggest avenues for future research.

Throughout the book, I occasionally refer to historical examples of international crises. These cases are intended to illustrate my arguments and to provide some empirical referents to an otherwise highly abstract exposition. These are not intended as empirical proof of any of my hypotheses. A brief case history of each case used is presented in the Appendix. I provide a brief synopsis of the historical record and then tell the story in the language of the model. I apologize to anyone offended by the simplified and superficial treatment of the cases—please understand that I am only taking from the historical record that which the theory says is important. My aim is limited to trying to show that the theory is not completely divorced from reality, but I do believe that the framework provided by the model offers some insight into how we can interpret these cases. If we have peeled away all but the most important aspects of each crisis and the simplified version leads to a fair (though not total) understanding, then we are well on the way to the goal of a general theory of crisis behavior.

CHAPTER 2

A Spatial Model of Crisis Bargaining

I argued in the previous chapter that one useful means of gaining insight into the causes of war is to draw on bargaining theory for analyses of international crises. These situations are instances of political conflict that either will be resolved through the strategic interaction (Young 1975, 5) of the parties involved or will result in war. Bargaining models are able to capture the essence of crisis situations in that while the primary focus is on bargaining behavior and outcomes, we may also determine the conditions under which we would expect negotiations to break down, resulting in war.

There exists a vast literature on bargaining theory, and numerous models of the bargaining process have been proposed. My purpose in this book is not to revolutionize this literature; rather, I intend to draw from the best aspects of a wide range of bargaining theory in my effort to devise a theoretical explanation for crisis outcomes. Thus, this chapter begins with a brief review of the previous research on bargaining in which I highlight the strengths and weakness of various approaches to the problem. Particular emphasis is placed on those aspects of this work that are incorporated into the model proposed below. Following this brief review, I set out the basic model used in the subsequent analysis.

Existing Models of Bargaining

Bargaining theory incorporates a wide variety of models that could be used to address the problem at hand. Each, of course, has its advantages and disadvantages in terms of how well it deals with various aspects of the bargaining problem. This discussion draws heavily from Snyder and Diesing (1977), who, in approaching essentially the same problem, provide a fairly thorough review of bargaining theory, and from Young (1975), who provides excellent analyses of various bargaining models in his chapter introductions. The literature on bargaining is exceedingly vast; therefore, a detailed review of all the models that have been proposed is impossible. For the purposes of this discussion, the literature is categorized on the basis of the general approaches followed.[1] Within each category, a few representative studies are discussed in some detail, and any important differences among the studies are pointed out.

Nonformal Approaches

Many, perhaps most, students of bargaining address the subject without the aid of a formal model. A number of such studies have been written by, or in consultation with, professional diplomats and are primarily concerned with teaching others the trade (see, e.g., Brown 1968; Winham 1979; Zartman and Berman 1982).[2] Since these pieces are often descriptive and generally consider the specific behavior of individuals involved in the bargaining process, they are of minimal use in the development of a general theory of bargaining. For the purposes of theory building, the chief contributions of these studies are the criticisms they make of academic bargaining studies. A consideration of these criticisms can contribute to the development of theory to the extent it leads to the incorporation of important factors previously overlooked.

The more common (and serious) of these complaints is that academics devote too little consideration to the issues involved in a bargaining problem and that internal bargaining (bureaucratic politics) is almost totally ignored (Brown 1968; Winham 1979). The heart of the first criticism rests in the tendency of bargaining theorists to reduce the values being bargained over to a single, usually utility, number. While this strategy enables us to model concessions in one respect, much is lost by not being able to consider tradeoffs across issues. We must recognize that some issues may be more salient to one party while other issues are more important to the other. Two bargaining situations that appear quite similar in a utility model may be quite different in terms of the tradeoffs the actors are willing to make across issues, and this difference can affect both the process and outcome of the bargaining.

The second criticism is based on the notion that the bargaining that occurs within nation-states affects the outcome of interstate bargaining as much as does the bargaining between the states' diplomats. This criticism is almost certainly valid. However, bargaining models, including the one proposed here, have not included internal bargaining for good reason. The goal is to develop a fairly simple, manageable model that can guide our analyses. Including only interstate bargaining leads to fairly complex models, and attempting to incorporate a large number of actors would lead to a model so complex that it would be nearly useless for the early stages of analysis.[3] In developing the model to be proposed here, I have taken these criticisms into account. The model focuses explicitly on the issues involved and is used to study the effects of issue linkages. Furthermore, while I adopt the "state as unitary actor" assumption, the model can accommodate any number of actors, which could be defined as subnational units, and can be used in future research that incorporates internal bargaining.

Also within this category are a number of studies dealing with strategic issues, such as deterrence, limited war, and coercive diplomacy (George,

Hall, and Simons 1971; Kahn 1965; Kecskemeti 1958; Kissinger 1957; Schelling 1966).[4] These studies bear on the question of bargaining by examining how best to use one's means of coercion to achieve national objectives. Little emphasis is placed on predicting likely outcomes in specific situations, other than asserting that if a certain course is followed, the outcome will be the most favorable. Similarly, little is said about the linkages among the variables purported to affect the bargaining. Yet this body of literature does provide several insights by demonstrating the importance of some key variables that determine bargaining outcomes. The two variables believed to be the central considerations affecting international bargaining are relative power (defined as the relative ability to manipulate costs and benefits) and relative resolve (defined as the relative saliency of the issues at stake).

Kecskemeti (1958) argues that, for states at war, relative military power is bargaining power and is used to increase the costs the opponent must pay to achieve its objectives. His main argument, that a defeated state can use its residual forces to extract some concessions from the enemy, can be extended to a wide range of cases. In general, the threat, or the actual imposition, of costs can be used to extract concessions from the enemy. The argument concerning resolve is simply that the participant for whom the issue at stake is more important should be willing to bear greater costs and thus be able to achieve a more favorable outcome. This argument frequently arises in discussions of deterrence, where it is often claimed that for a deterrent threat to be credible, it must be backed with the resolution to carry it out (Craig and George 1983, 172; George and Smoke 1974, 522–32; Jervis 1979, 315; Schelling 1966).

A number of empirical studies have tested propositions derived from bargaining theory. The majority of these studies focus on the power and resolve variables. In general, the hypotheses tested have not been logically deduced from a formal construction of the bargaining situation (for important exceptions, see Hopmann 1974 and 1978). The results of tests on bargaining outcomes that examine the effect of asymmetrical resolve are consistent in showing that the party for whom the issues at stake are more important generally obtains a favorable outcome (Hopmann 1978; Maoz 1983; Young 1968, 216). The findings concerning the impact of the balance of capabilities are less consistent: Maoz (1983) found little support for the notion that an asymmetry in capabilities leads to an asymmetrical outcome, while Hopmann (1978) found a great deal of support for the hypothesis. The divergence of these results is probably due to the nature of the cases examined. Maoz focused on militarized, bilateral disputes, while Hopmann examined a long-term, multilateral negotiation in a noncrisis situation. Thus, both variables are likely to influence bargaining outcomes, but their relative importance may depend on the nature of the situation.

The final set of studies that have adopted a nonformal approach are those that deal with social-psychological variables.[5] Sawyer and Guetzkow (1965) and Druckman (1973) have provided concise summaries of the social-psychological variables believed to affect the behavior of bargainers, so this discussion can be quite brief. Generally, these studies emphasize the effect on bargaining behavior of the psychological processes of decision makers and the social context in which decisions are made. The primary concerns are with determining what factors induce cooperative, as opposed to conflictual, behavior on the part of the bargainers and with providing an accurate description of the bargaining process. A number of empirical studies performed in the context of international relations have demonstrated the importance of incorporating these social-psychological factors (Hopmann 1972 and 1974; Leng 1983).

The advantages of nonformal analyses derive mainly from the flexibility provided by the absence of specific assumptions. Oversimplified assumptions are often required to keep formal models manageable. Without the burden of such assumptions, it is possible to construct more realistic descriptions of actual events and to account better for abnormal events by including or excluding variables as needed. Although nonformal studies can provide more realistic descriptions of bargaining processes, they are seriously deficient when it comes to producing theoretical analyses. Without a formal model, it is difficult to explain outcomes and to capture complex patterns of interactions among several variables. Since the issue addressed in this book requires a general theory of bargaining rather than descriptions of specific cases, a formal model is needed, albeit one in which the most important variables found in the nonformal studies are included. Thus, the problem in this book is identical to that Snyder and Diesing (1977) faced: What type of formal model is the most useful for understanding international crisis behavior?

Game Matrix Models

Probably the most commonly used formal models of bargaining are those that use the normal form representation of the theory of games. These models have been used as the basis for more elaborate models (Allan 1983) and as a guide in the analysis of specific cases (Zagare 1977 and 1981) as well as the basic framework for analyzing bargaining and international behavior more broadly (Jervis 1972 and 1978; Snyder 1972; Snyder and Diesing 1977). In general, the bargaining situation is represented by a matrix that represents two players, column and row, their respective strategy choices, and the payoffs to each associated with each possible combination of strategy choices. Figure 1 is a general example of such a matrix in which the players each have two strategies, c and d, providing four possible outcomes, generically labeled A–D.

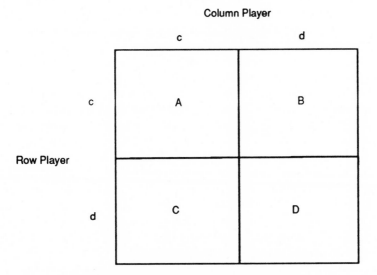

Fig. 1. The bargaining problem in normal form

The players are assumed to be rational self-interest maximizers with complete information regarding the structure of the game—including the opponent's preference ordering over possible outcomes.[6] Matrices are usually structured so that the players have two strategies, cooperative (c) and noncooperative (d). Although the game can incorporate any number of strategies, very few have been constructed to permit more than two. Certainly, nations in crisis have more than two options, but most of these can be classified as cooperative or noncooperative, and this matrix can provide a sufficiently accurate representation of most crisis situations (Snyder and Diesing 1977, 83).

Within this framework, the distinctive structures of various bargaining situations are represented by the players' preference orderings over the four outcomes. Bargaining is viewed as a situation of strategic interaction, in which the decisions made by each of two interdependent actors affect the payoffs going to both. The structure of a particular game can be used to determine what choices actors playing the game are likely to make and, by extension, provide insight into why actors behave as they do in the real-world situations that these models approximate. As an example of this type of analysis, we can refer to Snyder and Diesing's (1977, 90–92) treatment of the Agadir crisis as a Prisoner's Dilemma.[7]

The Agadir crisis came about when France began to establish full colonial control over Morocco. Prior to doing so, France had compensated Italy, Spain, and Great Britain. Germany felt it also had a right to compensation and that its exclusion by France was a blow to its prestige as a great power. The crisis was precipitated when Germany attempted to press its claim for compensation by sending a gunboat to Agadir. Snyder and Diesing (1977) characterize the situation as a Prisoner's Dilemma (see fig. 2) in which France and Germany can each choose to concede to the other's demands or stand firm. A primary consideration for each is the loss of prestige involved in backing down, which is the worst outcome. Both preferred war to humiliation but would rather have found some compromise. The available compromise, and ultimately the solution, was for the French to grant the Germans some territorial compensation in the French Congo in return for Germany's recognition of French supremacy in Morocco. Thus, the preference ordering of the participants created a Prisoner's Dilemma situation, and the outcome of the crisis was consistent with the outcomes of similar situations (Snyder and Diesing 1977, 482).[8]

The use of these models for analyzing bargaining behavior can be criticized on several grounds. First, the models actually tell us very little about bargaining. They are essentially models of decision making that rely solely on a characterization of the preference orderings of the parties involved to arrive at a solution. These models minimize the importance of the bargaining process as a determinant of outcomes and are relatively useless as a descriptive or predictive theory of this process.

The most common criticism of these models is that they simplify the problem to such an extent that meaningful analyses are impossible. Rarely are only two actors involved in an international crisis, and these actors generally have more than two options. Even though these may be classified as cooperative or noncooperative strategies, a model that incorporates a recognition of these distinct options is much more complete. In the Agadir case, for example, Great Britain played an important role, and the bargaining between Germany and France concerned how much compensation was to be paid. Assumptions concerning the information available to the parties are also suspect. Rarely does one party have complete knowledge about the other's preference ordering and yet have no information regarding the others' likely choice. A great deal of bargaining in the early stages of a crisis is aimed at uncovering information about the other's preference orderings, yet some estimations will always be required. As noted above, since choices are not made simultaneously and are not necessarily binding, information regarding the other's actions is available. Should one cooperate initially and later discover that the opponent has not, one's decision can be reversed. Thus, these games would come closer to representing the situations they are intended to represent if they were to allow for continuous play (Wagner 1983b).

The most serious shortcomings of these models are that it is difficult to incorporate other variables into the analysis and that they provide no means of

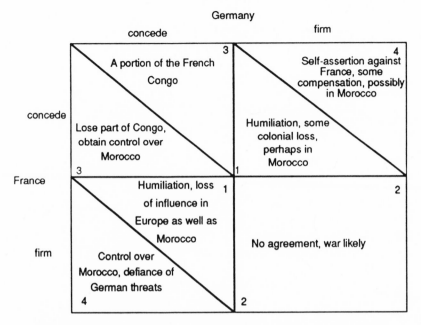

Fig. 2. Snyder and Diesing's representation of the Agadir crisis. (Adapted from Snyder and Diesing 1977, 90.)

specifying the theoretical linkages among variables that can be included. As noted in the previous section, resolve and power are two variables widely considered to have an impact on bargaining. These variables, and a number of others, are not excluded from the normal form models in that they presumably influence the actors' preference orderings over outcomes. For example, a state with a high probability of winning a war may prefer war to capitulation while its opponent's preference would be the reverse. However, the specification of how the power relationship affects the preference orderings is not made explicit in the model, and more important, there is no way to establish a linkage from the power variable to other variables, such as resolve, and show how they interact to determine preferences and, ultimately, choices. The theoretical gaps thus left by these models are fairly substantial and their explanatory power is sufficiently weakened to raise doubt concerning the possibility of basing an explanatory theory on such a model.

In short, game matrix models are too simplistic to provide an accurate representation of the bargaining process and, furthermore, cannot provide adequate predictions regarding bargaining outcomes since their construction allows for only four possibilities. Some attempts have been made to increase the complexity of these models, by increasing the number of choices available to the players or by considering the possibility of sequential choice, for example; however, these efforts are constrained by the construction of the models and actually add very little to their analytical power (Snyder and Diesing 1977, 60–61). Since these models essentially provide limited insight, another formalization may be more useful analytically.

Utility Models

Utility models of bargaining have been extensively used in economics but have been infrequently applied to international relations, although notable exceptions can be found in Pillar 1983 and Wagner 1983a. When faced with a bargaining problem, traditional economic theory predicts only that the outcome lies somewhere within the "range of practicable bargains" (Zeuthen 1968). The goal of utility models of bargaining is to arrive at a determinate solution to the bargaining problem by specifying the nature of the bargaining situation and the characteristics of the solution in such a way that the solution can be deduced from the specification. A variety of such models have been proposed, including game-theoretic models (Nash 1950), economic models (Zeuthen 1968), time-based models (Cross 1969), sociological models (Bartos 1977), and psychological models (Spector 1977), to name but a few. Nash's model is the most basic and will serve to focus this discussion.

Nash (1950) conceives of the bargaining problem as a game in which the players' strategies involve determining how much utility to demand. He represents the bargaining problem by a two-dimensional utility space in which each axis represents the utility of some agreement to one of the participants (see fig. 3). Within this context, Nash's task is to determine the solution to the game by specifying a number of assumptions regarding the nature of the outcome and deducing from these axioms the existence of a single solution point.

The first set of assumptions Nash (1950) makes establish von Neumann-Morgenstern utility functions[9] to represent the players' preference orderings among outcomes. Since these utility functions are invariant up to a positive linear transformation, any point can be set as the origin; thus, for simplicity, the functions are set such that the zero utility point for each player is at the origin.[10] Nash also assumes that the solution will be Pareto optimal—that is, a point in the bargaining space cannot be the solution if there exists some other point that provides at least one of the players greater utility without reducing the utility the other receives. The independence of irrelevant alternatives is also assumed, which means that if the solution point in a set, S, is included in a subset of S, T, then the solution to S is also the solution to T. The final assumption is that the situation is symmetrical with respect to the bargainers.

According to Nash, this assumption "expresses equality of bargaining skill" (1950, 159) and essentially means that the labeling of players makes no difference in the outcome.[11] Given these assumptions, Nash shows that the unique solution is the point on the efficient frontier that maximizes the product of the two players' utilities. This is point $c(S)$ in figure 3.

Although Nash's (1950) theory is analytically rich and provides a determinate solution that is intuitively reasonable, at least when his assumptions are met, it does have several shortcomings. Primarily, it does not provide an adequate conceptualization of the bargaining problem: the model tells us nothing about the bargaining process. In addition, bargaining concessions are simply not made in terms of utilities (Cross 1969, 43), and in real-world bargaining situations, his assumptions are seldom met—particularly symmetry and independence of irrelevant alternatives.[12] Furthermore, the theoretical linkages between important variables are not explicit. For example, the power and resolve relationship would presumably affect the utility functions of the players; however, the precise interactions of these two variables cannot be specified.

Several other utility models have been designed to remedy some of the shortcomings in Nash's (1950) model by, for example, focusing more directly on bargaining behavior. Those models referred to by Young (1975) as economic models are perhaps the best example of this effort. The first such model, proposed by Zeuthen (1968), actually predated Nash by several years. Zeuthen's model is constructed to reflect his interest in labor-management

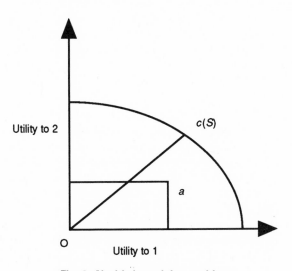

Fig. 3. Nash's bargaining problem

bargaining. According to Zeuthen, the minimum each side is willing to accept from a settlement is equal to the value it expects to receive from a "fight." Considering labor, for example, this would be the wage rate expected to result from a strike minus the costs of the strike. These minimums establish the bounds of the bargaining space, and Zeuthen's problem is to specify what determines bargaining outcomes within this range. Given his definitional assumption, he further assumes that the parties would also be willing to accept some probability of a fight for the opportunity to achieve a given increase in the minimum demand. Given the demands of the two sides, the party least willing to risk a fight should be the one to make a concession; furthermore, the amount of the concession should be such that the other side becomes less willing to risk a fight to achieve its demands. It will then make the next concession, and the process will repeat until agreement is reached. This model improves Nash's by providing some insight into the bargaining process; however, as Harsanyi (1956) has shown, it is mathematically equivalent to Nash's and thus subject to a number of the same criticisms.

Other scholars have drawn on these basic bargaining models and have incorporated into them other factors deemed important to bargaining theory. By far the most common adaptation is to include the effect of bargaining costs, incurred as a cost of, for example, communication (Hessel 1981) or, as is usually the case, of the time involved in reaching an agreement (Cross 1969; Rubinstein 1982). Pen's (1952) effort is of particular interest to this study. At the basis of Pen's theory is his concept of ophelimity functions. *Ophelimity* refers to the amount of satisfaction a bargainer receives from a given outcome and is therefore similar to the notion of utility functions. Pen conceptually improves on most utility bargaining models by pointing out that much of what constitutes bargaining are attempts to alter the opponent's ophelimity functions (by persuasion or other means) rather than assuming the functions to be predetermined and fixed (1952, 37). Pen also incorporates into his model the effect of the power relationship as a determinant of the limits of the bargaining range. The significance of Pen's theory is that the interplay of the factors determining bargaining outcomes is specified more explicitly than in other models. Also, Pen's (1952, 39) theory purports to incorporate every factor influencing the bargaining outcome, primarily as they affect the ophelimity functions. Herein lies the primary weakness in Pen's argument, however. First, the model allows the ophelimity functions to vary in the course of bargaining, and since these functions are unmeasurable because they incorporate so many factors, it cannot actually lead to a determinate outcome even though the equations constituting the model are exactly specified. More importantly, by claiming that every possible factor is accounted for, Pen weakens his argument that the linkages among factors are specified. It is quite difficult to conceptualize the theoretical linkages among what could be a large (perhaps infinite) number of variables. The construction of an elegant, parsimonious theory is better served when relatively few factors and their theoretical linkages are precisely specified.

Several recent studies have extended Nash's (1950) work by following an axiomatic approach while altering Nash's original axioms in various ways (Binmore 1984; Kalai 1977; Kalai and Smorodinsky 1975; Moulin 1984; Roth 1979; Roth and Rothblum 1982). These studies represent interesting generalizations of Nash's result, but they suffer from a number of the same deficiencies. In particular, they shed no light on the bargaining process. This is particularly troublesome for one wishing to apply the theory to the study of international crises because the nature of the abstractions are such that the models ignore precisely the variables presumed to influence crisis behavior. Clearly, some modifications are necessary if a utility model is to be used to study international crises.

A number of scholars have drawn on the basic bargaining models and have adapted them to incorporate other factors deemed important to bargaining. One common adaptation is to include the effect of bargaining costs (Bishop 1964; Cross 1969 and 1977; Foldes 1964; Hessel 1981; Rubinstein 1982; Shaked and Sutton 1984). As Cross (1969) has pointed out, if it does not matter when bargainers agree, it does not matter if they agree. Such models can also be used to represent other situations, such as those in which one side threatens to continue performing some costly act until the opponent agrees to come to terms; the U.S. refusal to sell nuclear fuel to India until India submits to international inspections is one such example (Wagner 1983a). In general, these models are also designed to arrive at a determinate equilibrium point representing the outcome. Interestingly, a common conclusion is that, under a condition of perfect information, the solution is for the party for whom delay is most costly to yield to its opponent's demands (Perry 1986; Rubinstein 1982). This conclusion arises from the fact that both parties recognize that the latter will be able to hold out longer than the former; thus, both are better off if the disadvantaged party acquiesces quickly. Since such outcomes are rare in actual cases of bargaining, some modifications are necessary to bring these models closer to reality.

Many of the more recent studies of bargaining theory have modeled the bargaining situation as a strategic game in extensive form and have based the analysis of bargaining outcomes on solution concepts developed for these games such as the perfect equilibrium concept (Selten 1975) and the related sequential equilibrium concept (Kreps and Wilson 1982). This approach holds the promise of being able to tell us more about the bargaining process than does the axiomatic approach because it does focus on a series of decisions made by the players rather than only on the properties that should characterize an outcome; but it is related to the Nash theory, in that its characterization of the bargaining process can motivate Nash's axiomatic system (Sutton 1986). Furthermore, since the solution is represented as an equilibrium in terms of strategies, rather than in terms of a unique outcome consistent with a set of axioms, it is sensible to incorporate into the model the probability that a player would make a mistake at each choice node. This facilitates empirical applications of the model because our predictions are not restricted to a single outcome point, which is unlikely to result unless the conditions reflected in the axioms are actually met. Because the models can allow for a range of outcomes, deviations from a solution point can be accounted for.

The application of such a model to the study of crisis behavior is problematic, however. These models are similar to the older utility models in that they are based on a highly abstract representation of the bargaining problem. At the very least, the application of such a model to international crises would require conceptual modifications to incorporate variables supposed to affect crisis behavior. A few such attempts have been made, but none is satisfactory for our purpose. As noted above, the efforts of Rubinstein (1982 and 1985) and others to incorporate into the model the fact that the time involved in bargaining is costly has led to the result that a bargaining game should take only one time period and be settled on terms favorable to the party for whom bargaining is least costly. Since there are very few cases of crises (probably none) that are resolved in this manner, it is not clear what such a result tells us about the problem in which we are interested. Perry (1986) has incorporated a notion of power into his analysis, but this notion refers to the ability of one party to decide who makes the first offer. Clearly, this is of little use for our purpose since the power that is supposed to affect crisis behavior refers primarily to military capabilities.

Summary

This review should indicate the strengths and weaknesses of available types of models. One must make tradeoffs between models that are conceptually meaningful and those that are analytically useful. A nonformal approach provides the best conceptualization and description of the bargaining process but is not analytically useful since the linkages among variables are not specified, nor can accurate predictions be made. Game matrix models are more analytically useful, but the characterization of the bargaining problem they provide is inadequate—bargainers simply do not simultaneously choose either to cooperate or not. Finally, utility models provide the most useful analyses because they allow for the full range of choices and outcomes and because the linkages among the important variables can be specified. Unfortunately, they are too abstract to provide conceptually meaningful descriptions of the bargaining situation and process.

Faced with this problem, Snyder and Diesing (1977) choose the middle ground. Focusing on the conceptual weakness of the utility models, they argue that the utility models must be "rejected for crisis bargaining" rather than being restructured (1977, 76) and thereby choose to employ game matrix models. However, I propose to restructure a utility-based model to more appropriately address the problem at hand. Very little, if any, additional insight into crisis bargaining can be provided by the game matrix models. If we are to continue to advance our knowledge, models other than those currently employed must be devised. In particular, the model proposed here represents a synthesis of utility-based bargaining theory with the spatial theory of voting and provides a considerable conceptual improvement over existing utility models.

These improvements become clear as the model is developed in the following sections; however, a few relevant comments are in order. Perhaps the most significant conceptual improvement the spatial model provides is that it shows how the bargainers' utilities are derived from the issues at stake. This feature enables us to describe the bargaining process in appropriate terms while retaining the usefulness of the utility functions for analyzing bargainers' decisions.[13] Furthermore, the predictions derived from the model are expressed as probability distributions. While it is true that the traditional view of the bargaining problem as being indeterminate within the range of practicable bargains is not very useful, it is also the case that determinate solutions are highly suspect. Not all factors (such as luck) affecting bargaining outcomes can be specified in any model; some uncertainty will always remain. In addition, determinate solutions have met with little empirical support. While we may not be able to determine which possible outcome within the bargaining range will be *the* solution, we can say that some should be more likely than others. Thus, the purpose of this model is to determine a probability distribution over all possible outcomes. This construction will also enable us to specify the theoretical linkages among variables affecting bargaining outcomes by demonstrating the influence variables such as the power relationship between the bargainers have on the distribution of outcomes. Finally, the model is constructed in such a way that it allows the incorporation of other factors. For example, the model can easily be extended to more than two actors, which permits the analysis of the impact of internal bargaining, and it can be extended to handle the effects of misperceptions (see Carlson 1992). In this book, however, the model will not be developed to its full generality. I am primarily interested in presenting the basic form of the model, in showing how some of the variables considered as important determinants of crisis outcomes are incorporated, in demonstrating that the model leads to reasonable predictions concerning the likely outcome of crisis situations in certain specific cases, and in briefly illustrating how the model provides a conceptual framework for describing the bargaining process.

A Spatial Model of Crisis Bargaining

My purpose in the remainder of this chapter is to present a spatial model of crisis bargaining. The variables comprising the model are identified and defined, and the basic structure of the model is explained. I show how the model can be used to provide descriptions of bargaining in actual crises and how, for analytical and predictive purposes, the model can be used to determine probability distributions over possible outcomes. In this chapter only the basic model is presented. The model is developed more fully in subsequent chapters where we see what insight the model can provide into the effects on bargaining of varying the conditions in which a crisis occurs as well as what the model can tell us about the bargaining process. One should remember that this model represents a synthesis of existing utility-based bargaining models with the spatial theory of voting—not a dramatic revolution in bargaining theory. For this reason, a portion of this chapter is devoted to demonstrating how this model corresponds with previous works.

The use of any formal model requires that a number of basic, simplifying assumptions be made. While most of these assumptions are more usefully presented and discussed as they are incorporated into the model, two—that nation-states are unitary and rational actors—will be discussed at this time. Since these assumptions have become somewhat controversial in international relations research (see, e.g., Allison 1971; Morrow 1988) and since they will be maintained throughout the book, a preliminary, fairly detailed discussion is warranted.

Although the rational actor assumption has been widely discussed in a number of bodies of literature, it is necessary to specify exactly what this assumption does and does not entail. I will follow Abrams (1980, 10) and define a rational actor as one whose preference ordering over a set of alternatives is transitive. This assumption implies nothing about the decision rules the actors use when faced with the problem of selecting from among several strategies under conditions of risk or uncertainty. A rational player may maximize expected utility, maximize the minimum payoff, or follow any of a number of other decision rules (Luce and Raiffa 1957, chap. 13). Similarly, the rationality assumption implies nothing about the information available to the players. They may have incomplete information regarding their opponent's preference orderings or the probabilities of outcomes associated with their choices. In fact, the model is constructed as a probability model in part because of these uncertainties. This assumption implies only that the actors have transitive preference orderings over possible outcomes.

Another aspect of the rational actor assumption that must be discussed is that it requires the adoption of a unitary actor assumption. If the "actor's" preference ordering is the product of the collective preference orderings of a number of subactors, it is entirely possible that the collective ordering will include intransitivities (Abrams 1980, 29). Thus, if the actor under analysis is a collection of individuals, we must make some assumption that removes the possibility of intransitivities in the collective preference ordering. This assumption can be quite restrictive, particularly if there are several issues at stake, in which case even the assumption of single-peaked preferences is not sufficient to ensure transitivity (McKelvey 1979; Plott 1967). Adopting a rational actor assumption thus requires that we assume that the actors are unitary, under the direction of a single dominant leader, or that any collection of individuals an actor comprises be homogeneous with respect to their preferences (Bueno de Mesquita 1981, 15).

In the international relations literature, this feature of the rationality assumption is generally taken to mean that rational models force us to adopt a "nation-state as unitary actor" assumption (Allison 1971). This assumption has opened the use of rational models to a great deal of, only partially justified, criticism. It is clearly the case that nation-states, or even the leadership of nation-states, are not characterized by homogeneous preference orderings among their members. This fact does not invalidate the use of rational models, however. There is, in fact, nothing inherent in the rationality assumption that dictates the choice of the nation-state as the actor. Subnational units could be the actors under consideration, as could individuals. The model developed here could be constructed in a manner that treats subnational actors as the unit of analysis; however, considerations other than the requirements of rational models will lead to a focus on nation-states as actors.

Perhaps the most frequent criticism of the use of rational models rests on the assertion that in the real world decisions simply are not always rational. In part, these criticisms are a product of a misuse of empiricism. It is an easy matter to enumerate decisions that, in retrospect, were irrational in the sense that some other action could have brought about a better outcome; however, given our definition of rationality, the situation at hand, and the decision rule in use, it is possible that these decisions were rational. A more damaging form of this criticism comes from the body of research showing the impact on decisions of bureaucratic, psychological, social psychological, and other nonrational factors (see, e.g., George 1980; Janis 1972; Jervis 1976; Quattrone and Tversky 1988). To the extent that these factors do influence decisions, rational models will lead to imperfect explanations and predictions of international behavior.

Rational models can be defended against these charges in a number of ways. One approach is to consider rational models to be "as if" models (Friedman 1968; Bueno de Mesquita 1981, 32). That is, we assume that actors behave *as if* they are rational even though they may not be so. The essence of such a defense rests in the premise that even if the actors are not rational, it is still possible that propositions derived from a model incorporating a rationality assumption could be borne out empirically. Thus, assuming the actors behave as if they are rational could lead to a useful explanatory and predictive theory. Other defenses are to claim that the models are prescriptive; they tell us how we should behave or that they are "approximately" descriptive, that is, in the aggregate people will more often than not behave rationally (Marschak 1974, 5–6). The basis for this argument is that the rationality assumption can lead to an ideal type model that serves as a standard against which we can evaluate actual behavior. The models can be used to determine what should be done or the extent to which what was done was rational.

I prefer a slightly different argument. We must keep in mind that the purpose of constructing a model of some social phenomenon is not to mirror reality exactly. Rather, the purpose is to provide a building block toward a theory of, in this case, the causes of war. This early step in the development of our understanding does not require that our assumptions precisely conform to the full complexity of the real world; in fact, since we wish to develop a parsimonious model, we are required to adopt some assumptions that oversimplify reality. Thus, to assume that the actors are rational should not be taken as an assertion that actors are rational, or even that they behave as if they are rational; it is merely a simplifying assumption imposed to make the model more manageable. To see the usefulness of such an assumption, it is necessary only to consider the alternative. It is a simple enough task to argue that nonrational factors play an important role in decision making, but constructing a model that incorporates these factors in explanations and predictions of behavior is another story. It would be necessary to specify what nonrational factors are important, under what circumstances they are important, how they interact, and precisely what effect they bring about. It is therefore better to begin with the simplifying assumption of rational actors while keeping in mind that we may later wish to relax this assumption to develop a more accurate model.

The second basic assumption underlying this study is that the nation-state is the appropriate unit of analysis. As noted above, this does create some difficulty in that nation-states are not unitary actors. The adoption of this assumption can be defended on two points. First, given the nature of the problem under consideration, this assumption actually does relatively little disservice to reality. Since we are dealing with cases in which vital national interests are at stake, it is likely that decision makers will unite behind a decision reached even though there may have been much disagreement before the decision (Bueno de Mesquita 1981, 20–29). Although there was much disagreement among American decision makers over the proper course of action during the Cuban Missile Crisis, once the decision for the blockade was reached, the members of the Executive Committee of the National Security

Council (EXCOM) presented a unified front. Thus, to the extent that there are intransitivities in the social preference ordering, any behavioral impact should be negligible. Particularly during crises, which are the focus of this study, the actions that occur can be viewed as having been taken by the nation-state.

Second, and more importantly, this assumption is adopted to keep the model manageable: the fewer the actors, the simpler the explication of the model. With three actors, the model remains fairly manageable; but as actors are added, it becomes increasingly complex. If subnational actors were the unit of analysis, the number of actors would increase dramatically, even in a two-nation conflict. Paige (1969, 467) has determined that there are regularly around fifteen decision makers involved in crisis decisions; thus, the analysis of a conflict between two nation-states would require the inclusion of some twenty to thirty actors in the model if each individual were treated as an actor. Although it is undoubtedly the case that a complete understanding of international behavior will require the consideration of within-nation bargaining as well as across-nation bargaining (McGinnis and Williams 1992; North and Choucri 1983), the necessity of keeping the initial model simple dictates that the focus in this book remain on the latter.

An Issue Space Representation of Conflict Situations

In at least one important respect, the study of voting addresses a problem similar to that faced in the study of international crises; that is, the situation is one in which there exists, among interdependent actors, a conflict of interests that must be resolved. The spatial theory of voting (Enelow and Hinich 1984; Hinich, Ledyard, and Ordeshook 1973; Hinich and Pollard 1981; Ordeshook 1976) has been developed primarily as a means for increasing our understanding of how individual preferences are aggregated into social choices when these choices are arrived at through some prespecified voting rule. Although the social choice mechanism electorates use differs from that crisis participants use, the theoretical representation of conflict situations that has proven useful for the study of voting can also be used to depict the situation in which crisis participants find themselves. In this section, I will show how the conflicts underlying international crises can be represented spatially.

The model represents the conflict situation through the use of an *m*-dimensional space where each axis represents one of the issues involved in the dispute. These issues will usually be the values under contention in the crisis (e.g., the number of Soviet missiles to remain in Cuba) or other issues brought into the bargaining for linkage purposes (the number of U.S. missiles to remain in Turkey). By definition, all possible solutions for a given issue are arrayed on the dimension representing that issue and, as will be discussed below, the ordering of the solutions is, in some sense, meaningful. Figure 4

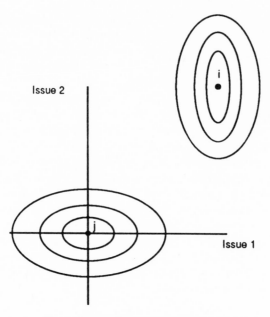

Fig. 4. A two-dimensional issue space

provides a hypothetical, two-issue example of a bargaining space. We will suppose for the purpose of discussion that issue 1 is the control over some parcel of territory and that issue 2 represents the amount of trade concessions in some colony controlled by player j that will be granted to player i.

It is important to note that the dimensions in this space may also represent intangible issues, such as the prestige or face of the bargainers. Thus, important considerations, such as these, that have been found to affect bargaining (Snyder and Diesing 1977) can be incorporated into the model. In principle, all factors influencing bargaining behavior and outcomes could be included. It is unlikely that all such issues could ever be identified, however, even for a simple case. Furthermore, the number of factors to be included in the model would become so large that any empirical applications would be impossible. Therefore, the analyses performed in this study will, for simplicity, deal with a restricted number of issues facing crisis participants.

It is assumed that for every issue involved in a conflict each participant has an outcome that is most preferred. We can locate a party to a crisis in the issue space by a point the coordinates of which represent its most preferred outcome on each issue. These points are referred to as the players' ideal points. In international crises, it is often the case that a player's true ideal point is recognized as being impossible to obtain. In the crisis leading up to the Austro-Prussian war, for example, the Prussians' most preferred outcome may have been to conquer and completely annex several of the smaller German states as well as Austria. Since they realized that the remainder of the European community would not have permitted this, no effort was made even to suggest that this outcome was being sought. Because crisis participants may often be constrained in the outcomes that feasibly can be achieved, the parties' ideal points will be taken to be their initial bargaining positions. It is undoubtedly the case that in many instances an initial offer will represent more than a bargainer hopes to achieve or less than desired. From the standpoint of the analyst, however, it is generally impossible to determine the bargainers' true ideal points; thus, it is reasonable to assume that bargainers' opening proposals represent the most they expect to achieve in the situation. In the hypothetical example provided in figure 4, there are two participants (i and j) located within the issue space. (Note that the space can contain any number of participants.) We may suppose that j, located at the origin, favors the status quo (whereby i has no trade concessions and j controls all of the territory) and that i favors certain changes (that i receives some trade concessions and some of the territory).

The Weighted Euclidean Distance Preference Rule

Just as each participant's most preferred outcome is located in the issue space by that participant's ideal point, every possible solution to the crisis can be represented in the space by a point that has, as its coordinates, the outcomes for all issues that comprise that solution. Bargaining occurs when the parties attempt to agree on a solution that is mutually acceptable, and it is assumed that a player's preferences for the various possible outcomes will affect its bargaining behavior. One important aspect of the spatial model is that the ordering of the points, which represent outcomes, in the issue space allows us to relate the distances between these points and the actors' preferences over outcomes.[14] This is accomplished through the use of the weighted Euclidean distance (WED) preference rule (Enelow and Hinich 1984, chap. 3). At this time, this rule will be explained and a number of related assumptions will be introduced.

The WED rule is best introduced by first referring to a simple example. Figure 5 represents a single-issue conflict in which the good under dispute is infinitely divisible. For the purpose of discussion, we will assume that two players, i and j, disagree about how a certain territory should be divided between them. Along the issue dimension are arrayed all possible outcomes. The end points, which represent all to j and all to i, are the players' ideal points. All intermediate points represent other divisions of the territory and are ordered such that as one moves from left to right on the dimension, i

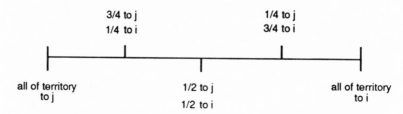

Fig. 5. A one-dimensional conflict involving an infinitely divisible good

receives an increasing proportion of the territory. If we adopt the reasonable assumption that each player always prefers an outcome in which it receives more territory to one in which it receives less, it is obvious that a player will prefer an outcome closer to its ideal point over one farther away. Stated mathematically, if x_i denotes player i's ideal point and if y and z are possible solutions to the conflict, i will prefer y to z if and only if $\|x_i - y\| < \|x_i - z\|$ where the $\| \ \|$ notation is used to denote the Euclidean distance between the points.[15] Thus, players' preference orderings over outcomes are represented by monotonically decreasing functions of the distances the outcomes are from their ideal points.

Before extending this analysis to multi-issue cases, a number of points must be addressed. First, the assumption of single-peaked preferences has been incorporated. That means that the outcomes for an issue can be arranged so that every player's preference function is monotonically decreasing in each direction from its ideal point. While an assumption of single-peakedness is not essential for the application of a spatial model, this assumption does simplify the analysis greatly. The results would be more general if all preference orderings were permissible; however, it is arguable that this assumption is reasonable and thus omits no actual cases. Virtually all of the issues in international crises involve a question of the division of some good,[16] and it seems likely that the actors will always prefer receiving more of the good to less. We can conceive of situations in which an actor prefers less of some good to more, but that is generally the result of the influence of other issues. If actor j, for example, prefers 60 percent of the territory to 80 percent, it will be because of its preferences on some other issue (e.g., the defensibility of borders) rather than because j receives more intrinsic value from the smaller area.

In this example, I avoid the question of whether the actors' preferences are symmetrical about their ideal points. Preferences over an issue are symmetrical when a player is indifferent between two points that are in opposite directions and equidistant from its ideal point. Consider another party involved in the dispute in figure 5, a mediator for example, whose ideal point is at (.5,.5). If this person is indifferent between (.6,.4) and (.4,.6), (.7,.3) and (.3,.7), and so on, his or her preferences are symmetrical. The question of whether players' preferences are symmetrical about their ideal points is not relevant for this particular example because it is a two-party conflict in which the parties' initial bargaining positions serve to limit the possible solutions. Since outcomes outside the interval delimited by the bargainers' opening proposals are not considered feasible, the bargainers' preferences for outcomes outside this range are irrelevant and the question of whether preferences are symmetrical is meaningless.[17]

The extension of this distance rule to several dimensions is fairly straightforward. Figure 6 represents a two-issue case that will guide the discussion, but the points to be made are generalizeable to any number of issues. In figure 6, issue 1 is identical to the issue in figure 5—a piece of territory must be divided between i and j. Issue 2 provides for the possibility of cash side payments and involves the amount of the sum of money involved that each player receives. The dimensions have been structured to specify the proportion of the relevant good (land or money) received by player i, and we will assume that j receives a proportion equal to 1.0 minus i's proportion. Each player's initial offer states that it shall receive all the land and all the money. We will assume that for either player and either issue, the distance-preference relationship is similar to that presented above. The problem is to specify the players' preference ordering over all possible outcomes on both issues; that is, we must reflect in the model the tradeoffs players are willing to make across issues.

The simplest rule by which we can characterize bargainers' preferences over outcomes in the issue space is the simple Euclidean distance rule, which is, in fact, an n-dimensional extension of the rule used in the single-issue case; that is, when comparing two alternatives, an actor will prefer the one that is closer in Euclidean (or straight line) distance to its ideal point. The distance between an actor's ideal point, x, and any other point in the issue space, y, can be expressed mathematically through the use of the Pythagorean theorem. The distance between two points $x = (x_1, x_2)$ and $y = (y_1, y_2)$ in a two-dimensional space can be expressed by

$$\|x - y\| = [(x_1 - y_1)^2 + (x_2 - y_2)^2]^{1/2} \qquad (2.1)$$

Naturally, this can be extended to n-dimensions. We can now extend the preference rule stated above to more than two issues. The ith player will prefer outcome y to outcome z if and only if $\|x_i - y\| < \|x_i - z\|$.

This representation of i's preferences implies that the two issues are equally salient for i. Note that, by definition, i is indifferent between any points equidistant from its ideal point. We can thus draw circles around i's

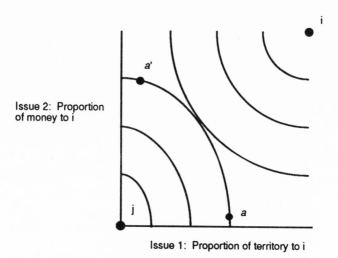

Fig. 6. Preferences in two dimensions

ideal point (actually quarter circles, since we consider only those outcomes in the feasible set) that represent i's indifference contours. We can see that, for any indifference contour, i can trade a given proportion of the territory for an equivalent proportion of the cash and will be indifferent between the two outcomes. Obviously, it is often the case that some issues will be more important than others to a player. Thus, we allow some issues to weigh more heavily than others in determining actors' preferences over outcomes through the use of the WED preference rule, which is a generalization of the simple rule presented above.

Using the WED preference rule, the distance between the points x_j (j's ideal point) and y in a two-space is defined as:

$$\|x_j - y\|_{A_j} = [a_{11}(x_{j1} - y_1)^2 + 2a_{12}(x_{j1} - y_1)(x_{j2} - y_2) + a_{22}(x_j2 - y_2)]^{1/2} \tag{2.2}$$

A_j is the two-by-two (in the two-dimensional example) matrix

$$\begin{bmatrix} a_{11} & a_{12} \\ a_{12} & a_{22} \end{bmatrix}$$

which, when multiplied by the equation providing the simple Euclidean distance, provides the weighting scheme that allows us to represent a player's different saliences for different issues. (Note that in this matrix, $a_{21} = a_{12}$.

Thus, for simplicity, I refer to both as a_{12}) The WED preference rule can now be stated as follows: A player will prefer alternative y to alternative z if and only if $\|x - y\|_A < \|x - z\|_A$. Note that if

$$A_j = \begin{bmatrix} 1 & 0 \\ 0 & 1 \end{bmatrix},$$

the identity matrix, the WED, and the simple Euclidean distances are equivalent, showing that the WED preference rule is a generalization of the simple rule used above.

If we consider cases in which $a_{12} = 0$ and $a_{11} \neq a_{22}$, we can see how the model accommodates the making of trade-offs among issues when they are not equally salient to the player.[18] Suppose that j is more concerned about maintaining control over the territory in question than about the money. This situation can be reflected by setting $a_{11} > a_{22}$, which causes j's indifference contours to be non-circular (but still elliptical) as shown in figure 6. Using figure 6 as an example, we can see that j is indifferent between points a and a'. This illustrates its willingness to forgo a relatively large proportion of the cash to gain a small segment of territory. In this manner, we can incorporate into our bargaining analyses that bargainers often are more concerned about one issue than the others. It may be the case that different issues are most salient to different actors, which, when recognized, could affect the course of bargaining by making logrolls available that can benefit all. The use of this model enables us to address this phenomenon directly. Other utility models do not disallow the possibility that the actors have different priorities across the issues at stake;[19] however, since they do not show how the utility space is related to the issues in dispute, they provide no means for directly analyzing trade-offs bargainers can make across issues of varying importance.

The calculation of the WED also enables us to consider cases in which the actors' preferences across issues are not separable. Preferences are defined as separable when an actor's preference ordering over the possible outcomes on one issue are not affected by an actual or anticipated outcome on another issue. Preferences are nonseparable when, for some reason, the actor's preference ordering on one issue depends on the outcome on another. It seems that preferences over issues involved in international crises generally are separable. As argued above, the issues can usually be interpreted as involving questions of division, and most actors seem to think that more is better on any issue, regardless of the outcome on other issues. In the Agadir crisis, for example, French preferences on the issue of German influence in Morocco did not depend on the outcome on the issue of how much tribute should be paid the Germans.

It is possible, however, to conceive of situations in which preferences are not separable. This generally occurs when some constraint exists (apart from the actions of the opponent) that prohibits an actor from achieving its most preferred outcome on all issues.[20] Thus, as the outcome moves closer to its ideal point on one issue, sacrifices must be made on others. A hypothetical example from international crises can be constructed. Suppose two issues under dispute involve the control of two different territories. Taken singly, a party to the conflict may prefer gaining more of a territory to less; however, there may be certain constraints that would make total control over both territories undesirable. Perhaps, for example, the actor's ability to rule and defend its possessions would be overextended if both were annexed. Even though we will generally assume separable preferences, it will be useful to show how the model can incorporate nonseparable preferences when that is appropriate. Figure 7 illustrates the indifference contours for a player with nonseparable preferences. We can see how these preferences can be incorporated into the model mathematically by recalling equation (2.2). Nonseparable preferences are represented by setting the interaction term to nonzero values, (i.e., $a_{12} \neq 0$). In this way, the interaction of an actor's preferences on the two issues are reflected in the weighted distances.

A Spatial Representation of the Bargaining Process

One of the more useful aspects of this bargaining model is that it provides a means of conceptualizing and describing the bargaining process. Bargaining, in general, consists of the participants' efforts to find some solution in the bargaining space to which all parties can agree. These efforts involve the making of concessions, which occur when a party moves toward its opponent by proposing an outcome closer to the opponent's ideal point, as well as attempts by each side to induce the other to accept an outcome closer to its own ideal point. These attempts to move the opponent can take any number of forms. Concessions can be made in the hope that the opponent will reciprocate, or one may try to persuade the opponent that making concessions would be in its own interest (i.e., either by convincing it that concessions on its part are necessary for a resolution to the conflict or by showing it that an outcome closer to one's own ideal point actually serves its interests better than its own proposal). In addition, uses of force short of war can be seen as attempts at inducing the opponent to move toward one's ideal point by increasing the costs involved in delaying, or failing to reach, an agreement. The issue space provides the means to trace the pattern of concessions as well as the means to show what bargainers hope to achieve, in terms of the issues involved in the conflict, by their actions.

The issue space also allows us to address a number of subjects important to the study (and practice) of bargaining that cannot be easily discussed within

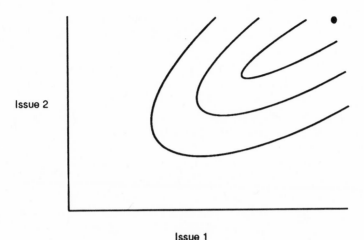

Issue 2

Issue 1

Fig. 7. Nonseparable preferences

the context of other utility models. For example, because we can specify how the actors' utility functions are related to their preferences over outcomes on the issues at stake, we can use the model to study linkage strategies. Furthermore, one aspect of bargaining over multiple issues that is often considered to affect outcomes is whether the issues are negotiated as a package or one at a time. Since this model does not conceptualize bargaining as occurring over total utilities, this topic can be addressed. These topics, and others relating to the bargaining process, will be addressed in subsequent chapters.

The Spatial Model and the Theory of Bargaining

Although actual bargaining occurs over the issues at stake, decisions to accept the opponent's proposal, make a counterproposal, or begin a war are made on the basis of the expected benefit derived from each option. While the issue space provides a useful means for representing a crisis situation and describing the bargaining process, the concept of utilities provides a useful theoretical construct with which to analyze the decisions that bargainers must make. The purpose of this section is to show how the utility space is derived from and related to the issue space.

This construction of the model represents actors involved in crises as having complete, transitive preference orderings over all possible outcomes to the conflict. I also assume that these preference orderings can be represented on an interval scale by von Neumann–Morgenstern utility functions. Thus, each outcome in the issue space can be characterized as providing a given amount of utility to each party in the conflict. This enables us to construct an n-dimensional (n = the number of actors) utility space into which every point in the issue space maps to exactly one point. We can then use this space to analyze the decisions facing bargainers.

Figure 8 can be used to illustrate the connections between the issue space and the utility space. We will, for the purpose of the example, assume two issues (generically labeled as 1 and 2) and two actors, i and j. We will also suppose that issue 1 is more salient for j and that i is more concerned with issue 2. We will set the utility functions so that when either party achieves its ideal point, the other receives 0 utility. Thus, the ideal points for i and j in the issue space map to points O_i and O_j, respectively, in the utility space. Since von Neumann–Morgenstern utility functions are invariant up to a linear transformation, that can be done without any loss of generality. Every point in the issue space maps to one point in the utility space; point a, for example, may map to $(U_j(a), U_i(a))$. It is possible, however, for more than one point in the issue space to map to the same point in the utility space. Both i and j are indifferent between a and a', so even though they actually represent different solutions to the conflict, we would expect the players to react identically to the proposition that point a be the solution and the proposition that a' be the solution. There does exist a set of points in the issue space that maps one to one to a set of points in the utility space. These are the points of tangency between the two players' indifference contours and are denoted in the issue space by the curve connecting the players' ideal points. These points are also the set of Pareto-optimal outcomes (and are analogous to a contract curve) and map to the points along the efficient frontier in the utility space.

A primary assumption of this study is that the behavior of crisis bargainers is partially motivated by the benefit they expect to derive from various possible outcomes. We can roughly categorize the responses that a crisis bargainer can make to an opponent's proposal as (1) accept the proposal, (2) continue the crisis bargaining, and (3) begin the war. Proposals that provide a bargainer with a great deal of utility are more likely to elicit response 1, while those that provide little utility are more likely to result in war. The benefit bargainers expect to receive from various possible settlements of the issues is not the only factor influencing their behavior, however. We must also consider the impact of a number of other variables, such as the background conditions in which the crisis occurs (e.g., the relative power of the participants). The problem facing the analyst is to determine which outcome(s) is most likely to be mutually acceptable to all participants, if any such outcome exists. Many previous students of bargaining have sought to accomplish this task by specifying a number of qualities that a solution should have and showing that a unique point is determined by these qualities. These axioms

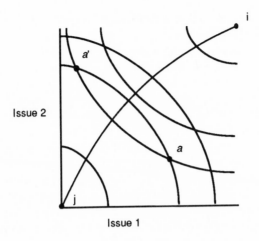

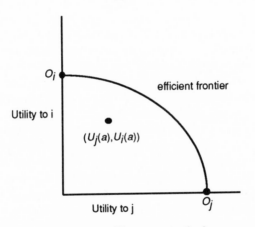

Fig. 8. Relating the utility space to the issue space

and outcomes are entirely related to the utility space, and we are forced to assume that any factor affecting bargaining behavior does so through its impact on the players' utility functions. The purpose here is to specify the impact these other factors have on crisis outcomes and to show how changes in these factors affect the predicted outcomes. In the discussion that follows, I turn to the task of showing how the model is used to arrive at its predictions regarding crisis outcomes, which requires that I introduce the other variables driving the model.

A Solution to the Bargaining Problem

The primary goal of most bargaining models is to determine a solution to the bargaining problem. In this context the term *solution* can have any of several meanings and thus can refer to a number of concepts. In some instances a solution is considered to be the value of the game, in the game-theoretic sense. As such, it specifies the amount of benefit each participant can expect to receive.[21] The solution may also be an ideal outcome in that it represents what would occur if all players behaved rationally. A slightly different but related way to view a solution is as a prediction that can be empirically verified. I take the position that this latter notion is the most useful. The model is intended to have some applicability to the real world, and one aim is to use the model to formulate testable predictions.

As argued previously, determinate solutions are not verifiable in practice. We must necessarily omit variables from the model, and there will likely be some random perturbations in bargaining outcomes. Therefore, we would expect a point prediction to usually be wrong, and we have no means by which to determine if the point prediction is good enough.[22] On the other hand, simply specifying a range into which the outcome is expected to fall is not very useful either. In this study, I will attempt to find the middle ground and construct the model in such a way that it provides a probability distribution over all possible outcomes.

This type of solution has a number of advantages over the others generally used. Since the probability of all possible outcomes is specified, the model can be used to determine the likelihood that no bargained solution, and therefore war, will result. This likelihood is exceedingly important for the purposes of this study because we are actually more interested in the question of whether a crisis will result in war than the question of what precise agreement will be reached through bargaining. This construction of the model also permits theoretical analysis of how changes in the various variables incorporated in the model affect the likelihood that war will result. Thus, to the extent that these variables are manipulable by the crisis participants, we have the potential to prescribe strategies that will enable crisis participants to avoid war.

This specification of the solution does enable us to make predictions regarding bargained outcomes, however, in that the probability distribution of all bargained outcomes is provided. We do wish to specify a point prediction so that the model can be compared to other bargaining models. For the purposes of this study, I will consider the point solution to be the point that is the most likely to be accepted by all parties (i.e., the mode of the probability distribution over outcomes). While this point will be the correct prediction more often than any other, it must be recognized that other criteria might provide better predictions (e.g., the least squares criterion would require using the mean of the distribution). The mode is used here because, as will be shown below, it is equivalent to the bargaining solutions provided by other models (Nash 1950; Zeuthen 1968). Another advantage of this model is that it can tell us what the distribution of outcomes around this point should look like. Thus, the model provides testable predictions in that we can determine if the actual distribution of outcomes matches the predicted distribution.

Finally, the construction of the model enables us to determine how changes in the variables driving the model affect the solution. We can tell not only whether a change in a critical variable moves the solution point toward a player's most preferred outcome but also how this change affects the distribution of outcomes. By focusing only on the solution point, it may appear that a certain action is advisable (because it moves the point toward one's own ideal point), whereas a focus on the entire distribution may show that this benefit comes at the expense of substantially increasing the probability of war.

To arrive at this solution, we will begin with the assumption that for every possible bargained outcome, there is some probability that each player would accept that outcome rather than go to war. For each player, we can determine a probability function over all possible outcomes that specifies the likelihood that that player will accept every solution. Once these probability functions are determined for every player, we can arrive at a joint probability distribution over all outcomes that will serve as the bargaining "solution" provided here. The point with the highest joint probability of acceptance will be our solution point, and we can determine the likelihood that no bargained solution, and therefore war, will occur. These probability of acceptance functions are determined by a number of factors, in addition to the player's utility functions over outcomes. The next section is devoted to presenting and defining those factors that will be incorporated into the model. Once that is accomplished, we will proceed with an explanation of how the probability of acceptance functions are derived and how the bargaining solutions are determined.

Variables Affecting Crisis Outcomes: Relative Power and Resolve

The solution to the bargaining problem that will be developed here requires that we determine for each possible outcome the probability that each actor would accept that outcome rather than resort to war. The variables driving the model therefore are those that affect the likelihood that an actor will accept any given proposal. Recall that the variables most frequently purported to affect bargaining outcomes are the relative resolve and power of the participants. These variables are introduced into this model as partial determinants of the willingness of bargainers to make concessions that thereby affect the probability that an actor will accept any particular outcome. Before demonstrating how we can model the effect these variables have on the probability of acceptance functions, we must define the concepts and provide, at an intuitive level, an explanation of how they should be expected to influence bargaining.

Providing clear definitions for resolve and power is not an easy task. There are numerous definitions for each in the literature, and the majority of these are ambiguous. A common fallacy, particularly when considering *power*, is to associate the term being defined with the outcomes we are trying to explain. Many analysts, for example, begin with the assumption that the most powerful bargainer wins and then proceed to define the most powerful party as having been the side that won.[23] If one follows this approach, the task of explaining outcomes either becomes tautological or involves determining what factors made one side more powerful than the other, in which case the concept of power is not especially useful because (1) it is too broadly conceived and (2) it is indistinguishable from whatever concept of *outcomes* we are using. In this book, I attempt to avoid this pitfall by isolating some of the more important aspects of these broad notions of power and resolve and providing more precise conceptual (and ultimately operational) definitions of those aspects to be used as theoretical constructs.

As noted above, a number of conceptualizations of *bargaining power* include anything that affects the chances of a bargainer's success. Whether a bargainer prevails over its opponent because it had more resources or because it was more resolved, we tend to say it won because it had more power. Following this reasoning, power is often generally defined as an ability to get what one wants even in the face of opposition (Russett and Starr 1985, 130). My claim is that such a notion of power is less useful than one that specifies *how* power affects an actor's ability to prevail. This notion requires that we define power much more narrowly, however, since a broad definition would require that we show how each aspect plays in the determination of a winner. Here, the conceptualization of *power* is closely linked to the expectation of how power should affect outcomes and, as we will see, the power variable is divided into its component parts.

The first thing we must recognize about power is that it is a characteristic of a relationship. It makes little sense to state that A is powerful, unless we specify in relation to whom. Furthermore, a power relationship is not a trichotomy; that is, it is not simply the case that either A and B are equal in power or one has greater power than the other. The power relationship is more usefully seen as comprising a continuum, so we can determine if A has 1.2 times the power that B has, or twice the power that B has, and so on. This conceptualization allows us to assume not that the more powerful will win but that as one party increases its power relative to the other, it increases the probability that it will win.

In this study we will consider two related but analytically distinct aspects of power (in addition to treating resolve as a separate variable). The immediate aim is to present intuitive arguments concerning how these variables are expected to affect bargaining behavior and outcomes and to show what constitutes these types of power for bargainers in international crises.

One important characteristic of international crises is that if the participants fail to reach an agreement through bargaining, war will result. The likely outcome of such a war will affect the parties' willingness to make bargaining concessions; thus, the parties' relative war-making capabilities are one aspect of their power relationship.[24] One way of viewing this relationship is that if one of the participants has a higher probability of winning a war, we would expect it to be less willing to make bargaining concessions. If it can, in fact, achieve all its objectives through war, it should be willing to make concessions only to avoid the costs inherent in fighting. Conversely, the other side would be better off with any negotiated settlement (since it could achieve none of its objectives through war and would also suffer the costs of fighting) and thus would be expected to concede much. Unfortunately, real-life situations are never so clear cut. In the first place, which side will win is seldom certain. Unless one side has an overwhelming share of the total military capabilities, many other factors, including luck, can affect the outcome of a war. In the second place, it is not entirely clear what *winning* even means. It is certainly not the case that the only possible outcomes of war are the parties' ideal points. Any of the feasible outcomes could result, and the outcome of war does not even necessarily have to have been in the bargaining set. The bargaining set is bounded by the players' initial offers, while, through war, one party may be able to impose a solution it prefers more than its original offer.

A more meaningful way to view this aspect of power is to assume that the likely outcomes of a war can be expressed as a probability distribution, the shape of which is determined by the relative capabilities of the disputants.[25] For the purpose of illustration, consider the single-issue conflict represented in figure 9. If the two parties have equal capabilities, this distribution of outcomes may be normal with an expected value at the midpoint between the two parties' ideal points. If j, for example, has greater capabilities than i, the expected value of the distribution will shift toward j's ideal point and the distribution will become skewed toward i. One such distribution is denoted by the dashed line in figure 9. We would expect that as this distribution shifts in one player's favor, that player will become increasingly less willing to make concessions simply because that player would stand to gain an increasing amount from a failure to agree and, for opposite reasons, the other would become more willing to concede. The model is constructed to reflect this expectation; however, the precise relationship remains an empirical question.

A second way in which a bargainer's power is often considered to affect

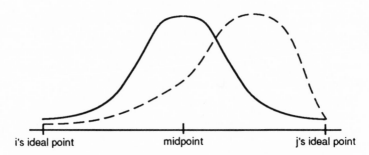

i's ideal point   midpoint   j's ideal point

Fig. 9. Possible probability distributions of war outcomes. Solid line represents situation in which capabilities are equal. Dashed line represents a case in which j has greater capabilities.

bargaining behavior and outcomes is through its ability to impose costs on its opponent and to resist the imposition of costs by the opponent. In international crises, the notion of *costs* generally refers to the parties' abilities to inflict damage on one another through military means (such as bombardments, ship sinkings, occupations of territory, etc.). The notion of exercising power through the imposition of costs is more general, however, and also refers to a player's ability to harm its opponent through economic sanctions, damaging its political reputation (perhaps, for example, by gaining support for a UN resolution condemning the opponent), and so on.[26] When one party is able to impose significant costs on its opponent (through both its own ability to do so and the opponent's inability to resist), the opponent should be willing to make bargaining concessions. The ultimate outcome is less valuable to a bargainer the longer it has to suffer these costs; thus, it should be willing to accept immediately something less than its ideal point simply to avoid paying the costs. The greater these costs are, the greater the difference between the ideal point and the proposal that would be immediately acceptable.

There are two important things to note about this aspect of bargaining power. First, the ability of one party to impose costs on its opponent is conceptually independent of the opponent's ability to impose costs on it. This aspect of power is still a characteristic of a relationship, but there are two components, each of which compares the ability of one player to impose costs to the ability of the other to resist. However, this aspect of power can change for one party without changing for the other. That is, i's ability to impose costs on j may increase (making j more prone to making concessions) while j's ability to impose costs on i remains constant. Thus, this element of power must be reflected in the model by two (for a two-party case) independent variables.

Second, while this aspect of power probably covaries with the probability distributions over war outcomes (since both largely depend on the same factors, such as military capabilities and economic strength), they are analytically distinct. We expect them to affect bargaining behavior in different ways, and we can see that any relationship between them is not perfect. In the Oregon boundary dispute, it was generally believed that the British position was indefensible and that they would probably lose the territory as a result of war. Because of the British mastery of the seas, however, they could have caused great harm to the United States (primarily through the disruption of trade but also by projecting their power to American shores), while the Americans could have done relatively little harm to the British (they could possibly have caused British prestige to suffer somewhat and inflicted some damage on, or through, Canada, but actually damaging Britain would have been impossible). Thus, while the Americans had an advantage in one type of power, the British had the advantage in the other. Since these aspects of power relationships between crisis participants are distinct, it will be useful to distinguish them in the model.

Coming to grips with the meaning of resolve and how bargainers' resolve affects crisis outcomes is a more arduous task than was dealing with power. *Resolve* is even less clearly defined in the literature and, in many respects, seems to correspond closely with other concepts. One way of viewing a player's resolve is in terms of the salience of the issues. That may be part of what we mean, but it is certainly not all of the concept. Many prescriptive arguments regarding resolve suggest that a bargainer should commit to a position to demonstrate, or even create, resolve. If resolve refers to the salience the issues have for the actor, it is intrinsic in the situation, and efforts to commit oneself to one's position would be at best worthless and at worst foolish (if the commitment resulted in tying one to a position on an issue that was actually unimportant). In any case, this aspect of resolve is incorporated into the model since the actors' preference orderings over possible outcomes are determined by how dearly they hold the values under contention.

Resolve may also refer, in some sense, to the risk orientation of a player. A highly resolved player may, in the hopes of achieving an ideal outcome, prefer to run the risk of war over settling for a certain, intermediate outcome. However, risk orientation also fails to capture the full essence of what we generally mean by *resolve*. An actor may be risk averse (defined in the standard sense) and still be determined to prevail. Such an actor may run the risk of war not because of risk acceptance but because it is necessary to achieve one's aims. In addition, we must recognize that in some cases war may be the least risky alternative. We may conclude that this too is part but not all of what we mean by resolve. In any case, the risk orientation of the actors is also reflected in the model through the shape of the actors' utility functions.

It may seem that we should equate resolve with determination. People generally seem to place great value on winning for its own sake. This value goes beyond the benefit gained from achieving one's aims on the issues (including intangible issues, such as prestige), and there seems to be another side to this value in that we also feel that losing, in itself, is costly—even beyond the value of the losses on the issues. This determination to get one's way can vary from actor to actor and even within the same actor across different situations.[27] Part of this determination to win (or to force a stalemate so that the opponent does not win) may be motivated by a desire to enhance one's bargaining reputation or prestige. Other motivations do come into play, however, and a great deal of a player's resolve as determination may be due solely to the values placed on winning and losing in and of themselves.

It would seem that each of these factors is one aspect of what is usually considered to be resolve. All but the last are already incorporated into the model in one way or another; thus, we need only to show how bargainers' determination affects their willingness to accept given proposals. This determination could be expressed in either of two ways—positively (bargainers are determined to win) or negatively (bargainers are determined not to lose). The latter actually seems more appropriate for crisis bargaining. It would imply that the bargainer is unwilling to accept outcomes close to the opponent's ideal point (even if the value of the outcome is higher than the expected value of war), whereas the former expression implies that a bargainer would be unwilling to make any concessions from its own ideal point. Since parties to international crises are able to claim victory even if the outcome is merely close to their ideal point, even a highly determined actor could make some concessions and the negative expression is more reasonable. The primary goal seems to be to avoid a situation in which the opponent can claim victory and one cannot; therefore, a bargainer's determination is to not accept an outcome too close to the opponent's ideal point. Thus, this aspect of resolve will be incorporated into the model through its effect on determining the possible outcomes that a bargainer would reject with certainty.

Determining the Bargaining Solution

To this point I have argued that the appropriate way to address the bargaining problem is to determine a probability distribution for all possible outcomes and that this distribution should be a function of the willingness of the bargainers to accept various proposals. I have introduced the variables that will be incorporated into the model, and I have shown how we expect these variables to affect bargainers' willingness to make concessions. We may now turn to the problem of illustrating how the model can be used to arrive at bargaining solutions. Although the model is designed to provide a probability distribution over all outcomes, we are particularly interested in two: the probability that war will occur and the most probable bargaining outcome. I will refer to the two-player example shown in figure 10. This analysis is generalizeable to situations involving more than two parties, but we will focus on this case to facilitate the presentation. Note also that only the utility space is presented. That is because this aspect of the bargaining analysis is performed entirely within the utility space; the issue space will be reintroduced below.

In using the model to derive bargaining solutions, we focus on the utility the bargainers receive from the various possible outcomes. We will suppose that for each proposal, π, in the utility space, we can determine the probability that each player would accept it rather than resort to war. Once that is accomplished, we can determine a joint probability distribution over all π that will specify the probability that each outcome will occur.[28] The π that maximizes this joint probability distribution will be our solution point, and we can calculate the probability that war will result. It should again be noted that nothing currently in the model specifies what offers, π, are made, when they are made, or by whom they are made. Any number of theories could be devised specifying particular patterns of offers, but each would be open to

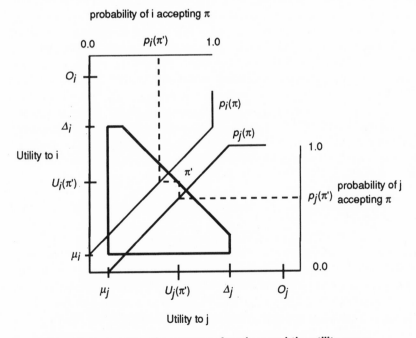

Fig. 10. Probability of acceptance functions and the utility space

criticism. My aim is to develop a theory of crises that is sufficiently general to subsume *any* such theory of moves so that the conclusions presented here will hold regardless of from whence specific offers derive. The cost, of course is that the theory cannot tell us much about the specific bargaining offers that should be expected in particular crises. Since my aim is to understand how the contexts in which crises occur affect their outcomes, this is not a severe cost, though it does point out an avenue for future research should the model prove useful.

Our first task is to specify, for each player, a function over all π that provides the probability of accepting each given π. This exercise is the same for each player; thus, it will be described only for i. Recall that a player's willingness to accept any given π is assumed to be a function of four things: the utility loss (relative to the constrained ideal point) associated with π, the costs involved in delaying or failing to reach an agreement, the probability distribution over war outcomes, and the player's resolve. Each of these will be discussed in turn.

The first factor that is assumed to influence a bargainer's willingness to accept any proposal is the amount of benefit it expects to receive from such a proposal. This benefit is reflected in the model by the player's utility functions, and we can see in figure 10 that I have represented the probability that a player would choose some π over war as a function of that player's utility for π. If we take some π in the utility space, we can determine the amount of utility it provides i on the vertical axis and the amount it provides j on the horizontal axis. Taking i as an example, we can then determine the probability that it would accept that π, or some other π that provided equal utility, by finding out what probability of acceptance is associated with such a utility payoff. Note, in figure 10, the dashed lines from π' to the probability of acceptance functions and then to the probability of acceptance scales, across the top for i and on the right side for j. The probability that i would accept π', or any other π that provides equal utility, is denoted by the point $p_i(\pi')$. We will assume that the probability that a player would accept some π always decreases (or at least remains constant) as the utility loss for π increases. A player will accept its initial offer (O_i or O_j) with certainty and will accept anything providing less utility with a $p \leq 1.0$.

By far the simplest construction of the model would be to adopt the assumption that the players are pure expected utility maximizers. Such a player would make a decision on the basis of a comparison of the utility provided by the proposed π with the expected utility of the alternative, war. We could then calculate the expected value of war by subtracting the costs of fighting from the value of the expected outcome and compare this expected utility with the utility of any π. The probability of acceptance function would take on one of two values—it would be 1.0 if $U(\pi) > EU(\text{war})$ and 0.0 if

$U(\pi) < EU(\text{war})$. I accept this model as the basis for the model presented here but incorporate a number of modifications that show the impact of other factors that affect bargaining.

Rather than assume that the utility that a player gets from a specific proposal determines exactly whether the proposal will be accepted (depending on its relationship to the expected value of war), I will adopt an assumption very similar to that used by Zeuthen (1968). A player will, with certainty, reject any π of less utility than the expected utility of war, but it will not necessarily accept with certainty any π of greater utility.[29] If π is less than the utility associated with its ideal point, the player will be willing to accept some probability of war to have a chance at obtaining a better deal. The closer the outcome associated with π is to the player's ideal point, the less chance of war it will be willing to accept (since little more could be gained by holding out) and thus the higher the probability that the outcome would be accepted.

The other factors presumed to affect bargaining behavior will determine the upper and lower limits as well as the shape of the probability of acceptance functions. We may suppose that there is some point at which the utility provided by π is sufficiently great that the player would accept π with certainty. Since it is inconceivable that a player would refuse its initial offer,[30] we know that for i, O_i would be accepted with certainty. Thus, we may set O_i as the upper bound for the probability of acceptance function. Since the act of holding out would definitely involve costs, it is likely that i would be willing to accept, with certainty, some πs that provide less utility than O_i to achieve an immediate settlement. It is at this point that we can introduce power, in terms of one party's ability to impose costs on the other, into the model. To the extent that j is able to make i suffer, i should be willing to accept less utility than its ideal point provides. The points representing the π providing the lowest utility a player would accept with certainty are denoted by Δ_i and Δ_j (for i and j respectively). The better able j is to impose costs on i (or the less able i is to resist), the further Δ_i will be from O_i. Recall, however, that O_i represents i's initial offer. It may be that O_i involves a significant loss of utility, compared with the true ideal point; therefore, Δ_i may equal O_i, even though j is able to impose significant costs on i. Δ_i actually represents the utility point equivalent to the utility of the costs j can impose on i subtracted from i's *true* ideal point. In the Cuban Missile Crisis, for example, Kennedy felt that removing the Soviet missiles was so imperative that he was unwilling to make any significant concessions. Thus, although the Soviets had the capabilities to impose significant costs on the United States, $\Delta_{us} = O_{us}$.

The lower bound, as stated above, is the point at which the utility provided by π becomes less than that provide by the expected value of war. This specification requires assuming that the players are risk neutral. This assumption somewhat simplifies the analysis. It is not essential to the model, and we may, in future research, wish to examine the effects of assuming risk-averse or risk-acceptant actors. There are situations in which πs providing more utility than $EU(\text{war})$ will definitely be rejected, however. Resolve has been defined as a bargainer's determination not to lose. This definition implies that a bargainer will, to the degree that it is resolved, be unwilling to accept outcomes that provide some greater utility than the expected value of war. This unwillingness is built into the model at this point by setting the point at which a bargainer will reject π with certainty, μ_i and μ_j, at $EU(\text{war})$ plus some factor that reflects the actors' resolve.

We have now established the bounds of the probability of acceptance functions. A player, i, for example, will accept any π providing utility greater than or equal to Δ_i with certainty and will reject (thereby accepting war[31]) any π providing utility less than μ_i. The shape of the probability functions remains to be determined. We know that the function will be monotonically decreasing from Δ to μ since any π providing less utility is less likely to be accepted than one providing more. If the function decreases rapidly near Δ_i, it would mean that i was very reluctant to make any concessions (since even points fairly close to Δ_i would have a low probability of acceptance). Conversely, if it decreases very slowly near Δ_i and more rapidly near μ_i, it would reflect a case in which i is fairly willing to concede much. We can thus use the shape of the functions to represent the power relationship in terms of whom is likely to prevail in war. Since the side more likely to win will be willing to concede little, its probability function will be convex with respect to its O. The other side must necessarily be willing to concede more, and its function will be concave with respect to its O. If the sides are equal in this aspect of power, both functions will be linear, like in figure 10. The infinite range of such power relationships can be reflected by altering the pairs of functions. As player i, for example, increases the likelihood it would prevail in war, we can increase the rapidity with which its function falls near Δ_i and decrease the rapidity with which its opponent's function falls near Δ_j.

In general, the probability of acceptance functions are in the form

$$p_i(\pi) = \left[\begin{array}{ll} 0.0, & \pi > \mu_i \\ -(b_{i1}\pi^n + b_{i2}\pi^{n-1} + , \ldots, + b_{in}\pi - a_i), & \Delta_i < \pi \le \mu_i \\ 1.0, & \pi \le \Delta_i \end{array} \right]$$

$$p_j(\pi) = \left[\begin{array}{ll} 0.0, & \pi < \mu_j \\ b_{j1}\pi^n + b_{j2}\pi^{n-1} + , \ldots, + b_{jn}\pi - a_j, & \mu_j \le \pi < \Delta_j \\ 1.0, & \pi \ge \Delta_j \end{array} \right]$$

Since we are primarily interested in the portion of these functions for which the probability of acceptance is greater than 0 and less than 1, however, I will generally consider these functions to be defined by the middle terms. Naturally, one must keep in mind that this specification only refers to the interval between a player's μ and Δ.

One important aspect regarding the probability of acceptance functions is that, at this point, the exact probabilities are exogenous to the model. I have not made any assumptions regarding, for example, the information available to the actors or the estimation procedures they use to evaluate an opponent's likely course of action, on which endogenous probabilities could be based. That simplifies the analyses performed in this book without limiting them in any way. The aim is to show how changes in the independent variables affect the probability distribution over outcomes; that is, our interest is *not* in determining precise probabilities but rather in determining how these distributions *change* with changes in the variables of interest. Since the results are fully general (i.e., they hold for any specific probability functions), they apply to any version of the model for which the probabilities are endogenously derived. Naturally, if the model is to be used for certain other types of purposes, such as identifying equilibrium strategies or specifying concession rates, some method for deriving the probabilities endogenously would have to be devised.

Now that I have shown, in general, how each player's probability of acceptance function is specified, it is time to show how these functions are combined to provide the "solution" to the bargaining problem. The product of these functions provides a joint distribution function over all possible outcomes, and we are particularly interested in two aspects of this distribution: the point most likely to be accepted by both parties and the probability that war will result. Note that there exists a set of points in which any negotiated settlement must be included. This set of proposals constitutes the range of practicable bargains and is called the bargaining set in this book. Any proposal not in this set could not be a negotiated settlement because it would definitely be rejected by at least one of the parties or because it would be impossible to obtain.[32] In figure 10, the bargaining set comprises those points within the triangle bounded by the efficient frontier above and those points providing utility equal to one or both players' reservation points, μ_i and μ_j, below and on the left. The specification of the two aspects of the solution distribution in which we are interested involves (1) finding the proposal within the bargaining set that is most likely to be accepted by both parties and (2) calculating the probability that no proposal in the bargaining set would be accepted by both parties, thereby leading to war.

Determining the point most likely to be accepted is a straightforward maximization problem. For each party i, we have defined a probability of acceptance function over the set of all possible proposals, Π ($\pi \in \Pi$), which can be denoted as $p_i(\pi)$. The product of the probability of acceptance functions provides the joint probability of acceptance function over all Π. Since the proposal, π', with the highest joint probability of acceptance will be our solution point,[33] we wish to find the π' that maximizes the joint probability that all players will accept it. For a two-party situation, this involves finding the π' within the bargaining set that satisfies

$$\left(p_i(\pi) \cdot \frac{\partial p_j(\pi)}{\partial \pi} \right) + \left(p_j(\pi) \cdot \frac{\partial p_i(\pi)}{\partial \pi} \right) = 0. \tag{2.3}$$

Naturally, this equation is generalizable to n players.

We can better understand this bargaining solution with reference to a simple example. Figure 11 represents a two-party situation in which an additional restrictive assumption is imposed—the division of the values under dispute is zero sum.[34] The zero-sum condition allows us to represent the utility any proposal provides to both players on a single axis since, by definition, once we know the payoff to one player, we can determine the payoff to the other. This assumption is made solely to simplify the visual representation of the situation. I will also arbitrarily assign numerical values to the parameters of the model and specify the probability of acceptance functions for the players in this example. That too is done solely to facilitate the discussion of the example; note that this in no way detracts from the generality of the solution presented above.

In figure 11 I have set the points at which the players would definitely accept π, Δ_i and Δ_j, as equal to 0.0 and 1.2, respectively.[35] The reservation points, μ_i and μ_j, which constitute the bounds of the bargaining set, have been placed at 0.2 and 1.0. The probability of acceptance functions are $p_i(\pi) = -\pi + 1$ (within the interval $[\Delta_i, \mu_i]$) and $p_j(\pi) = \pi - .2$ (within the interval $[\mu_j, \Delta_j]$). Given this construction, we can apply equation (2.3) to determine the solution point for this example. The joint probability distribution, $p_{ij}(\pi)$, is $(-\pi + 1)(\pi - .2) = -\pi^2 + 1.2\pi - 0.2$, the derivative of which is $-2\pi + 1.2$. Solving for $-2\pi + 1.2 = 0$, we find that π', the most likely negotiated settlement, equals 0.6.

There are two things particularly worth noting about this example. First, $|O_j - \Delta_j| = |O_i - \Delta_i|$, $|O_j - \mu_j| = |O_i - \mu_i|$, and the probability of acceptance functions are linear. Thus, the situation in which the bargainers find themselves is perfectly symmetrical. The solution point, π', is midway between O_i and O_j—exactly where our intuition would suggest the solution to a symmetrical situation should be. Second, recall that the bargaining solution is actually a probability distribution over all outcomes in the bargaining set. The shape of this distribution (which is given by the joint probability of acceptance function) for this example is illustrated in figure 11b. Notice that the symmetrical bargaining situation results in a symmetrical distribution of

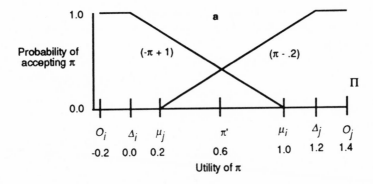

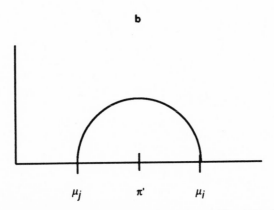

Fig. 11. *a)* **A utility space representation of a zero-sum conflict;** *b)* **Probability distribution of negotiated outcomes**

negotiated settlements. Since the notion of symmetry implies that the bargainers cannot be distinguished, we would expect the actual bargaining outcomes in such situations to be distributed symmetrically about the solution point.

We can now turn to the task of showing how the model specifies the probability that a crisis will end in war. Essentially, this task involves using the actors' probability of acceptance functions to determine the likelihood that neither player would accept a proposal that is minimally acceptable to the other. For some player, i, and any proposal in the utility space, π^*, we can interpret the probability of acceptance function as specifying the probability that π^* or some $\pi < \pi^*$ is the proposal providing the least utility that i would accept rather than run the risk of war. That is, if we consider a proposal, $\pi^* > \mu_i$, there is some probability that it is truly the least amount of utility that i would prefer to the chance of war. This probability is less than the probability that i would accept π^*, however, since some $\pi < \pi^*$ may be the true minimally acceptable point, in which case π^* would also be acceptable. Thus, for each $\pi^* + e$, the probability that it is the true minimally acceptable offer is marginally greater than the probability that π^* is such an offer. We can therefore equate the probability of acceptance functions with cumulative distribution functions. The derivatives of these functions would then be probability density functions (PDFs), and we can determine the proportion of each player's PDF that is within the bargaining range. The product of these proportions for all players would then provide the probability that the crisis would not end in war, and naturally, subtracting this probability from 1.0 would give us the probability that war would result. Using $p'(\pi)$ to represent the derivative of $p(\pi)$, we can state this mathematically for two-player, zero-sum cases such as that represented in figure 11 fairly simply:

$$
p(\text{war}) = 1 - \left(\frac{\int_{\mu_j}^{\mu_i} p_i'(\pi)}{\int_{\Delta_i}^{\mu_i} p_i'(\pi)} \cdot \frac{\int_{\mu_j}^{\mu_i} p_j'(\pi)}{\int_{\mu_j}^{\Delta_j} p_j'(\pi)} \right) \tag{2.4}
$$

The determination of the probability of war is generalizeable to non-zero-sum cases; however, a single function that would provide an algorithm to determine this probability in every case would be quite detailed. The precise functional form is contingent on a number of factors, primarily concerning which sections of an actor's PDF are within the bargaining range, so a complete function would require a specification of the probability of war for every possible combination of factors. I will not attempt to specify such a function here;[36] suffice it to say that the calculations for any specific case are a straightforward matter of determining the proportion of each player's PDF that is within the bargaining range and subtracting the product of these proportions for all players from 1.0. The determination of this aspect of our solution is also generalizeable to cases in which there are more than two actors. This calculation simply involves determining the proportion of each actor's PDF that is within the bargaining set and subtracting the product of all such proportions from 1.0.

Equations (2.3) and (2.4) constitute the heart of the specification of the model. They represent the mathematical statement of the assumptions I have made regarding how certain variables characterizing crisis situations affect crisis outcomes. I have tried to justify the particular specification as consistent with a reasonable conceptualization of the variables included, but I recognize that the manner in which I have specified these assumptions is open to question. One might argue, for example, that the impact of the distribution of capabilities variable should be reflected in the location of the μs rather than through the shape of the functions. Much of the problem stems from the fact that I am trying to offer specific assumptions regarding concepts that, though commonly found in the literature, are extremely ambiguous. Thus, my understanding of *power* or *resolve* may not jibe with someone else's. While I believe that my specification of the assumptions is reasonable, the justification for the model ultimately rests with the conclusions it produces. If the model increases our understanding of international crises and if its expectations are supported by the empirical evidence, then we may conclude that the specific assumptions are better than alternative constructions. One purpose of subsequent chapters is to establish this point.

Comparing the Spatial Bargaining Model to Previous Models

The purpose of this chapter to this point has been to present the basic model used in this study. I have discussed the variables that the model comprises, the manner in which the model represents bargaining situations, and how the model is used to make predictions regarding bargaining outcomes. It remains for me to show how this construction can be used to deduce testable propositions regarding the effects changes in the key variables have on the crisis outcomes. Before turning to these analyses, however, it will be useful to discuss how this model corresponds with, and diverges from, other formal bargaining models. The discussion in this section will focus on showing how this model improves our ability to conceptualize and analyze bargaining in international crises.

The most obvious improvement made by the model proposed here is the use of the issue space to represent the conflict situation underlying a crisis. Previous models assume that actors' preference orderings over possible outcomes can be represented by utility functions, but they do not explicitly establish a direct linkage between the issues under dispute and the utility functions used in the analyses. Pen (1952) comes closest to showing how the issues involved affect bargaining in that the basis of his model are his ophelimity functions. In the process of describing these functions, he shows (in an abstract way) how the concerns of the bargainers are related to the concessions they are willing to make. By constructing his model so that "all factors" influencing bargaining are included, however, he precludes the possibility of specifying the exact relationship between the actors' positions on the issues and their preferences over outcomes. Thus, we are still unable to use his model to deduce any hypotheses relating the actors' issue positions to bargaining behavior and outcomes.

The use of the issue space in this model provides two particular benefits. First, it provides for the description of specific cases within the conceptual framework provided by the model (examples can be found in the Appendix). This description helps to establish a link between the model and the real world, which, by making our analyses less abstract, increases the conceptual usefulness of the model. Second, the specificity of the linkage between the issues and the bargainers' utility functions enables us to analyze important aspects of the bargaining situation. In particular, we are able to deduce hypotheses concerning the effects of issue linkages and of the importance of the order in which issues are settled. We can, for example, use this model to make predictions concerning the effect on bargaining of such events as the United States' offer to settle the Oregon Boundary Dispute on terms favorable to the British in exchange for British help in acquiring a portion of California from Mexico. Other models would presumably treat such linkage attempts as partial determinants of the bargainers' utility functions, but they do not directly specify the impact on the actors' preferences brought about by such an offer.

The benefit brought about by directly incorporating actors' issue positions into the model does involve a cost, however. By using a less abstract model, we are unable to assume that all factors influencing the bargainers' utility functions are incorporated. For this reason, our bargaining solutions cannot be determinate. Since such solutions are essentially unverifiable, this cost is slight, particularly in relation to the benefit of having a model that can lead to testable hypotheses concerning a number of additional phenomena.

In comparing the bargaining solutions provided by the various models, we find a great deal of similarity with the differences that do exist being a product of how *solution* is conceptualized. Harsanyi (1956) has shown, for example that the Nash (1950) and Zeuthen (1968) solutions are mathematically equivalent. Since the Nash solution is so intuitively reasonable for the situations in which his assumptions apply, it is useful to show that the model presented in this book provides an identical solution when similar conditions are imposed. Were it to provide a different solution in such a situation, the utility of the model would be highly suspect.

To show that this model can provide a solution equivalent to Nash's when his axioms are met, I will once again refer to the zero-sum example presented in figure 11. For the purposes of this discussion, we may ignore the numerical values previously assigned to the parameters and treat this as a general zero-sum, symmetrical case. Notice that all of Nash's axioms are met: (1) In constructing my model I have assumed that actors' preferences can be represented by von Neumann–Morgenstern utility functions. (2) The zero-sum assumption implies Pareto optimality. (3) The situation is, by construction, symmetrical. (4) Given that the bargaining set must be convex and compact (Nash 1950) and the symmetry assumption, independence of irrelevant alternatives is implied.[37] We can best see that the solutions are equivalent by pointing out that one way of viewing Nash's model is directly analogous to the construction of my model. In figure 11, the horizontal axis represents the utility each player will receive, and the functions for each player provide the probability that they would accept a given amount of utility (represented on the vertical axis). We can view this figure as a representation of Nash's model, however, by interpreting the horizontal axis to represent what each player would receive on a given issue and the functions for each player as providing the utility that player would receive from a given outcome on the issue (see Hopmann 1978). My solution point is the point that maximizes the probability that both players would accept the given amount of utility (where the functions intersect), whereas Nash's solution point is the point that maximizes the product of the players' utility function (when the no-agreement point is assigned a utility of zero for each actor)—the identical point. That this model can provide a solution identical to that provided by other models when their axioms are met points out that the solution concept is intuitively reasonable.

A few other points regarding the model are worth considering. Note, for example, that while the solution does not require that we assume Pareto optimality, the solution point is always Pareto optimal. We can see that this is the case with reference to figure 10. If we take any point π^* in the bargaining set that is not on the efficient frontier (Pareto optimal), we can easily see that it cannot be the solution point. Since each player has a higher probability of accepting some π that provides that player with more utility than does π^* and since any time we can increase the probability that one player would accept π without reducing the probability of acceptance of the other we increase the joint probability of acceptance, any π closer to the efficient frontier than π^* would have a higher joint probability of acceptance than π^*, meaning that π^* could not be the solution point. However, π is limited by the efficient frontier, suggesting that the solution point must be Pareto optimal.

We thus get the benefit of the reasonableness of the assumption (i.e., that the players will consume all available utility) without having to make the implicit assumption that the players have perfect information regarding all participants' utility functions. In a similar vein, the probability distributions over all outcomes provide a means of predicting the likelihood that a Pareto-optimal outcome will not result. These benefits are made possible by the fact that the solution used here does not provide a determinate outcome. Some would consider this an enormous price; however, I believe that this solution is more realistic and empirically sound and therefore more useful. Note also that the independence of irrelevant alternatives assumption is not needed. Finally, symmetry is not assumed, which, as will be argued more fully below, allows us to develop hypotheses regarding the effect on the bargaining solution brought about by changes in the relationship among the actors.

The primary difference between the solution used in this book and that presented by others is that this solution is not determinate; rather, this model is constructed to provide probability distributions over all possible outcomes. Some would argue that this is a considerable shortcoming (Nash 1950); however, to address the topic of primary concern in this research adequately, a nondeterminate outcome is essential. We are actually less concerned with the predicted bargaining outcome than with determining the probability that no bargained outcome, and thereby war, will result. The other models seem to assume, at least implicitly, that if the bargaining set is nonempty, a negotiated settlement will be reached. The explanation for the occurrence of war that follows from such an assumption would be that the bargaining set was empty. On the face of it, this seems to be a reasonable assumption since, by definition, if the bargaining set is nonempty, all players would be better off with some outcome in the set than with no agreement. However, there is abundant empirical evidence to suggest that a nonempty bargaining set does not automatically lead to a negotiated settlement (Raiffa 1982). In a great number of strike situations, law suits, and wars, both parties would have been better off with a negotiated settlement. Furthermore, it is often the case that one side has offered a solution acceptable to the other, who has in return rejected the offer solely in hopes of attaining even more through the fight. The solution concept provided here is thus more useful for the purposes of this study than the others because it provides the probability that the actors will choose to forgo a negotiated settlement and take their chances in war.

The final comparison among the models to be made involves an examination of the kinds of variables included in the models and the manner in which these variables are treated. A distinguishing characteristic of the model proposed in this book is the major emphasis it places on the *power* and *resolve* variables and the linkage among these variables and crisis outcomes. In other models, these variables are presumably reflected in the actors' utility functions; however, how they affect bargaining is never made explicit. Therefore, the model proposed in this book is unique in that it will enable us to deduce hypotheses relating the power and resolve of the participants to crisis behavior.

Naturally, there are some variables excluded from this model that are included in others. Specifically, the basic model tells us nothing about concession rates, the effect of time pressures on bargaining, or the importance of information conditions and the ability of bargainers to learn. My intent in excluding these variables from the analysis is not to suggest that they have no impact on bargaining behavior—they undoubtedly do. Rather, my aim is to construct a parsimonious model explaining outcomes of international crises, a goal that necessitates the exclusion of important variables. While the model would certainly provide a more complete explanation were these variables to be included, it is desirable at this point to keep the model manageable.

My claim is that the model presented here is more useful for understanding bargaining in international crises than are previous models because the variables it includes are more important for an understanding of the phenomena of interest than are those variables included in other models. As noted earlier, the relative power and resolve of states are frequently claimed to have a major influence on crisis bargaining. The other variables, while important, are expected to explain less of the variance in crisis behavior and outcomes. Of the variables excluded, time is probably the one believed to have the greatest impact on crisis behavior; in fact, it is often included in definitions of *crisis*. The time factor is obviously important in any bargaining situation in that if it does not matter when the parties agree, it does not matter if they agree (Cross 1969). One aspect of the time factor that has been incorporated into models of bargaining is the reduction in the players' payoffs that occurs when agreement is delayed. This aspect of time is indirectly incorporated into my model through defining one of the power variables as the ability to impose costs variable. I treat this variable less as a function of time, however, than as a factor that is manipulable by one's opponent.

Note also that this model has been constructed in such a way that it can be expanded to incorporate additional variables. It is thus intended to serve as a general framework that can be used to guide our study of international crises, not as a complete specification of a theory of crisis behavior. For example, additional assumptions would enable us to use the model to analyze concession rates. If we assume that decision makers follow a certain decision rule (e.g., they are expected utility maximizers) and that they follow certain estimation procedures regarding their opponent's utility functions, reservation points, and so on, then we can determine an optimal concession rate for that actor. We could also use this construction to incorporate learning into the analysis by showing how decision makers' estimates about their opponents change as a result of new information. Finally, this model can be used to analyze the effects of other variables as well. Recent work by Carlson (1992), for example, uses this model in an investigation of the effects of certain types of misperceptions. Thus, this model does not require the assumption of complete information and can include at least one nonrational factor often purported to influence the likelihood of war. The important point is that while certain variables have been excluded from the basic model, it is sufficiently flexible to allow many of them to be included in future analyses.

CHAPTER 3

Power and Resolve in Crisis Bargaining

In the previous chapter, I presented the basic model to be used in this book, and I argued that this model is more useful for the analysis of crisis bargaining than are other formal bargaining models. One of the reasons that this model is more useful is that it explicitly incorporates variables that most students of international crises believe to be important determinants of crisis behavior— the relative power and resolve of the participants. In this chapter, I turn to the task of using the model to derive hypotheses relating these variables to crisis outcomes. We are interested in determining the effect of changes in these variables on the probability distribution of crisis outcomes. Particular attention is paid to the shifts brought about in our solution point and to the changes in the probability that war will result.

Before turning to the task at hand, a number of preliminary points must be made. The analysis to be performed in this chapter is concerned with the impact of the power and resolve variables on the probability distribution of outcomes and therefore is carried out solely within the utility space. We are interested in linking variations in our independent variables to changes in the distribution of negotiated outcomes as well as to changes in the likelihood of war. This discussion can be fruitfully carried out without reference to the specific issues in dispute. It would be possible to translate the predicted bargaining outcomes back into the terms of the issues at stake, but that would add relatively little to this analysis and would add significantly to the length of the discussion. For this reason, the issue space, which will be reintroduced in the analysis performed in the next chapter, is mentioned only in passing.

These analyses involve determining what the model implies regarding the theoretical relationship between changes in the independent variables and the probability distribution over possible outcomes. We are primarily interested in two aspects of this distribution: the negotiated settlement most likely to be reached and the probability that war will occur, as specified by equations (2.3) and (2.4). Therefore, the nature of the analysis will be to use these equations to see how changes in the independent variables affect, first, the most likely negotiated settlement (e.g., does increasing the resolve of one actor shift the solution point in that actor's favor?) and, second, the probability of war (e.g., does increasing the resolve of one actor increase the likelihood of war?). The first type of analysis involves determining whether changes in the independent variables cause the π' that satisfies equation (2.3) to shift toward one player's ideal point. The second type involves determining how changes in the independent variables affect the proportion of each player's PDF that is within the bargaining set. The exact nature of these changes and the precise manner in which they are reflected in the model will be discussed more fully below.

Two aspects of these analyses are important to note. First, we should be aware that the model has been developed at a level of specificity unlikely to be realized in any data we may obtain with which to test our hypotheses. We could, for example, use the model to derive hypotheses suggesting that x units of change in the probability that i would win a war brings about as large a shift in the bargaining solution as do y units of change in i's resolve. Obviously, we are unlikely ever to be able to test such a specific hypothesis, especially since it would involve measuring the power and resolve variables in comparable units. For the hypotheses we derive to be meaningful and testable, they will be presented in a much less specific form. We can, for example, hypothesize that if we increase the resolve of one player, the probability of war increases (i.e., the units of change involved are not specified) and have some hope of subjecting the hypothesis to an empirical test.

Second, the analyses in this chapter are restricted to two-actor, zero-sum situations. This restriction reduces the generality of the results, but it also considerably simplifies the discussion. Although the results are generally derived for zero-sum situations, much of the explication focuses on specific, hypothetical examples. The pictorial representations of these examples are important components of the exposition and must be as simple as possible to convey the ideas contained in the argument. Since the figures must be presented in more than two dimensions if we assume non-zero-sum situations, the restriction makes the argument much easier to visualize and follow. This restriction will be dropped, however, as the model is further developed in subsequent chapters. In any case, the loss of generality is not as problematic as one might imagine. Recall that the nature of the bargaining solution point is such that it will always be Pareto optimal. Since a significant portion of this analysis will be concerned with examining the effects of changes in the power and resolve variables on the location of the solution point, performing the analysis in its full generality would still imply Pareto optimality. Thus, much (though not all) of the additional restrictiveness implied by the zero-sum assumption is incorporated into the model in any case. More importantly, the type of analysis we are performing is such that the hypotheses we derive should not differ significantly under non-zero-sum conditions. We are essentially interested in how changes in the power and resolve relationship of crisis bargainers will affect their willingness to make bargaining concessions or begin a war. It is likely that the relationship among these particular variables would not significantly depend on whether the situation is zero sum, particularly given Pareto optimality. Thus, the hypotheses we derive can be assumed to be fairly general.

I begin by considering each of the variables singly. For each, I state the hypotheses linking it to crisis outcomes and provide a general discussion outlining the logic behind the argument. Specific, hypothetical examples will be used to represent the arguments visually; therefore, much of the discussion will focus on a series of zero-sum situations that are modifications of the case represented in figure 11. The conclusions do not rest on these specific examples, however, and formal, mathematical derivations of the hypotheses follow the general discussions. While the logic leading to the hypotheses is to be found in these formal derivations, the reader can skip these sections without significant loss. Following the analysis of each variable taken alone, I focus on allowing the variables to vary simultaneously (i.e., the ceteris paribus assumption characterizing the initial analyses is dropped). I then turn to the cases presented in the Appendix in an effort to provide more concrete illustrations to the points being made. These cases are not intended as empirical tests of the model, but some emphasis will be placed on demonstrating that the cases are consistent with the theoretical expectations. The concluding section of the chapter is devoted to an evaluation of the results in light of the international relations literature. The results presented in this chapter bear on a number of debates in the crisis management literature. I also refer to a number of empirical results that are consistent with the expectations derived from the model and demonstrate that the model can, in fact, reconcile some apparently contradictory empirical findings.

Hypotheses on Crisis Outcomes

Before turning to the task of deriving hypotheses relating the power and resolve of crisis participants to crisis outcomes, it is useful to restate the specific, hypothetical case that will serve as the basis for the examples. The basic situation presented in figure 11 is reproduced in figure 12. Recall that since the situation is assumed to be zero sum we can use a single scale to represent the utility accruing to both players. For the sake of convenience, we allow the utility scale presented in figure 12 to provide the utility of a proposal to player j. We can then determine the utility to i by subtracting this quantity from zero.

We have three points specified for each player. O_i represents the utility provided by the ith player's opening proposal. The point providing the least utility that a player would accept with certainty is represented by Δ. The ability of the actors to impose costs on each other are reflected in these points.

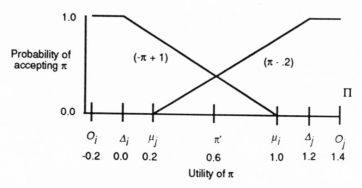

Fig. 12. A utility space representation of a zero-sum conflict

If, for example, we increase the ability of j to impose costs on i, Δ_i will move away from O_i, indicating a greater willingness by i to avoid paying costs by making concessions. The point representing the least utility a player could possibly accept is denoted by μ. The resolve of the parties is reflected in these points—as, for example, j becomes less willing to allow i to get its way, μ_j will shift toward O_j. In figure 12, O_i, Δ_i, μ_i, O_j, Δ_j, and μ_j have been set at $\pi = -0.2$, 0.0, 1.0, 1.4, 1.2, and 0.2, respectively.

We must also specify a probability of acceptance function for each player. These functions specify the probability that the players would accept a proposal of any given utility. The upper and lower bounds ($p = 1.0$ and $p = 0.0$) of these functions are Δ and μ, respectively. The probability that a player will accept a given proposal is assumed to be a monotonically decreasing function of the utility associated with the proposal, and the shape of the function reflects the likelihood that the player would win a war should negotiations fail. When the players are equally likely to win such a war, the probability of acceptance functions are linear, like in figure 12. As one player increases the likelihood that it could win a war, its probability of acceptance function becomes convex with respect to its O and the opponent's function becomes concave with respect to its O. Keep in mind that the hypotheses to be derived will generally apply to two-actor zero-sum bargaining games and the specific example will be used only as a visual aid to our understanding.

Bargaining Costs and Crisis Outcomes

Our first task is to consider the effect on crisis bargaining brought about by an increase in the ability of one side to impose costs on the other. Recall that the ability of the actors to impose costs is reflected in the model through the location of the Δs, the points of least utility that the parties would accept with certainty. As, for example, the ability of j to impose costs on i increases, Δ_i will move away from O_i. Figure 13 will serve as an illustration to guide this discussion. Notice that our initial situation, represented by figure 12, is included in this figure along with four additional probability of acceptance functions for i. Each additional function, together with the initial function for j, reflects a new situation in which the ability of j to impose costs on i is increased, while all other variables are held constant.

Consider the original probability of acceptance functions $p_j(\pi) = \pi - .2$ and $p_i(\pi) = -\pi + 1$ as well as two additional functions for i, $p_{i2}(\pi) = -1.25\pi + 1.25$ and $p_{i3}(\pi) = -1.67\pi + 1.67$. These later two functions correspond to situations in which j has increased its ability to impose costs on i so that $\Delta_{i2} = 0.2$ and $\Delta_{i3} = 0.4$. In the original case, $p_{ij}(\pi) = -\pi^2 + 1.2\pi - .2$. Setting the derivative of this to 0 gives π', the most likely negotiated outcome. In this case, $p'_{ij}(\pi) = -2\pi + 1.2$, so $\pi' = .6$. In the next case, $p_{ij}(\pi) = -1.25\pi^2 + 1.5\pi - .25$, $p'_{ij}(\pi) = -2.5\pi + 1.5$, and $\pi' = .6$. Similarly, we can see that $\pi' = .6$ in the third case. Thus, our examples suggest that as one party's ability to impose bargaining costs on the other increases, the expected negotiated settlement does not change. Note that there is a limiting condition to this result. Once the bargaining costs imposed on i have been increased to the point that i would accept with certainty some π that provides i with less utility than does the original π', π' will be shifted in favor of j. Under this condition, the new π' will be equivalent to the new Δ_i. We can easily see that this is the case with reference to figure 13. Notice that Δ_{i5} has been set at $\pi = \pi'$. For any $\pi < \Delta_{i5}$, $p_i(\pi) = p_i(\Delta_{i5}) = 1.0$ and $p_j(\pi) < p_j(\Delta_{i5})$, so the joint probability of accepting any $\pi < \Delta_{i5}$ is less than the joint probability of accepting Δ_{i5}.

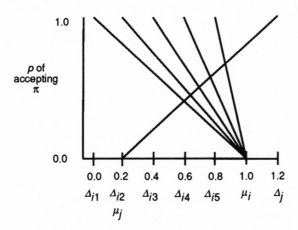

Fig. 13. The effect of bargaining costs on crisis outcomes

The examples in figure 13 also suggest hypotheses relating changes in the cost-imposing abilities of one party to the probability of war. In the original case, $p_i(\pi) = -\pi + 1.0$ and $p_j(\pi) = \pi - .2$, the derivatives of which are -1 and 1, respectively. The parameters are set so that $\Delta_i = 0.0$, $\mu_i = 1.0$, $\Delta_j = 1.2$, and $\mu_j = 0.2$. The probability of war is given by

$$p(\text{war}) = 1.0 - \left(\frac{\int_{0.2}^{1.0} -1 \quad \int_{0.2}^{1.0} 1}{\int_{0.0}^{1.0} -1 \quad \int_{0.2}^{1.2} 1} \right) = 1.0 - \left(\frac{.8}{1.0} \cdot \frac{.8}{1.0} \right) = .36.$$

If we increase the ability of j to impose costs on i so that $\Delta_i = 0.2$, $p_i(\pi)$ will become $p_i(\pi) = -1.25\pi + 1.25$ and $p_i'(\pi) = -1.25$. The only component of the probability of war function to change will be the term specifying i's PDF, which will become

$$\frac{\int_{0.2}^{1.0} 1.25}{\int_{0.2}^{1.0} 1.25} = 1.0.$$

The probability of war will become $1 - (1.0 \cdot 0.8) = .2$. This probability suggests that increases in the ability of one side to impose costs on the other serve to decrease the probability of war. Note also that at this point $\Delta_i = \mu_j$ so that all of i's PDF is within the bargaining range. Thus, additional increases in j's ability to impose costs on i cannot bring about further decreases in the probability of war.

The examples in figure 13 suggest two hypotheses:

HYPOTHESIS 1. *In symmetrical situations, negotiated crisis outcomes should be unaffected by the level of bargaining costs that each actor imposes on the other (up to the limiting condition noted above).*

HYPOTHESIS 2. *In symmetrical situations, the greater the bargaining costs that can be imposed by one actor on the other, the lower the probability that war will result.*

Formal derivations of these hypotheses are presented below, but we can see the general logic of these arguments by referring to figure 13. We hold constant the bargaining costs for j, so the probability of acceptance function pictured for j does not change. As the costs for i increase, shifting Δ_i away from O_i, the effect on i's probability of acceptance function is to increase the probability that i would accept each π within the bargaining range. This suggests that all possible negotiated settlements will become more likely to occur; however, as long as the probability of acceptance functions are linear, the maximum of their product will remain constant (to the point at which Δ_i is to the right of the original π'). Although the most probable negotiated settlement does not change, the likelihood that *some* negotiated settlement will occur increases.

One plausible interpretation of these results suggests that increasing the bargaining costs an actor must pay serves to hasten the bargaining process by increasing the incentives for that bargainer to reach some agreement quickly. This interpretation appears fairly intuitive, but it is not obvious that this scenario should lead to no change in the most likely negotiated settlement or a decrease in the probability of war. In the first place, it would seem that increased bargaining costs would lead to greater concessions by the party suffering those costs, which would provide a bargaining advantage to its opponent. It might be the case, however, that the increased costs create an incentive not to make more concessions but to make already acceptable concessions more quickly. Since increased bargaining costs do not necessarily make the actor willing to sell itself short, there is no definite advantage to the opponent in terms of being able to achieve a settlement close to its own O. The opponent does benefit, however, in that outcomes within the bargaining range close to its O are more likely to be achieved than in the lower cost condition and the probability of achieving some settlement the actor prefers to war is increased while the probability of war decreases.

Furthermore, it is not intuitively obvious that increased bargaining costs should decrease the probability of war. Especially if greater bargaining costs do not create an incentive for the party to make greater concessions than would otherwise be the case, it might be argued that there is a tendency to jump into war more quickly than when the crisis can drag on at little cost. The reason that this argument fails, however, is that it overlooks the fact that going to war does not save one from paying the costs of delaying a settlement of the issues. To be sure, fighting a war *increases* the costs of failing to agree; so resorting to war, rather than eliminating the bargaining costs, serves to increase and perhaps prolong the suffering. High bargaining costs, which are probably an omen of an extremely costly war, thus provide an incentive to settle quickly, not an incentive to attack. Note too that this tendency is enhanced if the bargaining costs are great for both parties. As a practical matter, imposing costs on the opponent usually involves a cost to oneself (economic sanctions deprive oneself, as well as the enemy, of the benefits of trade, and one must usually expend political capital to impose diplomatic sanctions). Thus, we might expect the level of bargaining costs to one side to be correlated with the level of costs to the other. Our expectation is that high-cost crises should be resolved quickly, that war has a low probability (though the probability is not zero), and that the level of costs should little affect the terms of a negotiated settlement. It should be remembered, however, that all other variables have been held constant. Depending on the values of these variables, we might observe particular crises characterized by high bargaining costs in which the probability of war was relatively high. This result only suggests that this probability would be even higher if the bargaining costs were low.

Mathematical Derivations

Determining the effect increases in j's ability to impose costs on i have on the solution point involves calculating the changes in π', the proposal that maximizes the joint probability of being accepted, that are brought about by changes in i's probability of acceptance function associated with the increased ability of j to impose costs. Linear probability of acceptance functions, as assumed, can be specified generally as $p_i(\pi) = a_i + b_i\pi$ and $p_j(\pi) = a_j + b_j\pi$.[1] The point within the bargaining set at which the derivative of the product of these functions equals zero will be π'. Generally, $p_{ij}(\pi) = b_ib_j\pi^2 + (a_ib_j + a_jb_i)\pi + a_ia_j$; thus, $p_{ij'}(\pi) = 2b_ib_j\pi + a_ib_j + a_jb_i$. Solving for $p_{ij'}(\pi) = 0$, we find that

$$\pi' = \frac{-(a_ib_j + a_jb_i)}{2b_ib_j}.$$

Our task is to determine what happens to π' when a_i and b_i are altered to reflect the increased ability of j to impose costs on i. Since a_j and b_j will be held constant, I will set them as 0 and 1, respectively.[2] We can now simplify the equation for π' to

$$\pi' = \frac{-a_i}{2b_i}.$$

To define a_i and b_i generally for the original probability of acceptance function, we can specify two points that must be on this function: $[\pi_1, p_i(\pi_1)]$, which is at μ_i and, by definition, $p_i(\mu_i) = 0.0$, and $[\pi_2, p_i(\pi_2)]$, which is at Δ_i and, again by definition, $p_i(\Delta_i) = 1.0$. We can see that

$$b_i = \frac{0 - 1}{\pi_1 - \pi_2} = \frac{-1}{\pi_1 - \pi_2}.$$

Since

$$a_i = p_i(\pi) + \frac{\pi}{\pi_1 - \pi_2},$$

inserting $(\pi_1, 0.0)$ into the equation, we have

$$a_i = \frac{\pi_1}{\pi_1 - \pi_2}.$$

Thus, i's probability of acceptance function in the initial condition is defined by

$$p_i(\pi) = \frac{\pi_1}{\pi_1 - \pi_2} - \frac{\pi}{\pi_1 - \pi_2}.$$

We can define another such function for i that would reflect j's threat to impose greater costs on i by following a similar procedure using $[\pi_3, p_i(\pi_3)]$, where $\pi_3 = \pi_2 + \epsilon$ and $p_i(\pi_3) = 1.0$. In this case we find that

$$b_i = \frac{-1}{\pi_1 - (\pi_2 + \epsilon)}$$

and

$$a_i = \frac{\pi_1}{\pi_1 - (\pi_2 + \epsilon)}.$$

We may use these values for a_i and b_i to determine the effect on π' associated with j's ability to impose greater costs on i. In the original case,

$$\pi' = \frac{\dfrac{-\pi_1}{\pi_1 - \pi_2}}{\dfrac{-2}{\pi_1 - \pi_2}} = \frac{\pi_1}{2}.$$

When j's ability to impose costs on i is increased,

$$\pi' = \frac{\dfrac{-\pi_1}{\pi_1 - (\pi_2 + \epsilon)}}{\dfrac{-2}{\pi_1 - (\pi_2 + \epsilon)}} = \frac{\pi_1}{2}.$$

Thus, the ability of one actor to impose greater costs on the other will not change the most probable negotiated settlement.

We may now turn to the problem of determining how j's ability to impose greater costs on i affects the probability that war will result. The probability of war is given by

$$1.0 - \left(\frac{\displaystyle\int_{\mu_j}^{\mu_i} p_i'(\pi)}{\displaystyle\int_{\Delta_i}^{\mu_i} p_i'(\pi)} \cdot \frac{\displaystyle\int_{\mu_j}^{\mu_i} p_j'(\pi)}{\displaystyle\int_{\mu_j}^{\Delta_j} p_j'(\pi)0} \right).$$

By construction, the denominators of the terms within the parentheses will be equal to 1.0, so this can be simplified to

$$p(\text{war}) = 1.0 - \left(\int_{\mu_j}^{\mu_i} p_i'(\pi) \cdot \int_{\mu_j}^{\mu_i} p_j'(\pi) \right).^3$$

In the linear case, $p_i(\pi) = a_i + b_i\pi$ and $p_j(\pi) = a_j + b_j\pi$, so $p_i'(\pi) = b_i$ and $p_j'(\pi) = b_j$. Since μ_i, μ_j, and $p_j(\pi)$ remain constant, the changes in the probability of war will depend entirely on

$$\int_{\mu_j}^{\mu_i} p_i'(\pi).$$

We can solve for

$$\int_{\mu_j}^{\mu_i} p_i'(\pi)$$

by finding the antiderivative of p_i', call it G, and solving for $G(\mu_i) - G(\mu_j)$. In this case

$$\int_{\mu_j}^{\mu_i} p_i'(\pi) = b_i(\mu_i) - b_i(\mu_j).$$

From the prior discussion, we know that increasing j's ability to impose costs serves to increase the magnitude of b_i. We also know that $\mu_i > \mu_j$. Thus, an increase in b_i will increase $b_i(\mu_i) - b_i(\mu_j)$. Returning to the equation for the probability of war, we can see that an increase in b_i will increase the product of the terms within the parentheses and thereby decrease the probability of war. According to the model, we would expect that an increase in the ability of one side to impose costs on the other would be associated with a decrease in the probability of war. ∎

Resolve and Crisis Outcomes

Our next task is to determine the effect on bargaining outcomes brought about by an increase in an actor's resolve. This increase is reflected in the model by moving the point at which the actor would definitely prefer war away from the opponent's initial offer. That is, the actor's reservation point, μ, moves closer to its own O. Figure 14 illustrates this discussion. Notice that included in figure 14 are the original example and three cases in which j's resolve has been increased.

In our example, $p_i(\pi) = 1.0 - \pi$, $p_{j1}(\pi) = -0.2 + \pi$, and $p_{j2}(\pi) = -0.5 + 1.25\pi$. The formal derivation of the previous hypotheses revealed a simple computational formula for π' when the probability of acceptance

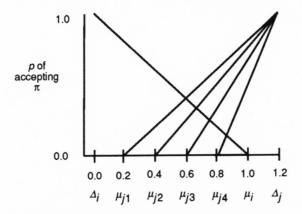

Fig. 14. The effect of resolve on crisis outcomes

functions are linear. If we generally specify $p_i(\pi) = a_i + b_i\pi$ and $p_j(\pi) = a_j + b_j\pi$,

$$\pi' = -\frac{a_i b_j + a_j b_i}{2 b_i b_j}.$$

Recall that for our initial case, $\pi' = .6$. In the second case,

$$\pi' = -\frac{(1.0)(1.25) + (-0.5)(-1.0)}{(2)(-1.0)(1.25)} = .7.$$

This suggests that greater resolve on the part of an actor will lead to a negotiated outcome more favorable to that actor. To be more specific, in this case increasing μ_j by .2 increases π' by .1. Again, we can see that there is an upper limit to this relationship, which is reached when $\mu_j = \mu_i$. At this point, the only possible negotiated settlement is μ_j (or μ_i), and further increases in either player's resolve would make war a certainty.

Turning to what the examples suggest about the effect of resolve on the probability of war, first recall from the previous section that for the initial situation in our example, the probability of war is .36. Using μ_{j2} in figure 14, we have $\Delta_i = 0.0$, $\mu_i = 1.0$, $p_i(\pi) = 1.0 - 1.0\pi$, $\Delta_j = 1.2$, $\mu_j = 0.4$, and $p_j(\pi) + -0.5 + 1.25\pi$. For this situation,

$$p(\text{war}) = 1 - \left(\frac{\int_{0.4}^{1.0} 1.0 \int_{0.4}^{1.0} 1.25}{\int_{0.0}^{1.0} 1.0 \int_{0.4}^{1.2} 1.25} \right) = .55.$$

From this, it appears that an increase in j's resolve leads to an increase in the probability of war.

Two hypotheses are suggested by these examples:

HYPOTHESIS 3. *In symmetrical situations, higher levels of resolve by one actor will be associated with a higher probability that that actor will achieve a favorable negotiated settlement.*

HYPOTHESIS 4. *In symmetrical situations, higher levels of resolve by one actor will increase the probability that a war will occur.*

Again, the formal derivations of these hypotheses will be presented below. The logic behind these arguments can be seen with reference to figure 14. This time, hold the parameters for i constant while allowing j's resolve to increase (i.e., μ_j shifts toward O_j). While the probability of accepting each π remains constant for i as j's resolve is increased, the probability that j would accept π decreases for all proposals. This decrease is not constant over all π and is greatest for those proposals nearest to O_i. Thus, the probability of occurrence decreases less for π close to O_j, and this difference is sufficient to cause a shift in π' favorable to j. However, increases in j's resolve also decrease the size of the bargaining range, so a smaller proportion of i's PDF is included, which clearly leads to an increase in the probability of war.

The implications of this result are fairly clear and intuitive. The most obvious interpretation suggests that as an actor's resolve increases, it tends to bargain tougher. Since that actor is willing to make fewer concessions, a negotiated settlement, if one is reached, is likely to be more favorable to that actor than would otherwise be the case. This result comes at the expense of a higher probability of war because, first, the actor whose resolve is increased is no longer willing to accept some proposals that could avoid war and, second, since increasing one side's resolve does not make the other more willing to make concessions, the former's tougher bargaining will make the latter more likely to resort to war.

Mathematical Derivations

We can determine the effect that increasing j's resolve has on π' in a manner similar to that used above. Since we will hold a_i and b_i constant and can specify any reasonable values for them, I will set them at 1.0 and -1.0, respectively. Thus,

$$\pi' = -\frac{a_i b_j + a_j b_i}{2b_i b_j}$$

reduces to

$$\pi' = \frac{b_j - a_j}{2b_j}.$$

An initial, linear probability of acceptance function for j can be defined by specifying two points: $(\Delta_j, 1.0)$ and $(\mu_{j1}, 0.0)$. We can calculate that

$$b_{j1} = \frac{1}{\Delta_j - \mu_{j1}}$$

and

$$a_{j1} = -\frac{\mu_{j1}}{\Delta_j - \mu_{j1}}.$$

In this case,

$$\pi' = \frac{\dfrac{1}{\Delta_j - \mu_{j1}} + \dfrac{\mu_{j1}}{\Delta_j - \mu_{j1}}}{\dfrac{2}{\Delta_j - \mu_{j1}}} = \frac{1 + \mu_{j1}}{2}.$$

Allowing j's resolve to increase causes μ_j to shift to the right. Therefore, the new probability of acceptance function will be defined by the points $(\Delta_j, 1.0)$ and $(\mu_{j1} + \epsilon, 0.0)$. Solving for a_{j2} and b_{j2} shows that

$$b_{j2} = \frac{1}{\Delta_j - (\mu_{j1} + \epsilon)}$$

and

$$a_{j2} = -\frac{\mu_{j1} + \epsilon}{\Delta_j - (\mu_{j1} + \epsilon)}.$$

Here,

$$\pi' = \frac{\dfrac{1}{\Delta_j - (\mu_{j1} + \epsilon)} + \dfrac{\mu_{j1} + \epsilon}{\Delta_j - (\mu_{j1} + \epsilon)}}{\dfrac{2}{\Delta_j - (\mu_{j1} + \epsilon)}} = \frac{1 + \mu_{j1} + \epsilon}{2}.$$

Thus, increasing μ_j by ϵ will increase π' by $\epsilon/2$, suggesting that as j's resolve increases, j can expect to achieve a more favorable negotiated outcome.

Turning to the probability of war, we see that, in the linear case, equation (2.4) can be rewritten as

$$p(\text{war}) = 1 - \left(\frac{b_i(\mu_i) - b_i(\mu_j)}{b_i(\mu_i) - b_i(\Delta_i)} \cdot \frac{b_j(\mu_i) - b_j(\mu_j)}{b_j(\Delta_j) - b_j(\mu_j)} \right)$$

where b_i and b_j represent the slopes of the players' probability of acceptance functions. We may use this construction to determine the effect an increase in j's resolve has on the probability of war. Such an increase is reflected in an increase in μ_j, which causes b_j to increase since Δ_j is held constant. Consider the first term inside the parentheses (which reflects the proportion of i's PDF that is within the bargaining range). The only part of this term that varies with an increase in j's resolve is $b_i(\mu_j)$, which will, obviously, increase. Thus, the numerator of this term will decrease, as will the entire term. We can also see that the second term (reflecting the proportion of j's PDF within the bargaining range) will decrease. Since every component of this term is the product of b_j and some other parameter, the value of the term will not be affected by the value of b_j and we can reduce this to

$$\frac{\mu_i - \mu_j}{\Delta_j - \mu_j}.$$

We know that, by construction $\mu_j \leq \mu_i \leq \Delta_j$.[4] Therefore, we can see that an increase in μ_j will either decrease the value of the second term or hold it constant if $\mu_j = \Delta_j$. Since an increase in j's resolve will reduce at least one of the terms within the parentheses and can increase neither, the product of these terms will necessarily decrease. Thus, $p(\text{war})$ will increase, and we may conclude that an increase in one actor's resolve will raise the likelihood of a crisis ending in war. Naturally, the limit to this is reached when the probability of war becomes 1.0. ■

The Likelihood of Winning a War and Crisis Outcomes

The final variable to be considered is the probability that each side would win a war should one occur. This probability is incorporated into the model through the shape of the probability of acceptance functions. As one party increases the likelihood that it would prevail in war, its probability of acceptance function will become increasingly convex with respect to its O, and its opponent's function will become increasingly concave with respect to its O. Therefore, at this stage of the analysis, we must drop the assumption of linear probability of acceptance functions. The functions will now be of the form $p_i(\pi) = a + b_1\pi + b_2\pi^2 + \ldots + b_n\pi^n$, where n will increase as does the discrepancy in war-fighting capabilities. Obviously, the linear functions represent a special case of the more general form in which the war-fighting capabilities are equal. Note that when $n > 2$, the functions can curve more than once. However, since we are dealing with only a monotonically decreasing segment of this function, that will not complicate the analyses.

Figure 15 contains three pairs of probability of acceptance functions. The first are the linear initial conditions used in the previous examples. The other pairs represent situations in which $n = 2$ and $n = 3$. In the first, $p_i(\pi) = 1 - \pi^2$

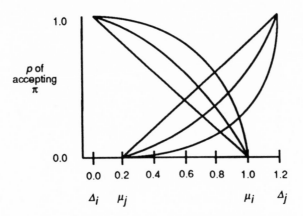

1.0

p of
accepting
π

0.0

0.0	0.2	0.4	0.6	0.8	1.0	1.2

Δ_i μ_j μ_i Δ_j

Fig. 15. The effect of the distribution of capabilities on crisis outcomes

and $p_j(\pi) = (\pi - .2)^2$, while in the second, $p_i(\pi) = 1 - \pi^3$ and $p_j(\pi) = (\pi - .2)^3$. Whereas $\pi' = .6$ in the initial case, it shifts to .76 when the square functions are used and .83 for the cube functions. The calculations are fairly straightforward for the case in which the square functions are used. Setting $p_{ij'}(\pi) = 0$ gives $2\pi^2 - .2\pi - 1 = 0$, which can be solved by use of the quadratic equation:

$$\pi' = -\frac{(-.2) \pm \sqrt{-.2^2 - (4)(2)(-1)}}{(2)(2)}$$

Note that this solution will actually provide two values for π'; however, only one, $+.76$, will be within the interval $[\mu_j, \mu_i]$. Since the calculations of π' become exceedingly complex as n increases, the value for π' when $n = 3$ has been determined by a simple, iterative process using a computer program. The conclusion following from these examples suggests that as the disparity in war-fighting capabilities increases, the most probable negotiated outcome will increasingly favor the stronger party.

Turning to the relationship between relative war-fighting capabilities and the probability of war, recall first that, as we have seen above, $p(\text{war}) = .36$ in our initial condition. In the mathematical derivation that follows, it is shown that, given the values of the μs and Δs that we are assuming, the probability of war can be given by the simple computational formula, $p(\text{war}) = 1 - [(\mu_i^n - \mu_j^n) \cdot (\mu_i - \mu_j)^n]$. Thus, when $n = 2$, $p(\text{war}) = 1 - \{[(1)^2 - (0.2)^2] \cdot (1 - 0.2)^2\} = .39$, and when $n = 3$, $p(\text{war}) = 1 - \{[(1)^3 - (0.2)^3] \cdot (1 - 0.2)^3\} = .49$. From this, we are led to conclude that increases in the disparity of war-fighting capabilities lead to increases in the probability that a crisis will end in war.

The final bivariate hypotheses can be stated as follows:

HYPOTHESIS 5. *The greater the disparity in military capabilities, the greater the probability that the more capable will achieve a favorable negotiated settlement.*

HYPOTHESIS 6. *The greater the disparity in military capabilities, the greater the probability that the crisis will end in war.*

Not surprisingly, having an advantage in terms of war-fighting capabilities increases the likelihood that an actor will achieve a more favorable negotiated settlement. The stronger actor is less likely to make concessions because it has a greater expectation of getting what it wants through war, while the weaker actor is more willing to make bargaining concessions because it can expect to lose a war. Many will find it surprising that such disparities lead to a higher probability of war, however. It seems obvious that the probability of war would be increased by the more powerful side's increased willingness to resort to force, but we might expect this increase to be more than offset by the weaker side's decreased willingness to fight. This hypothesis suggests that the weaker side is less willing to fight, but not sufficiently so to overcome the stronger's greater willingness. Since I do not assume that the stronger side will win a war (only that it has a greater chance of winning), it is not necessarily unreasonable for the weaker to fight, particularly if there is much to be gained. We might further suspect that an actor engaging in a crisis with a stronger party has already considered the power disparity and values the stakes sufficiently to risk a losing war. Thus, we can expect power disparities to increase the likelihood of a crisis ending in war.

Mathematical derivations
To determine the impact on the solution point brought about by a change in the probability that each side would win a war, we must first note that regardless of the magnitude of n, $p_i(\pi) = 1 - \pi^n$. That is because the nature of von Neumann–Morgenstern utility functions allows us to set any point as the origin (here Δ_i) and any interval as the unit length (here $\mu_i - \Delta_i$). Furthermore, by the symmetry assumption $\|\Delta_i - \mu_i\| = \|\Delta_j - \mu_j\|$, so $p_j(\pi) = (\pi - \mu_j)^n$. From this, we can see that $p_{ij'}(\pi) = \{(1 - \pi^n)[n(\pi - \mu_j)^{n-1}]\} + [(\pi - \mu_j)^n(-n\pi^{n-1})]$. The solution point, π', is the π at which this equation will equal 0.0; therefore, our task is to determine how π' must change as n increases.

To find the general solution, we can rewrite the equation as $0 = (1 - \pi^n)(\pi - \mu_j)^{n-1} - (\pi - \mu_j)^n(\pi^{n-1})$. Algebraic manipulation allows us to rewrite this as $2\pi^n - \mu_j\pi^{n-1} - 1 = 0$. We know that, by construction, $\mu_j \leq \pi' \leq \mu_i = 1.0$; thus, if π is held constant and n increases, the term to the left will become less than zero. To maintain the equality, π must get larger, which suggests that as j becomes increasingly likely to win a war, the solution point will shift toward O_j.

Turning to the problem of calculating the probability of war, we see that equation (2) can be written as

$$p(\text{war}) = 1 - \left(\frac{-n \int_{\mu_j}^{\mu_i} \pi^{n-1} \quad n \int_{\mu_j}^{\mu_i} (\pi - \mu_j)^{n-1}}{-n \int_{\Delta_i}^{\mu_i} \pi^{n-1} \quad n \int_{\mu_j}^{\Delta_j} (\pi - \mu_j)^{n-1}} \right).$$

The terms inside the parentheses can be solved by using

$$\frac{\mu_i^n - \mu_j^n}{\mu_i^n - \Delta_i^n}$$

and

$$\frac{(\mu_i - \mu_j)^n - (\mu_j - \mu_j)^n}{(\Delta_j - \mu_j)^n - (\mu_j - \mu_j)^n},$$

respectively. By construction, $\Delta_j > \mu_i = 1.0 > \mu_j > \Delta_i = 0.0$, and by the symmetry of this problem $\mu_i^n - \Delta_i^n = (\Delta_j - \mu_j)^n = 1.0$. Since $\mu_j - \mu_j = 0$, the probability of war can be given by $1 - [(\mu_i^n - \mu_j^n) \cdot (\mu_i - \mu_j)^n]$.

The question at hand involves determining what happens to the probability of war as n increases. Consider first the term representing the proportion of i's PDF that is within the bargaining range. Since $\mu_i = 1.0$ and $1.0 > \mu_j > 0.0$, as n increases, μ_j^n will decrease, and the entire term will increase. This suggests that as j increases its war-fighting capabilities, i becomes more willing to accept a negotiated settlement, which serves to lower the likelihood of war. However, this tendency is offset by j's increased willingness to resort to war, indicated by the fact that $(\mu_i - \mu_j)^n$ will decrease as n increases. In fact, increases in n serve to increase the probability of war. That is because at $n = 1$, $(\mu_i^n - \mu_j^n) = (\mu_i - \mu_j)^n$. As n increases, the difference between the terms will increase, causing the product to decrease;[5] and as the product of the terms within the parentheses decreases, the probability of war increases. ∎

Interaction Effects among the Variables

To this point, I have used the spatial model to derive a number of hypotheses relating our independent variables to crisis outcomes. According to the model, we expect the following: (1) As one party increases its ability to impose bargaining costs on its opponent, the bargaining solution point remains constant; however, the probability that the crisis will end in war decreases. (2) As one side increases its resolve, the solution point shifts in that party's favor, but the probability of war increases. (3) As the probability that one party would win a war increases, the solution point shifts in its favor and the probability of war increases. In each case, however, the result is achieved by holding the other variables constant at particular values. In this section, I shall show how the variables interact by allowing them to vary simultaneously; that is, I am dropping the symmetry assumption that has characterized the analysis to this point.

If we consider cases in which we hold the probability that each side would win a war at .5, we can easily see the effects of allowing the other two variables to vary in combination. Since the results regarding the ability of each side to impose costs on the other and those regarding the resolve of the parties are generalizable to all cases in which the probability of acceptance functions are linear, these, perhaps obvious, hypotheses are a direct extension of those presented above. For example, we can see that if the resolve of both parties is increased, the probability of war will increase substantially while the solution point shifts relatively little, if any.[6] Similarly, as the cost-imposing abilities of both players increase, the probability of war will rapidly decrease, but the solution point will not shift. Thus, we expect crises in which both parties are highly resolved to have a high probability of ending in war, while war is unlikely in those crises where both parties face high costs for failing to agree.

However, our ability to discuss the interaction effects of the two variables acting in combination is limited by the fact that we are unable to measure them in comparable units. For example, if j's resolve and j's ability to impose costs on i are increased, we cannot say whether the probability of war will increase, decrease, or stay the same without more information regarding the magnitude of the changes. We can draw some conclusions, however, even without precise information regarding the magnitude of changes in the variables. In this particular case, we know that the solution point will move toward O_j, and we know that any change in the probability of war brought about by the more important variable will be mitigated by the other. Thus, a party seeking to improve its bargaining position by increasing its resolve may temper the cost involved (in terms of increasing the chance of war) by also increasing its ability to impose costs on its opponent.[7]

Of greater interest are analyses that consider the effects of increasing resolve or the ability to impose bargaining costs when the players are not equally likely to win a war. Because the probability of acceptance functions are not linear, the effects of changes in the other variables may be modified. Figure 16 will be used to guide the discussion. This figure pictures three probability of acceptance functions for each actor. Player j is assumed to be more likely to win a war should one occur, and square functions are used. For both players, the original function (pictured in figure 15) is included, as are two additional functions—one depicting an increase in the player's resolve, the other depicting an increase in the ability of the opponent to impose bargaining costs.

We can specify the general form of the probability of acceptance functions as $p_i(\pi) = -\pi^2 + b_i\pi + a_i$ and $p_j(\pi) = \pi^2 + b_j\pi + a_j$. The solution point, π', for any two functions can be found by setting the derivative of the product of the functions, $p_{ij'}(\pi) = -4\pi^3 + 3(b_i - b_j)\pi^2 + 2(a_i + b_jb_i - a_j)\pi + (a_jb_i + a_ib_j)$, equal to zero. Our analytical task involves determining what shifts in π' are brought about by changes in the parameters a_i, b_i, a_j, and b_j, which are associated with changes in our variables of interest. Since deriving this result in full generality is exceedingly complicated,[8] I follow a different procedure for this discussion. Table 1 presents the π' values for sixty-one pairs of probability of acceptance functions and is organized in a way that allows us to see any trends in the movement of π' as our variables are altered. The nine π' values for the various pairs of functions depicted in figure 16 are marked by an asterisk. These values for π' have been generated through the

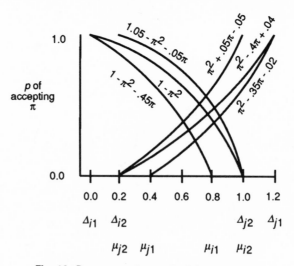

Fig. 16. Power, resolve, and crisis outcomes

use of a computer program that follows an iterative process. By examining the trends in shifts in π' brought about by changes in our variables, we can draw some conclusions about the effect the variables have when acting in combination. While we must have less confidence in these conclusions than in a mathematical result in full generality, they are sufficiently interesting to warrant discussion. Furthermore, our confidence in the validity of these findings can be raised by using a wide range of hypothetical cases, which has been done here.

Notice first that in table 1 the cell in the upper left corner, cell 1,1,

TABLE 1

Values of π' for Various Pairs of Probability of Acceptance Functions.

	Initial Condition	Increase i's Resolve			Increase j's Ability to Impose Costs on i			Alter Both
	1	2	3	4	5	6	7	8
	$\Delta_i=0.0$ $\mu_i=1.0$	$\Delta_i=0.0$ $\mu_i=0.8$	$\Delta_i=0.0$ $\mu_i=0.6$	$\Delta_i=1.0$ $\mu_i=0.4$	$\Delta_i=0.2$ $\mu_i=1.0$	$\Delta_i=0.4$ $\mu_i=1.0$	$\Delta_i=0.6$ $\mu_i=1.0$	$\Delta_i=0.2$ $\mu_i=0.8$
Initial Condition								
1 $\Delta_j=1.2$ $\mu_j=0.2$	.76[a]	.61[a]	.47	.33	.76[a]	.76	.75	.61
Increase j's resolve								
2 $\Delta_j=1.2$ $\mu_j=0.4$	.77[a]	.64[a]	.51	.40[b]	.77[a]	.77	.77	.64
3 $\Delta_j=1.2$ $\mu_j=0.6$	.83	.71	.60[b]	—[c]	.83	.82	.82	.71
4 $\Delta_j=1.2$ $\mu_j=0.8$	.90	.80[b]	—[c]	—[c]	.90	.90	.90	.80[b]
Increase i's ability to impose costs on j								
5 $\Delta_j=1.0$ $\mu_j=0.2$	.72[a]	.57[a]	.44	.33	.72[a]	.71	.71	.57
6 $\Delta_j=0.8$ $\mu_j=0.2$	.69	.56	.42	.31	.69	.69	.68	.55
7 $\Delta_j=0.6$ $\mu_j=0.2$	.68	.54	.42	.30	.67	.67	.66	.54
Alter both								
8 $\Delta_j=1.0$ $\mu_j=0.4$	.76	.63	.51	.40[b]	.76	.75	.75	.63

Note: The general forms for these functions are $p_i(\pi) = -(\pi^2) + b_i\pi + a_i$ and $p_j(\pi) = \pi^2 + b_j\pi + a_j$.

[a] These are the π' values for pairs of functions represented in figure 16.

[b] In these cases $\mu_i = \mu_j = \pi'$; that is, there is only one point in the bargaining set.

[c] In these cases the bargaining set is empty; therefore, $p(\text{war}) = 1.0$.

provides the π' for the initial case using the square functions that is presented in figure 15. As we move to the right, across columns 2, 3, and 4, we have the π' values for cases in which i's resolve is increased and the other variables are held constant (i.e., μ_i shifts from 1.0 in column 1 to 0.8, 0.6, and 0.4). Similarly, as we move downward, through rows 2, 3, and 4, we have the π' values for cases in which j's resolve is increased. Cases in which j's ability to impose costs on i, or i's ability to impose costs on j, is increased are reflected as we move across columns 5, 6, and 7 and down rows 5, 6, and 7, respectively. We can determine the effect on π' of the interaction of two variables either by examining the values of π' as we move through the table diagonally (e.g., the effect on π' of increasing both parties' ability to impose costs on one another can be determined by moving from cell 5,5 to cell 7,7) or by examining column 8 and row 8, in which i's resolve and j's ability to impose costs (or vice versa) are simultaneously altered. Notice that as we move from cell to cell, the relevant parameter is altered by 0.2 units (e.g., as we move from row 1 to rows 5, 6, and 7, Δ_j shifts from 1.2 to 1.0, 0.8, and 0.6); thus, if we can measure, for example, i's resolve and j's resolve in comparable units, we can compare the effect on π' produced by similar changes in each.

A number of interesting patterns emerge from table 1. First, notice that as a player's resolve is increased, the solution point shifts in that player's favor. Furthermore, if both players increase their resolve to any great extent, the bargaining set becomes empty and war becomes a certainty. That is fully consistent with the results regarding resolve that were presented earlier for the linear functions, and the finding is consistent regardless of the values taken by other variables. That is, as we move from column 1 to column 4 (or from row 1 to row 4), π' decreases (or increases) whichever row (or column) we examine. Of greater interest is a comparison of the effects of increases in i's resolve with the effects of increases in j's resolve. Moving from column 1 to column 4, a 0.6 unit shift in i's resolve, shifts π' from .36 units to .43 units, depending on the row. A similar change in j's resolve, from row 1 to row 4, moves π' at most .19 units. This suggests that a stronger party (in the sense of being more likely to win a war) has less to gain by increasing its resolve than does a weaker party. A reasonable interpretation of this result is that a weaker party trying to decide how much of a concession to make will be more concerned with the fact that it is likely to lose a war than with the opponent's resolve. For the stronger party, however, the resolve of the opponent is of relatively greater importance.

Turning to the question of how π' shifts as the ability of the parties to impose costs on one another changes, we find a rather surprising result. Recall that when linear probability of acceptance functions are used, changes in Δ_i or Δ_j did not alter π' at all. When j is more likely than i to win a war, however, increases in i's ability to impose bargaining costs on j result in a shift in π' in i's favor. This shift is rather modest in that changing Δ_j from 1.2 to 0.6 results in at most a .12-unit shift in π' (from cell 1,1 to cell 7,1) and, at least within the limits of the examples, the shift does not overcome the advantage j has by being more likely to win. While the costs i can impose on j do not seem to be as important of a consideration as does i's resolve, increases in this variable do seem to provide i with some bargaining advantage.

More surprising is that these results seem to suggest that increasing j's ability to impose costs on i also provides a bargaining advantage to i. While the shift in π' is extremely modest (moving from $\Delta_i = 0.0$ to $\Delta_i = 0.6$ brings about, at most, a .015-unit shift in π'—in row 7), this finding does deserve some explanation. The key can be found by examining figure 16. Consider one probability of acceptance function for j, say the one defined by $\Delta_j = 1.2$ and $\mu_j = 0.2$. Also consider two functions for i: the first defined by $\Delta_i = 0.0$ and $\mu_i = 1.0$; the second, reflecting an increase in j's ability to impose costs, defined by $\Delta_i = 0.2$ and $\mu_i = 1.0$. Since altering j's ability to impose costs affects only i's probability of acceptance function and because the joint probability that any π would be accepted is given by $p_j(\pi) \cdot p_i(\pi)$, any change in the joint probability of acceptance must be a result of changes in $p_i(\pi)$. By looking at the two functions for i, we can see that an increase in j's ability to impose costs on i increases the probability that i would accept *any* π within the bargaining set. It is also apparent, however, that this increase is not constant across all π in $[\mu_j, \mu_i]$. In fact, the increase in the probability of acceptance is greater for πs closer to Δ_i, which in turn will increase the joint probability of acceptance more for π close to Δ_i than for π closer to μ_i (although the latter will still be increased). We can now see why π', the point most likely to be accepted, would decrease as j's ability to impose costs increases. If we consider two points, the original π' and $\pi' - \partial$, we know that increasing j's ability to impose costs on i will cause the joint probability of acceptance for both points to increase, though the increase will be greater for $\pi' - \partial$. If ∂ is small enough and the additional increase for $\pi' - \partial$ is large enough, it is possible for $p_{ij}(\pi' - \partial) > p_{ij}(\pi')$ in the new joint probability of acceptance functions. That is precisely what happens in our case.

It should be noted that this rather odd finding does not call the model into question. Recall that the model actually provides much more information than we are using in our discussion of the solution point. Specifically, it provides a probability distribution over all possible outcomes, of which we are considering only the modal point. This focus does, in general, provide a useful indicator of the shifts in the distribution and is much more manageable than discussing every aspect of the changing distribution. In this instance, however, this focus is somewhat misleading. Increases in j's ability to impose costs on i do not make it less likely that j will achieve a favorable solution. In fact, j has a better chance of obtaining a solution it prefers to the original π' because of these increases, but the probability of achieving a negotiated settlement less favorable than π' increases more. However, these increases come at the expense of decreasing the probability of war, not at the expense of decreasing the probability that j could achieve a more favorable outcome.

One aspect of these findings is consistent with those when changes in resolve were considered. If the parties are not equally likely to win a war, further advantages (in terms of increased ability to impose costs or increased resolve) are less beneficial for the party more likely to win. In each case, the side less likely to win can at least partially overcome this handicap during negotiations through other advantages, whereas the stronger party has little, if any, extra to gain.[9] That may suggest that once an actor has decided to confront a much more powerful adversary, other considerations about the adversary become relatively unimportant. To the stronger side, who may have expected the weaker to avoid the crisis in the first place, questions regarding the opponent's other advantages may be important in deciding how hard to push.

Insight into the effects changes in these variables have on the probability of war can be studied by examining figure 16 directly. The probability of war is given by

$$1.0 - \left(\frac{\int_{\mu_j}^{\mu_i} p_i(\pi)}{\int_{\Delta_i}^{\mu_i} p_i(\pi)} \cdot \frac{\int_{\mu_j}^{\mu_i} p_j(\pi)}{\int_{\mu_j}^{\Delta_j} p_j(\pi)} \right)$$

The terms within the parentheses specify the proportion of the actors' PDFs that are within $[\mu_i, \mu_j]$. In essence, the denominator of each term defines the unit of the PDF as being the area under the curve and bounded by a player's reservation point, μ, on one side and the least utility that would definitely be accepted, Δ, on the other. The numerator specifies the area under the curve that is within the bargaining range. For each actor, this provides the proportion of the area under the PDF that is within the bargaining range and thus specifies the probability that some proposal will be accepted. By looking at any two functions for a given player in figure 16, we can tell for which the proportion of that player's PDF within the bargaining range is greatest. For example, consider the functions $p_i(\pi) = 1 - \pi^2$ and $p_i(\pi)^* = 1 - \pi^2 - .45\pi$ with $\mu_j = 0.2$. The total area under $p_i(\pi)$ is larger, but relatively little of this increase is within $[0.0, 0.2]$. Furthermore, we can tell that the size of the bargaining range is less when $p_i(\pi)^*$ is used, so that if $p_j(\pi)$ is held constant, a smaller proportion of the area under j's PDF would be within the bargaining range. Therefore, the probability of war is greater under $p_i(\pi)^*$ (which is associated with greater resolve on i's part) than under $p_i(\pi)$.

Once again, this type of analysis does not provide a fully general result as would a formal derivation. Our conclusion will be reasonably general, however, in that each specific example from which we draw our conclusions is actually one of a family of cases, all of which have similar characteristics. For example, there are other functions between $p_i(\pi)$ and $p_i(\pi)^*$ that follow the same general pattern but differ in the degree to which i's resolve is changed (e.g., $\mu_i = 0.81, 0.82$, etc.). Our conclusion drawn by comparing $p_i(\pi)$ and $p_i(\pi)^*$ will hold for any pair of functions in this family. More important, this method is much simpler and much easier to understand than is a fully general derivation.

We have seen that when j is more likely to win a war, should one occur, the probability of war becomes greater as i's resolve is increased. We may now determine the effect on the probability of war when j's resolve is increased. For this, consider the functions $p_j(\pi) = \pi^2 - .4\pi + .04$ and $p_j(\pi)^* = \pi^2 - .35\pi - .02$, the latter representing the case in which j's resolve is greater. First we see that the bargaining range is decreased since $\mu_j < \mu_j^*$. Thus, less of i's PDF is within the bargaining range, increasing the chances of war. Furthermore, we can see that, like for player i, as j's resolve increases, the proportion of its PDF within the bargaining range decreases. The total area under j's PDF is less, but the greater amount of the decrease is within the bargaining range. Thus, the probability of war increases as j's resolve is increased.

These results can be illustrated with reference to the specific cases shown in figure 16. Recall that in the initial case, where $p_i(\pi) = 1 - \pi^2$ and $p_j(\pi) = \pi^2 - .4\pi + .04$, the probability of war was .39. Consider first an increase in i's resolve using $p_i(\pi)^* = 1 - \pi^2 - .45\pi$. The probability of war is given by

$$1 - \left(\frac{\int_{0.2}^{0.8} - (2\pi + .45)}{\int_{0.0}^{0.8} - (2\pi + .45)} \cdot \frac{\int_{0.2}^{0.8} (2\pi - .4)}{\int_{0.2}^{1.2} (2\pi - .4)} \right) = 1 - (.87 \cdot .36) = .69.$$

Next, let $p_j(\pi)^* = \pi^2 - .35\pi - .02$, and once again use $p_i(\pi)$. The probability of war is

$$1 - \left(\frac{\int_{0.4}^{1.0} - 2\pi}{\int_{0.0}^{1.0} - 2\pi} \cdot \frac{\int_{0.4}^{1.0} 2\pi - .35}{\int_{0.4}^{1.2} 2\pi - .35} \right) = 1 - (.84 \cdot .58) = .51.$$

In both cases, as expected, the probability of war increased.

It is particularly interesting to compare the results of these two examples. In each case, the resolve of one party was altered by 0.2 units. While it is unlikely that we could measure resolve this precisely, let alone measure the resolve of two actors in comparable units, the general nature of these findings is informative. The probability of war increased by a greater amount when the party least likely to win a war, i, increased its resolve. This result would suggest that situations in which a relatively powerful state confronts a weaker but highly resolved adversary are particularly prone to erupt in war. It may be that the weaker side is determined not to make concessions in spite of the preponderant power of its opponent while the stronger side feels no need to make concessions. It often seems that observers are somewhat amazed by instances in which a weak state fights a hopeless war against a stronger aggressor, as did Poland and Finland in 1939. If we assume that a state whose territory is threatened would be highly resolved, these results suggest that such behavior would be the rule rather than the exception.

Turning to the effects of increasing the costs that one bargainer can impose on the other, we can see from the figure that, regardless of the side for whom the bargaining costs are increased, the probability of war declines. First note that the area under a party's PDF that is within the bargaining range remains constant as that player increases its ability to impose costs on the opponent. That is because the bargaining range remains fixed, as does that player's probability of acceptance function. Thus, all changes in the probability of war will result from changes in the PDF of the actor for whom the costs of bargaining have increased.

Consider two functions for i, $p_i(\pi) = 1 - \pi^2$ and $p_i(\pi)^* = 1.05 - \pi^2 - .05\pi$. The latter function represents a case in which j's ability to impose costs has been increased. From figure 16 it is obvious that as j's ability to impose costs increases, the proportion of the area under i's PDF that is within the bargaining range increases. In fact, for the example provided, all of i's PDF is within the bargaining range. Similarly, consider two functions for j, an initial function, $p_j(\pi) = \pi^2 - .4\pi + .04$, and another, $p_j(\pi)^* = \pi^2 + .05\pi - .05$, that represents an increase in i's ability to impose costs on j.[10] Again, the probability of war decreases through an increased willingness of j to accept a negotiated settlement. Thus, as when the parties are equally likely to win a war, an increase in the ability of one to impose costs on the other results in a decreased probability of war. Note that, once again, there is an upper limit to this result. Once all of a player's PDF is within the bargaining range, further decreases in the probability of war must come through changes in the other's probability of acceptance function.

We can easily see that our specific examples conform to our expectations. In the initial case, using $p_i(\pi)$ and $p_j(\pi)$, the probability of war equalled $1 - (.96 \cdot .64) = .39$. Since in each of our specific examples, one of the players'

PDFs is entirely within the bargaining range and the proportion of the other's that is within the range does not change, the probabilities will be given by $1 - (1.0 \cdot .64) = .36$ when j's ability to impose costs on i is increased and $1 - (.96 \cdot 1.0) = .04$ when i's ability to impose costs on j is increased.

Note that providing further advantages (in terms of the ability to impose bargaining costs) to the side more likely to win a war has less of an impact than does increasing the other side's ability to impose costs. In this case, our specific examples provide a fairly straightforward intuitive explanation for this result. The side less likely to win a war is already reluctant to risk a fight, and additional disadvantages can change this reluctance little. On the other hand, the party more likely to win a war is initially relatively willing to risk war. As the costs of these risks increase, however, this actor will become less and less willing to bear them. Since this party's willingness to risk war can be reduced a great deal, the probability of war can also be substantially reduced.

Case Studies

In this section I use the case studies presented in the Appendix to provide historical illustrations of the results derived above. These case studies are not intended to be an empirical confirmation of the hypotheses; rather, my purpose is to provide examples that merely establish the plausibility of the results. Clearly, the nature of the exercise prohibits definitive conclusions. There are too few cases to provide a high level of confidence in any results, and the values of the variables have not been established by rigorous, systematic coding procedures and are thus open to question. However, I have tried to characterize each case reasonably and in a manner consistent with the historical record (the justification for each coding decision can be found in the Appendix and will not be repeated here), and the cases have been selected to provide a great deal of variation in the variables of interest. Thus, the degree to which the theoretical derivations are consistent with the case histories should suggest the empirical applicability of the theory. Detailed chronologies of the cases are not repeated here. Rather, I provide brief, and admittedly simplistic, profiles of each crisis in terms of the variables with which we are concerned. I treat each as a two-party conflict and focus only on the primary, original disputants. I then outline the expectations regarding the outcomes of these crises that are drawn from the model. These expectations are expressed in terms of which, if any, of the three factors indicate a high probability of war and which indicate that a negotiated settlement will favor one side. These *postdictions* are stated quite generally for negotiated settlements (i.e., that the settlement should either favor one side or be roughly equal) and, in the end, comparatively for the probability of war (i.e, I specify which crises, according to the model, were most likely to have ended in war).

The Oregon Boundary Dispute involved the United States and Britain in a crisis over the boundary line between the Oregon Territory and Canada. Both parties saw the issue as relatively unimportant (as crisis issues go). The area was far removed from the population centers of both countries, and because of overtrapping, the economic value was believed to be declining. The resolve of both was relatively low, though because the disputed territory was on the North American continent, the United States was moderately resolved. The dispute had actually gone without resolution for several years, and the costs of continued nonagreement were fairly low. Although the crisis occurred at the height of British power, the perception on both sides was that the United States would have a very slight advantage in a war. Oregon was extremely difficult to reach from Britain, and supply would have been nearly impossible. The British were less concerned about the American military than about the American residents of Oregon, who were essentially seen by the British as well-armed, well-nourished savages perfectly suited to the environment. The only factor leading to an expectation of war is that the bargaining costs were low, and this is the least important factor. The resolve of the parties and their relative war-fighting capabilities suggest a negotiated settlement slightly in favor of the United States or about even. The actual settlement gave the United States what is now Washington State but not British Columbia, suggesting a split-the-difference outcome, and followed the Forty-ninth parallel, rather than the Columbia river, to the sea, suggesting a slight advantage to the United States. This settlement appears entirely consistent with the expectations of the model.

The crisis preceding the Seven Weeks War between Prussia and Austria was characterized by moderately high resolve on the part of both parties. The territories involved were not particularly crucial, but the settlement of the crisis had serious implications for the actors' ability to dominate in greater Germany and for their reputation as great powers. The bargaining costs were low to moderate. Few international costs were being paid, neither was suffering from heavy sanctions, and no unbearable military pressure was applied or expected, but the domestic political and economic situation in both countries produced some pressure for a settlement. The result of the war showed that Prussia had far greater military capabilities, though Austria had expected to be victorious.[11] I code this as a moderate disparity in war-fighting capabilities favoring Prussia. In this case, all three factors lead us to expect war, though this is somewhat mitigated by the moderate bargaining costs and the only moderate disparity in military capabilities. On the basis of the military disparity, a negotiated settlement would have been expected to favor Prussia slightly. The model accounts for the war that occurred.

Britain saw the French force at Fashoda as a serious threat to British prestige and the colonial empire. The French were preoccupied with domestic problems, and many relevant government officials did not approve of the Marchand mission in any case. Thus, the British were highly resolved in the crisis while the French hoped for a way out. The bargaining costs were moderate for the French, primarily because the crisis complicated the French domestic political scene. Though the crisis slowed the British efforts to reestablish colonial control along the Nile, it involved relatively low costs. The threat of military action was taken seriously and was seen as potentially costly for both parties. In terms of military capabilities, the British were vastly superior, both at the sight of the crisis and in the world; they enjoyed what has come to be called *escalation dominance*—in short, there was a clear disparity in war-fighting ability favoring the British. The high resolve of the British and the disparity in war-fighting capabilities suggest that war was a serious possibility, but the probability was lowered by the bargaining costs, the low French resolve, and the fact that the more powerful state was also the more resolved. Both the resolve factor and the military capability factor strongly favored the British, leading to the expectation of a negotiated settlement resembling a French capitulation. The actual outcome is consistent with this expectation, though the model might indicate a probability of war somewhat higher than was actually the case.

In the Agadir crisis, both France and Germany were moderately resolved. Both essentially accepted that French control over Morocco would be enhanced and that France would compensate Germany. At issue were only the precise terms of compensation. The exact compensation was not seen as a most critical issue by either, though both perceived that some prestige was at stake. The bargaining costs were relatively low for both, though they were significant in comparison to the values at stake. However, the potential costs of military action were great. The parties were approximately equal in war-fighting capabilities. Both were great powers, and while the Germans were probably superior in a one-on-one comparison, the French had a greater expectation of receiving assistance from allies. None of the factors lead to an expectation of war, and all suggest a compromise outcome. This expected outcome is what was observed. The probability of war in the actual crisis was higher than suggested by this analysis, but that is because Germany actually came much closer to going to war with Britain than it did with France. In this case, in particular, ignoring additional parties is somewhat misleading.

The crisis leading to the Winter War between Finland and the Soviet Union was characterized by high resolve on the part of the Soviets and by very high resolve on the part of the Finns. The Soviets sought Finnish territory that the Finns were most reluctant to surrender and that the Soviets believed to be necessary for an expected defense against Germany. The bargaining costs were fairly high for both parties, especially for the Soviets in that the longer it took to acquire the territory, the less time there was to prepare the defenses.

Clearly, there was an enormous disparity in war-fighting capabilities favoring the Soviet Union. The high resolve of both parties and the disparity in war-fighting abilities both suggest a high probability of war. Note also that in this case the weaker side was the more (and greatly) resolved. This was a situation that the model suggests is most likely to end in war. The only mitigating factor is that the costs of delaying an agreement were quite high. Soviet military strength provided some bargaining advantage, but the Finns had the edge in resolve and in terms of the bargaining costs. This situation suggests that an expected negotiated settlement would have given the Soviets much of what they sought but that they would have had to make large concessions, perhaps as side payments, in exchange. (It is interesting in this regard that the Soviets did offer substantial concessions, particularly in terms of offering to exchange territory.) Again, the outcome of the crisis was consistent with what the model would lead us to expect.

Finally, the Cuban Missile Crisis provides another case in which resolve was asymmetrical. The Soviets were somewhat determined not to be humiliated, but the United States perceived the missiles as a significant deterioration in the status quo. Furthermore, the site of the crisis was only 90 miles from the United States, so the Americans were highly resolved with the Soviets less so. The bargaining costs were high in that significant military operations were underway and the risks of an accidental war were seen to be great. The expected costs of large-scale military moves were incalculable. The United States enjoyed a large disparity in war-fighting capabilities, both in terms of forces at the site of the crisis and in terms of strategic capabilities. The high level of resolve and the disparity in war-fighting capabilities suggest that the probability of war was fairly high, though this probability was reduced by the high bargaining costs and the fact that the more resolved party was also the stronger. The asymmetries in the resolve variable and in the military capabilities both suggest that a negotiated settlement would be expected to favor the United States strongly. These expectations are fully consistent with the outcome of the crisis.

In comparative terms, the model suggests that the probability of war was quite low in the Oregon and Agadir crises, it was moderate (but significant) in the Fashoda and Cuban crises, it was somewhat higher in the Austro-Prussian crisis, and it was very high in the Russo-Finnish crisis. These results seem to be consistent with the historical record. The cases in which the probability of war was deemed to be the highest did in fact end in war, and the record suggests that the prospects of peace were greater in the Austro-Prussian case. The record suggests that the probability of war in the Oregon crisis was quite low, as it was in the Agadir crisis (if Britain is ignored). War appeared to be a very real possibility in the Cuban crisis, though the model probably exaggerates the likelihood of war in the Fashoda crisis. With the exception of

Fashoda, the ranking of the cases in terms of the probability of war assigned by the model appears quite consistent with what one would conclude from the historical record.

Clearly, we must be circumspect regarding this type of analysis, and we cannot safely draw any empirical inferences. This analysis cannot be seen as an empirical test of the model, particularly since the outcomes of the crises were known before the variables were coded. This exercise is valuable, however, in that it provides some empirical referent to the highly abstract derivations presented above. These examples show that the model can plausibly represent real-world crises, and they do give reason to be optimistic that the model is empirically useful. It is especially suggestive that, by starting from the spatial model of crisis bargaining and using only three variables, we can construct plausible explanations (admittedly in a highly stylized fashion) for the outcomes of these crises.

Summary and Discussion

In this chapter the spatial model of crisis bargaining has been used to derive hypotheses linking the power and resolve of crisis participants to the outcomes of international crises. Some of the conclusions the model provides are fairly intuitive. The conclusions suggest, for example, that highly resolved crisis participants possessing vast military capabilities can expect favorable negotiated outcomes. That is not surprising, however; we would justifiably question a model that led to contrary conclusions. Placing such obvious hypotheses within the context of a well-integrated theory of crises is valuable in itself, but the model has led to a number of hypotheses that are either non- or counterintuitive. More important, the results suggest that the theoretical linkages among the variables might be more complex than is commonly believed. If we consider the hypotheses associating a participant's resolve to crisis outcomes as an example, the model implies (1) that higher levels of resolve should lead to more favorable negotiated outcomes (which conforms to the conventional wisdom); (2) that higher levels of resolve should increase the probability that war will result (a question over which the conventional wisdom is divided and ambiguous); and (3) that the precise impact of the resolve variable will depend on the relative war-fighting abilities of the disputants (a point on which the conventional wisdom is mute).

The question with which I am most concerned has to do with what these results tell us about the likelihood that various crises will end in war. The impact of the variables taken singly is fairly straightforward. When resolve is high, the disparity in war-fighting capabilities great, and the costs of disagreement low, the probability of war is high. The interaction effects are particularly interesting, however. The most dangerous crises, in terms of the probability of war, appear to be those involving military unequals with the weaker party being highly resolved. The crises least apt to end in war are those between military equals who are both able to inflict enormous bargaining costs.[12] Even without deriving hypotheses at the level of mathematical precision that is possible with this model, the results improve our explanatory and predictive power. The model can account for the outcomes of historical crises, and by considering the general profiles of any future crises, we have some ability to anticipate whether they will be peacefully resolved.

The primary contribution of this chapter has been to frame the debate regarding the impact of three presumably important variables in terms of a formally specified theory. I have also shown, however, that the conclusions drawn from the model are consistent with the outcomes of several historical crises, which suggests that the model can provide, at the very least, plausible explanations for the outcomes of these cases. The usefulness of this theory must ultimately be judged on the basis of a systematic empirical test of the hypotheses presented. While such a test is beyond the scope of this book,[13] we can see that these conclusions bear on a number of arguments found in the international relations literature.

First, these results bear on a number of empirical studies that have sought to determine whether war is more likely between states of equal power or between states of unequal power (Garnham 1976; Weede 1976). These studies generally suggest that war is more likely between states of relatively equal power; however, this model indicates that crises are less likely to erupt into war when the participants are of roughly equal power—which would seem to be disconfirmed by the empirical evidence. The source of this incongruity might be that the relationship between power parity and war is more complicated than is reflected in these empirical studies. It is possible that crises are less likely to end in war when the sides are fairly equal in power but that crises are much more likely to occur among states of equal power. It is thus possible for the results of the empirical studies to be correct regarding the fairly simple association between power parity and war and for the model to be correct in its more complex representation of crises. If that is the case, we would expect that those crises involving states of disparate power that did occur would be more likely to escalate to war than those crises occurring between states of roughly equal power. Although the data sets used in the earlier studies were not appropriate to test this hypothesis, new data that are appropriate have recently been collected. Research by Siverson and Tennefoss (1984) using data on the escalation of international conflicts tends to support the conclusions of the model presented here. They have found that a disproportionate number of conflicts between states of unequal power have escalated.

Second, the results in this chapter can provide a theoretical basis for interpreting and reconciling some of the empirical research regarding the effect of nuclear weapons. Organski and Kugler (1980) note a number of instances in which nonnuclear powers have gone to war with nuclear powers, from which they infer that nuclear weapons do not deter war. Stoll (1982), on the other hand, found that major power–major power disputes have been less likely to escalate to war in the nuclear age than they were previously, indicating that nuclear weapons do have some inhibiting effect on war. These seemingly contradictory findings are actually both consistent with the results presented here. If we assume that the presence of nuclear weapons serves to increase the costs associated with delays in the resolution of a dispute and that the major power–minor power distinction indicates which side is more likely to win a war (with the parties in a major-major dispute being relatively equally likely to win a war), we can reconcile these empirical results. First, since the model indicates that in crises between military equals, increasing the costs of disagreement serves to decrease the probability of escalation to war, we can see that Stoll's finding is clearly consistent with the model. Second, note that Organski and Kugler focused on disputes involving a nuclear power against a nonnuclear power. Given the cases they examined, however, this distinction coincided perfectly with a major power–minor power distinction. Although we expect the nuclear weapons to inhibit escalation to war (but not completely), this expectation is countered by the expectation that crises between military unequals are more likely to escalate. Thus, Organski and Kugler's findings are also consistent with this model.

Third, the derivations of this model are consistent with much of the recent empirical work on extended deterrence by Huth and Russett (1984 and 1988) and Huth (1988). Since their cases are obviously a subset of the cases to which this model applies and there are some conceptualizations over which the two bodies of research are not entirely commensurate, we cannot treat their work as a completely satisfactory empirical test of this model. However, their work does contribute to our confidence in the empirical validity of the model by showing that results from a closely related empirical domain support the hypotheses; and the results derived from this model provide one theoretical basis from which to understand their findings. Space does not permit a complete comparison of the implications of the spatial model with the empirical results provided by Huth and Russett, but a few brief comments are instructive.

Their findings in the earlier study support the conclusion that the probability of deterrence success is increased by "close economic and political-military ties between the defender and its protégé" and by a "Local military superiority for the defender and its protégé" (Huth and Russett 1984, 523). These findings appear to support the hypotheses that high levels of resolve and greater military capabilities are associated with a higher probability of achieving a favorable crisis outcome. They also discovered that a military alliance between the defender and protégé was associated with deterrence failure, but in that study *failure* was seen as either not achieving one's aims or war. Since the spatial model suggests that resolve should be associated with a higher probability of a favorable outcome and a higher probability of war, this latter result might not contradict the model. In fact, their data do indicate that the alliance variable is associated with a greater likelihood of a favorable negotiated outcome and a higher probability of war (Morgan 1988), which is consistent with the spatial model.

In a more recent study, Huth and Russett (1988) have focused on the possibility that the variables that are most important in determining whether a deterrent threat is challenged might not also be the most important in determining whether war occurs. Among these results are those indicating that all forms of military capabilities do not have similar effects. A favorable short-term balance is more important for deterrence success than is a favorable long-term balance. That suggests that treating *power* as having two analytically distinct components, as is done in this model, can be theoretically useful. Furthermore, they interpret this finding as implying that "Deterrence by denial, rather than deterrence by threat of punishment, seems more important" (Huth and Russett 1988, 42). That is consistent with the results based on table 1 that indicate that a great ability to impose bargaining costs on the opponent is a less important determinant of crisis outcomes than is the ability to prevail in war. In addition, their results suggest that military capabilities (which are important determinants of nonwar deterrence failure) are less important for determining if war occurs than the "nature and strength of the linkages between the defender and protégé" (Huth and Russett 1988, 43). This conclusion is consistent with the simple hypothesis that the higher the resolve of an actor, the greater the likelihood of war. The more complex nature of this empirical result is also consistent with the spatial model's implications regarding the interaction effects among the variables. Consider the specific π' values and probabilities of war associated with the examples in figure 16. Using the square functions (indicating j's superior military capability) shifts π' from .6 in the linear case to .76 and increases the probability of war from .36 to .39. When we then also increase j's resolve, π' increases further to .77 and the probability of war rises to .51. Thus, given j's superior military capability, greater resolve on j's part should contribute relatively little to the likelihood of a favorable negotiated settlement while significantly increasing the likelihood of war, a hypothesis the Huth and Russett study bears out.

The results presented here are also relevant to the debate regarding how best to behave when involved in a crisis. Schelling (1966, chap. 2), for one, has argued that a useful bargaining tactic is to commit oneself to one's position by taking some action that makes it impossible for one to make further concessions. This tactic, according to the argument, will force the opponent to give in. We can see that the results derived from the spatial model suggest that this might not be a good strategy.

To develop the argument, let us first consider how to put Schelling's (1966) suggestion in the language of the model. Consider a situation in which two actors must divide some good, say territory, and assume that the bargaining set contains more than one solution. Schelling's advice to a player, say j, would be to take some action that would make it impossible for j to accept less than a given amount of the territory without a fight. For Schelling's suggestion to make sense, the position j commits to must provide j greater utility than μ_j (for j is already committed to this position). Furthermore, it must provide j with equal or less utility than μ_i, lest it cause the bargaining set to be empty, assuring war. Schelling adopts the assumption, at least implicitly, that if the bargaining set is nonempty, then a negotiated settlement will be reached. Thus, the optimal strategy for j is to commit itself to μ_i. Presumably, Schelling would agree that the committing action cannot be *soft* (i.e., j cannot later concede more than its commitment allows). Therefore, the process of making a commitment involves introducing a new, nonnegotiable issue into the bargaining that serves to shift j's reservation point in the utility space closer to Δ_j; that is, j's resolve is increased.

We have seen that the results derived from the spatial model tend to support Schelling's (1966) prescription in one respect: increasing a player's resolve shifts the most likely negotiated outcome in that player's favor. An examination of the entire probability distribution of outcomes suggests that the strategy might be less than wise, however. Although the solution point will shift in j's favor, the probability of war will increase. If j follows this strategy of commitment and commits itself to μ_i, the result would be an extremely high probability of war (since the probability that i would accept is near 0) and j would have foreclosed at least one alternative that it initially preferred to war. A player making such a commitment might thus be risking a high probability of war over an issue of relatively little importance. Furthermore, since the relative war-fighting capabilities of the parties have not been considered, the risk might be of a disastrous war.

The different prescriptions regarding the wisdom of making commitments is due to one assumption. If one assumes that an agreement will be reached if the bargaining set is nonempty, then the risk of war associated with Schelling's (1966) prescription is nonexistent as long as j does not commit to a position that provides i less utility than does μ_i. This model is not based on such an assumption. Rather, I assume that the probability of war varies directly with the size of the bargaining range, ceteris paribus. On the basis of this assumption, which I believe to be more reasonable, a strategy of commitment would be wise only in situations in which the potential for gain in the negotiated settlement far outweighs the increased probability of war (see

Morgan and Dawson 1992 for a formal analysis of this issue). Furthermore, an optimal commitment strategy, should one exist, might not be for j to commit to μ_i. Balancing the gains with the costs might lead to a different optimum strategy. In general, however, it would seem that a player's resolve should be inherent to the situation, not created.

At this point it seems fairly clear that the spatial model of crisis bargaining has the potential to provide a great deal of insight into international crisis outcomes. The model serves to reduce some of the ambiguity surrounding the relationships among power, resolve, and crisis behavior by incorporating, in a precise, systematic fashion, these variables that are often purported to affect crisis outcomes. We have also seen that the results of a number of empirical studies found in the literature lend support to the hypotheses derived from the model; furthermore, the implications of the model provide a means for reconciling some apparently contradictory empirical findings. Finally, the model, by specifying the probable consequences of particular strategies of coercive diplomacy, appears to have policy relevance. That suggests that this model can serve as the basis for a relatively powerful explanatory theory. While the hypotheses derived in this chapter are interesting and useful, they paint an incomplete picture of crisis bargaining. We have ignored the issues at stake, the analyses tell us nothing about bargaining strategies, and we have considered only two-actor, zero-sum situations. In the following chapter, I shall reintroduce the issue space and begin the process of using the model to study more complex questions.

CHAPTER 4

Bargaining Agendas in International Crises

One advantage of the spatial model relative to other formal bargaining models is that it permits some analyses of bargaining processes. The issue space is particularly important in this regard because it focuses our attention directly on the bargainers' stances on the issues, the relative salience of the issues for the bargainers, and the possible strategies bargainers can adopt to bring about a settlement. While there are a number of processes important to crisis bargaining, in this chapter, I apply the spatial model to the analysis of agenda setting. I have chosen to focus initially on agenda setting because many bargaining theorists and practitioners consider it to be the most critical facet of the bargaining process. Thus, there exists a well-developed body of theory on which to draw for this analysis. In particular, questions regarding bargaining agendas are common in all types of bargaining literature, as well as the literature that is concerned with describing international events, and spatial models have been used to address the question of agenda setting in the study of committee and legislative voting (Enelow and Hinich 1984).

The analyses in this chapter will proceed in two stages. The first stage will be devoted to demonstrating that the order in which issues are considered can affect crisis outcomes. I shall show that when the issues in dispute are considered sequentially, the order in which they are addressed can determine the nature of a negotiated settlement. I shall also show that whether the issues are addressed sequentially or simultaneously can affect the nature of negotiated settlements and the probability that war will result. The second stage will examine whether bringing additional issues into the bargaining for linkage purposes has an impact on crisis outcomes. I shall demonstrate that, theoretically, linking issues should increase the probability of a negotiated settlement. Since there is ample evidence that such tactics do not always work, however, a major portion of this chapter is devoted to developing hypotheses associating various conditions with the success, or failure, of issue linkage.

Before turning to an examination of the hypotheses regarding bargaining agendas to which the spatial theory leads, a number of preliminary points must be made. First, some of the simplifying assumptions made in the previous chapter will be retained. In particular, I continue to consider cases involving only two bargainers. However, some of the more restrictive assumptions are relaxed at various points in the analysis. We will no longer assume the situation regarding the division of the values at stake is zero-sum. This assumption must be dropped to make sense of an examination of the trade-offs across issues that actors are willing to make. In addition, the assumption of separable preferences will also be relaxed at some points. This change will allow us to derive a few more interesting and general hypotheses regarding the linkages actors make across issues. Finally, it should be noted that most of the discussion in this chapter will focus on the issue space. Some references to the utility space will be made, but since our major concern is with the effect on bargaining of the way in which the issues are addressed, the questions of interest are more fruitfully analyzed within the issue space.

Is the Agenda Important?

Bargaining in the initial stages of international crises almost always concerns the setting of the agenda. Before proposals regarding specific outcomes on the issues are made, the bargainers must determine what issues are open for negotiation and in what order they will be considered. Furthermore, questions regarding the agenda often arise during the course of a crisis as parties propose additional issues to be included. Casual observers often attribute this practice to pettiness or bad faith on the part of the bargainers, but in fact, agenda setting is serious business. It may not be an exaggeration to suggest that decisions about what issues to include and in what order are more important determinants of bargaining outcomes than are decisions regarding threats or concession rates.

Probably the clearest example of the importance placed on agenda setting can be found in the bargaining involved in the Fashoda crisis of 1898. The primary issue revolved around the presence of the French forces under Marchand at Fashoda, which the British interpreted as an act of hostility. From early in the crisis, it was fairly obvious to many in the French government that their position was untenable, and most, unlike their British counterparts, were unwilling to go to war over the issue. The French strategy quickly came to be aimed primarily at using Marchand as a lever to extract some concessions from the British in regard to clarifying the location of colonial boundaries in Africa. The bargaining at the height of the crisis focused on whether Marchand's exit from Fashoda would be negotiated only in conjunction with the border issues, would occur on a formal commitment by the British to negotiate on the borders, or would occur before the British would even consider other issues. Clearly, this bargaining was aimed at deciding which issues were open for negotiation and in what order they would be addressed; and as the parties well knew, the outcome of the bargaining over the agenda would substantially determine the nature of the final settlement.

Had the French been able to link Marchand's withdrawal to a settlement of the colonial boundaries, they would have had a significant bargaining chip with which to extract British concessions. Since the resolution of the agenda question called for Marchand to abandon Fashoda before the boundary questions would even be discussed, the British were able to achieve a highly favorable settlement.

In spite of the widespread recognition that agendas are important determinants of crisis outcomes, there have been no formal theoretic studies of agenda setting in international bargaining (though, as I shall discuss below, there have been analyses of issue linkage). A number of studies have formally addressed questions of agenda setting in voting situations, however. The majority of these have shown that the order in which issues are voted on has an impact on outcomes (e.g., Levine and Plott 1977; Plott and Levine 1978). More important for our purposes, Enelow and Hinich (1984) have used spatial theory to show that whether issues are voted on sequentially or simultaneously can influence the outcome of committee decisions, as can the order in which issues are considered. In the remainder of this section, I draw on this work to demonstrate that the bargaining agenda can affect crisis outcomes. I develop the argument in two stages. First, I show that even in extremely simple cases, settling the issues one at a time can produce different outcomes than does settling the issues simultaneously. I then show that when the issues are considered sequentially, the order in which they are considered can affect the outcome.

We can focus on an example to demonstrate that crisis outcomes can be affected by whether the issues are negotiated sequentially or simultaneously. Consider the situation represented in figure 17 where two parties must determine how to divide two pieces of territory. For the sake of simplicity, the example has been constructed so that, for both players, the amount of territory gained maps directly to utility. Thus, the issue space and the utility space can be represented in a single dimension. In addition, I suppose that the bargainers are identical in every respect, except that j places more value on territory 1 than on territory 2 and that i values territory 2 more than territory 1. Notice the effect that this supposition has as we move from issue 1 to issue 2: The only parameters defining the actors' probability of acceptance functions that change are Δ_i and Δ_j. Obviously, the shape of the functions remains constant since the probability that each would win a war does not change. Furthermore, given constant resolve, the actors' reservation points, μ_i and μ_j, are unchanged. Though the value of a settlement at, for example, μ_j would be less relative to the costs of war for j on issue 2 than on issue 1, the expected utility of war would be reduced by a similar amount. For each player, however, Δ will be farther away from O on the issue of less importance. That is because on the less important issue, the utility loss associated with surrendering a

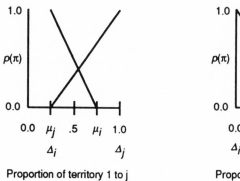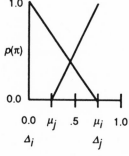

1.0

$p(\pi)$

0.0

0.0 μ_j .5 μ_i 1.0

Δ_i Δ_j

Proportion of territory 1 to j

1.0

$p(\pi)$

0.0

0.0 μ_j .5 μ_i 1.0

Δ_i Δ_j

Proportion of territory 2 to j

b

O_j

c   b

π'

Proportion of
territory 2 to j

d

a

O_i

Proportion of territory 1 to j

Fig. 17. Combining issues and crisis outcomes: *a*) Settling one issue at a time; *b*) Settling the issues simultaneously

given proportion of territory is reduced relative to the utility loss associated with the costs of bargaining. Therefore, an actor will be willing to concede immediately a greater portion of the less important territory to avoid the bargaining costs.

For the bargaining over territory 1, $p_j(\pi) = 1.33\pi - .33$ and $p_i(\pi) = -2\pi + 1.5$. Thus, $p_{ij}'(\pi) = -5.32\pi + 2.66$; and setting $p_{ij}'(\pi) = 0$, we find that $\pi' = .5$. From the result in the previous chapter, we know that changing the Δs will not affect the solution, so π' on the second issue is also at .5. If the issues are considered separately, the negotiated settlement most likely to be achieved is for j and i to each receive half of each territory.

Figure 17b shows the issue space representation of this conflict when the issues are addressed simultaneously. For any given proposal, the proportion of territory 1 going to j is reflected by the proposal's x coordinate and the proportion of territory 2 going to j is reflected by the y coordinate. Recall that by the weighted Euclidian distance preference rule, the distances between the actors' ideal points, $O_j = (1,1)$ and $O_i = (0,0)$, and a proposal (x,y) are given by $[(1 - x)^2 + (1 - y)^2]^{1/2} {}_{A_j}$ and $[(0 - x)^2 + (0 - y)^2]^{1/2}{}_{A_i}$ for j and i, respectively. An actor's salience matrix,

$$A_i = \begin{bmatrix} a_{11} & a_{12} \\ a_{12} & a_{22} \end{bmatrix},$$

reflects the trade-offs the actor would be willing to make across issues. Since we are assuming the separability of issues, $a_{12} = 0$ for both i and j. Issue 1 is more important to j, so in A_j $a_{j11} > a_{j22}$. Likewise, since issue 2 is more important to i, $a_{i11} < a_{i22}$ in A_i. Thus, in figure 17b, the actors' indifference contours are elliptical.[1] Notice that three such contours have been drawn for each actor, one passing through each actor's reservation point,[2] labeled a and b for j and i, respectively, and one passing through π', the solution point when the issues were separated.

We can easily see from figure 17b that the solution point will change when the issues are linked. We know that the theoretical solution point will be Pareto optimal, and we can see that π' is not in the set of Pareto-optimal outcomes (which is denoted by the curve connecting O_i and O_j). Both i and j prefer any proposal in the shaded area below and to the right of π' to π'. Therefore, any of these outcomes would have a higher probability than does π' of being accepted. In this particular case, the solution point is such that each side receives about two-thirds of the territory it values most and one-third of the territory valued least. Not only can considering the issues simultaneously lead to a different outcome, but both players will prefer the new outcome to the old.

Figure 17b also shows that considering the issues together can reduce the probability of war, a point that will be addressed more fully in the section that follows. Recall that as the number of points in the bargaining set increases, ceteris paribus, the probability of war decreases. When the issues are considered singly, each party would definitely prefer war to granting the opponent more than 75 percent of either territory. In figure 17b, the bargaining set this produces is denoted by the square *acbd*. When the issues are linked, the bargaining set is bounded by the players' reservation contours and the feasible set boundaries. This set is denoted by the heavy lines. Since the former set is entirely contained in the latter, we know that the probability of war is less when the issues are linked. In fact, it is interesting to note that some outcomes that both parties prefer to the original π' are not even in the original bargaining set (i.e., those points in the shaded area outside *acbd*).

Next, I shall demonstrate that when the issues are considered sequentially, the bargaining outcome can be affected by the order in which they are addressed. It is necessary only to demonstrate the existence of at least one case in which the order of settlement affects the bargaining outcome to establish this possibility result. Thus, we can focus the discussion on a single example, which will be depicted in figure 18.

We will again suppose that i and j are involved in a dispute regarding the division of two territories and that 1 is the more important to j while 2 is the more valuable to i. Specifically, set $a_{j11} = 2$, $a_{j22} = 1$, $a_{i11} = 1$, and $a_{i22} = 2$. Furthermore, for this discussion, we will assume that the issues are not separable for j. This means that j's preferences on one issue partially depend on the outcome of the other. It may be the case, for example, that j's reservation point on either issue would be at .25 but that over both issues, j must do better than (.25,.25). For example, if j accepts .25 of territory 1, it may then refuse to accept any less than .75 of territory 2. In addition, if it accepts .25 of territory 2, it may refuse less than .5 of territory 1 (this reflects the greater value j places on 1). This is represented in the model by setting $a_{j12} \neq 0$.

The particular case to be used here is pictured in figure 18a. I have set $a_{j12} = 2/3$, so the weighted Euclidian distance between $O_j = (1,1)$ and a proposal, (x,y), is given by $[(2)(1 - x)^2 + (2)(2/3)(1 - x)(1 - y) + (1 - y)^2]^{1/2}$. Note that the axes of j's indifference contours are no longer parallel to the issue space axes. The new reservation contour for j is represented by the heavy curve. We can determine from this what j's reservation point on one issue is, given that the other issue has been resolved. For example, if issue 2 has been resolved at .5, j's reservation point on issue 1 would be at about .35.

We can now consider how the solution is affected by the order in which the issues are considered. Figures 18b and 18c provide the illustrations for when issue 1 is considered first and when issue 2 is considered first, respectively. Notice that for i, all parameters are identical to those in figure 17a, regardless of which issue is considered first. For j, we are faced with the

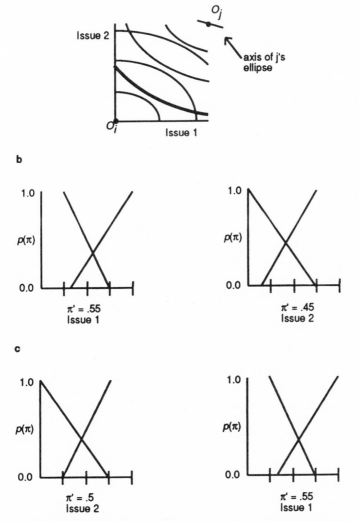

Fig. 18. Order of issue consideration and crisis outcomes: *a*) The 2-issue example—j's preferences nonseparable; *b*) Issue 1 settled first; *c*) Issue 2 settled first

problem that its reservation point on the issue to be settled first will depend on its expectations regarding the outcome of the issue to be discussed last. Virtually any assumption regarding j's expectations would be questionable, and j's expectations will, in fact, affect the solution point.[3] To establish this result, however, any assumption regarding j's expectations can be made. I will arbitrarily assume that j will expect the issue to be settled at .5.

First, suppose that issue 2 will be considered only after issue 1 is settled. Since j will expect issue 2 to be resolved at .5, μ_j will be at about .35. Thus, $p_j(\pi) = 1.5\pi - .5$ and, as before, $p_i(\pi) = -2\pi + 1.5$. Solving for $p_{ij'}(\pi) = 0$, we find that $p_{ij'}(\pi) = -6\pi + 3.25$ and $\pi' = .55$. Turning to issue 2, j knows that issue 1 was settled at .55, so $\mu_j = .15$. From this, we can determine that $p_j(\pi) = 1.66\pi - .25$, $p_i(\pi) = -1.33\pi + 1$, and $p_{ij'}(\pi) = -4.4\pi + 2$. In this case, $\pi' = .45$. Thus, when issue 1 is settled before issue 2 in this situation, the solution is at $(.55, .45)$.

We can follow a similar procedure to determine the result when issue 2 is considered first. Since j expects issue 1 to be resolved at .5, $\mu_j = .25$. Note that this is identical to the situation in figure 17a, so we know that $\pi' = .5$. Furthermore, we have just seen that when the solution on issue 2 is at $\pi' = .5$, the solution for issue 1 is $\pi' = .55$. Thus, when issue 2 is considered first, the solution is at $(.55, .5)$. This establishes the possibility that when issues are addressed sequentially, the order of consideration affects the solution.

The results presented thus far in this chapter show the possibility that the nature of the bargaining agenda can affect the outcome of international crises. Crisis bargainers have long known that outcomes are, to an extent, determined by what issues are open for negotiation and how these issues are packaged and ordered. In every crisis described in the Appendix, the initial stages of bargaining were aimed, at least in part, at setting the agenda. Establishing the result that the agenda can matter is useful, particularly in that it provides a theoretical basis for the conventional wisdom; but it tells us little about what determines how the agenda is set or what the precise impact on outcomes will be. In the next section, I shall begin to address this question with a fairly detailed examination of the factors that affect the success or failure of issue linkage strategies.

Issues and Issue Linkage

In a number of international crises, a peaceful resolution has become possible only after an issue not originally in contention is brought into the bargaining for linkage purposes. In the Cuban Missile Crisis, for example, the willingness of the Soviets to remove their missiles was linked to Kennedy's public promise not to invade Cuba and his private assurance that U.S. missiles would be removed from Turkey. Similarly, in the Agadir crisis of 1911, Germany agreed to a French protectorate in Morocco only after France compensated Germany with a section of territory in the Congo. Both crises were resolved peacefully when the participants included additional issues that led to an exchange of benefits, permitting both sides to achieve some positive results.

That such exchanges occur should not be surprising given the frequency with which such behavior is extolled in the international relations literature. Traditional balance of power theorists have suggested that "compensations" provide one means of lessening tensions and conflict between great powers (Gulick 1955), and a number of the more recent perspectives on international relations have explicitly focused on the issues over which conflicts occur and have considered the possibility of linking issues as a means of resolving conflict (Keohane and Nye 1977; Mansbach and Vasquez 1981). Students of foreign policy and diplomacy have recognized the importance of "tactical linkages" in resolving international disputes (see, e.g., Haas 1980; Iklé 1964; Kissinger 1979; Oye 1979; Wallace 1976), and recent theoretical work in international relations has shown that issue linkages can improve the chances of cooperation in international disputes (McGinnis 1986; Morrow 1986 and 1992; Sebenius 1983; Tollison and Willett 1979). Furthermore, scholars in other disciplines, such as social-psychology, have provided theoretical arguments and experimental evidence regarding the benefits of issue linkage in a wide range of bargaining contexts (see, e.g., Deutsch 1973; Pruitt 1981; Rubin and Brown 1975).[4]

The cloud around the silver lining of such a broad consensus is that in many cases linkage attempts are unsuccessful. Failure usually occurs when one party refuses to consider an exchange across issues. That occurred during the bargaining preceding the Seven Weeks War when Austria refused to consider cash side payments from Prussia in exchange for the rights to Schleswig-Holstein and from Italy in exchange for Venice. Similarly, in the negotiations prior to the Winter War of 1939, Finland would not exchange the territory that the Soviets coveted for a segment of Soviet territory. Linkage failures have also occurred in crises that did not end in war. During the Oregon Boundary Dispute of 1846, which was resolved peacefully, the British refused an American offer to draw the Oregon boundary as the British desired if the British would then support the Americans in acquiring part of northern California from Mexico.

The extent to which such linkage failures occur in the face of a significant consensus regarding the benefits of exchange suggests that, at best, the theory of issue linkage in international conflict is underdeveloped. The remainder of this chapter is devoted to the development of this theory by focusing specifically on those factors that affect the likelihood of linkage success, or failure, in international crises. This discussion will contribute to our knowledge in a positive sense by highlighting the conditions under which linkages will be useful and by suggesting linkage strategies that may contribute to the peaceful resolution of international crises. The argument will proceed as follows: First, I shall demonstrate why we expect issue linkages to facilitate conflict resolution. I shall then discuss a number of explanations for linkage failure that can be found in the literature, and I shall show why these are inadequate, at least when applied to crisis bargaining. Finally, I shall use the spatial model to determine when linkage attempts should be expected to fail and I shall discuss some implications for crisis management strategies suggested by these results.

The Spatial Model and Issue Linkages

Earlier in this chapter we considered a crisis involving two issues and found that the probability of war decreased when they were addressed simultaneously. At this point, I shall demonstrate that bringing additional issues into the bargaining for linkage purposes can, theoretically, be expected to decrease the probability of war. The results to be derived from the spatial model are essentially identical to those produced by Tollison and Willett (1979) and Sebenius (1983), who have used microeconomic techniques to show that issue linkages can facilitate agreement in international bargaining situations. I shall use a simple example, depicted in figure 19, to paraphrase their argument. In figure 19 there are two actors, i and j, involved in a crisis over how to divide a piece of territory between them—issue 1. The second issue, which might be used for linkage purposes, represents a cash side payment that i will pay to j. Each point on issue 2 is associated with a given proportion of the total cash amount being considered. Note that i is located in the space such that it receives all of the territory and pays no cash while j is located such that it receives all of the territory and all of the cash. Note that the example is constructed such that i is more concerned with the territory than with the cash while j places greater value on the cash.

With this simple construction we can paraphrase the Sebenius (1983) and Tollison and Willett (1979) argument. First note the curve connecting O_i with O_j in figure 19. This curve passes through the points of tangency between the actors' indifference contours and denotes the Pareto set. For any outcome, π, not in the Pareto set, there is at least one outcome, π', in the Pareto set such that π' is preferred to π by at least one actor and the other actor either prefers π' to π or is indifferent between them. We can thus expect any negotiated settlement to be an element of the Pareto set. Now consider what the negotiated settlement is likely to be if issue 2 is not brought into the bargaining. For this example, suppose that the parties are indistinguishable in terms of power, resolve, and any other variable that might affect the bargaining. If issue 1, the division of the territory, is decided singly, the spatial model suggests that we

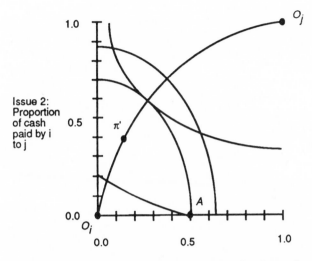

Issue 1: Proportion of disputed territory to j

Fig. 19. A spatial model of issue linkage

should expect the parties to divide the territory evenly. The outcome would thus be at point *A* in figure 19—each side gets half the territory and no cash changes hands. Now suppose that one of the parties suggests that issue 2, the cash, be introduced into the bargaining as a linkage candidate (j may make the suggestion, hoping to trade some territory for the more desirable cash, or i may bring this up, hoping to buy some of the more desirable territory). With the possibility of an exchange of territory for cash, the bargaining solution shifts to approximately π'. Since both parties prefer π' to point *A* , we can see that both sides can profit by introducing the issue for linkage purposes, and since both are happier with the outcome, we can assume that the likelihood of a negotiated settlement, rather than a war, is increased.

Why Linkages Fail: Traditional Explanations

This general result suggests that issue linkages should be a pervasive phenomenon in that for virtually any dispute, there should be an issue, or a set of issues, that would lead to a settlement by being incorporated into the bargaining. Yet that is not what we observe. While linkages are a factor in many dispute resolutions, there have also been many crises in which linkage attempts have failed to prevent escalation to war. Even more perplexing, in light of the relatively straightforward and powerful theoretical result, are cases like the Oregon Boundary Dispute, in which the conflict was resolved peacefully even though a linkage attempt was refused. Several reasons for such failures can be culled from the issue linkage literature. Three such reasons predominate and are worthy of discussion. As will be seen, each is unsatisfactory, at least for explaining linkage failures in international crises.

While setting out his version of the above theoretical result, Sebenius (1983) introduced a number of arguments concerning the conditions under which a linkage attempt would not be beneficial. The crux of each argument essentially is that if the bargaining set is empty when the additional issue is introduced, then the linkage will not facilitate agreement. Recall that the bargaining set is defined as the set of outcomes that are at least minimally acceptable to all parties. Clearly, if the bargaining set is empty in an international crisis situation, war is preferred to any proposed outcomes by at least one of the parties, so the linkage could not lead to an agreement. Thus, for example, any issue proposed for linkage purposes that either does not create sufficient additional benefit to overcome an impasse on the initial issue or that creates an impasse in its own right would lead to a linkage failure.

This argument undoubtedly accounts for some linkage failures and does specify a minimum requirement that must be met by a linkage attempt. It falls short in several respects, however. One problem is that the explanation for linkage failures is actually tautological—failures occur when the bargaining set is empty, and we know the bargaining set was empty when a failure occurs. More importantly, a fairly strict assumption regarding rational behavior underlies this explanation. It is assumed that if the bargaining set is nonempty then a settlement will be reached because, by definition, there is at least one outcome that both sides prefer to war. Following Zeuthen (1968), the model proposed in this book incorporates the much weaker assumption that a nonempty bargaining set is a necessary condition for an agreement but that it is not sufficient. When presented with a proposal that is better than minimally acceptable, most bargainers will accept some risk that negotiations will break down in the hope of achieving an even better outcome. The actor may believe that such risks can be managed and that in the face of imminent war, the minimally acceptable proposal could be accepted. However, events do occasionally get out of control, especially when war is a possibility. Since there is often an advantage to striking first and by surprise, a war may be initiated by the opponent who perceives that no bargaining range exists and that war is inevitable. If this rationale is accepted, we must also explain linkage failures that occur when the bargaining set is not empty.

In addition, there is some empirical evidence that linkage attempts fail even when a bargaining range exists. The strongest such evidence is provided by cases such as the Oregon Boundary Dispute, in which linkage attempts were rejected and yet the conflict was resolved peacefully. Clearly, acceptable outcomes were present (hence the agreement), so how can we explain the failure to increase overall welfare by including another issue? One could argue that the additional issue would have destroyed (not enhanced) a zone of agreement that existed on the original issue, but that is not likely given the particular situation. The linkage (presumably acceptable to the Americans, since they proposed it) would have benefited the British by providing them their ideal point on the original issue (which they did not receive) and would have required no direct concessions, only diplomatic support for the Americans versus Mexico. Austrian behavior preceding the Seven Weeks War also suggests that the "empty bargaining set" argument is incomplete. For example, they refused a cash payment from Italy in exchange for Venice even though they desperately needed the funds. That the surrender of Venice was negotiable is proven by the fact that Austria agreed to cede Venice to France with the understanding that it would be turned over to Italy. As will be seen below, the spatial model can account for such behavior without asserting that the bargaining set was empty.

Another explanation for linkage failures can be found in the work of Fisher (1964), who has argued that the chances of agreement are greater when the issues are "fractionated." He suggests that linking issues creates the impression of a large-scale confrontation, which decreases the willingness of the parties to make concessions, while separating issues makes the negotiations more manageable and easier to comprehend. Fractionating enables the parties to reach agreement on relatively minor points first, which contributes to a spirit of cooperation and makes the parties unwilling to break off negotiations and abandon progress already made. Fisher's argument rests on psychological factors and would account for linkage failures even in cases in which the bargaining set is nonempty and in which including the additional issue greatly increases the potential benefits to both sides.

Fisher's (1964) arguments are plausible for bargaining situations involving a great number of complex issues, such as labor-management disputes or arms control negotiations; but an explanation drawn from his work that accounts for linkage failures is substantially weakened by the context of international crises.[5] First, the vast majority of crises involve very few issues (often one), and these issues are usually not overly complex. Fractionating, if possible, cannot make the dispute significantly more understandable and manageable, nor does adding an issue significantly increase the complexity of the conflict. Second, crises are, by definition, situations of intense hostility that involve perceived vital national interests. It is unlikely that settling minor issues will greatly reduce the impression of a large-scale conflict or make the parties more willing to make concessions on remaining issues just to preserve agreements already reached. Furthermore, since trust is likely to be low, neither side is likely to be willing to make a concession on one issue in the hope that it will be reciprocated on a subsequent issue. It is more likely that linkages will reduce the need for trust by explicitly connecting concessions. Finally, since time pressures are often great in international crises, bargainers may not be able to enjoy the leisurely pace that fractionating would seem to require. In any case, the explanation for linkage failures to be provided below is much more powerful theoretically. As an extension of the theory presented in the previous section, it can account for linkage successes (which Fisher cannot) as well as failures.

The argument that may be most important for linkage attempts in international crises can be found in Deutsch (1973) and Pruitt (1981). They have focused on the nature of the issue that is a potential linkage candidate and have suggested that a necessary condition for linkage success is that "the parties have different priorities across the issues at hand" (Pruitt 1981, 153). This condition can be interpreted as requiring that the initial issue be more salient than the linkage issue for one party while the other party sees the additional issue as of greater salience, or in the language of the model, that one of the ratios a_{i22}/a_{i11} and a_{j22}/a_{j11} be greater than 1.0 and that the other be less than 1.0.[6] This condition would seem to hold some promise for explaining linkage failures in crisis situations. If a successful linkage attempt requires that an issue be found that is of greater salience than the initial issue for one party and of lesser salience for the other, then the absence of such an issue would lead to a failure while its availability would lead to success. Since crises generally occur over issues that are extremely important to both parties, it may be difficult to find an issue that is more salient for one and only one participant.

This argument fails because all that is necessary for a linkage to provide a basis for exchange is that $a_{i22}/a_{i11} \neq a_{j22}/a_{j11}$; that is, it is only necessary that the relative salience of the two issues not be exactly equal for the parties. The technical derivation of this result is somewhat complex and is included, along with the formalization of the general result, below. The general logic of the argument can be seen in the illustration provided in figure 20. Here we have two actors, i and j, and two issues, generically labeled issue 1 and issue 2. Notice that issue 1 is more salient than issue 2 for both actors but that $a_{j22}/a_{j11} > a_{i22}/a_{i11}$. This inequality is sufficient to ensure a curved Pareto set (rather than a straight line connecting the actors' ideal points), indicating that the possibility of such an exchange does increase the total benefit available. Thus, even when both sides consider the same issue as most important, it is possible for a linkage to increase the total benefit available and thereby facilitate a negotiated settlement. Although both sides in the Cuban Missile Crisis probably were more concerned with the Soviet missiles in Cuba than with the U.S. promise not to invade, the exchange provided the basis for a settlement. It should be noted that the Deutsch (1973)/Pruitt (1981) argument could be interpreted in a less restrictive sense that is consistent with this result. This condition is exceedingly minimal, however, in that it is hard to imagine that,

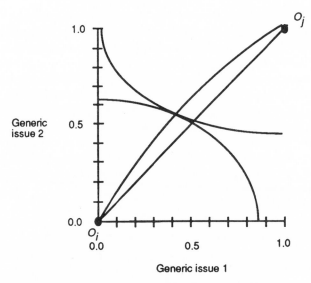

Fig. 20. Relative issue salience and issue linkage

with any great frequency, disputing parties would have exactly the same relative preferences for every possible pair of issues. Thus, this explanation is unlikely to account for more than a few linkage failures.

Why Linkages Fail: Insight from the Spatial Theory

Thus far, we have seen that issue linkages should theoretically provide a means for resolving international crises; that empirically, linkage attempts can fail; and that traditional explanations for linkage failures are incomplete. In this section, I draw from the spatial model in constructing a more general explanation of linkage failure. I also show how the beneficial aspects of the traditional explanations are incorporated into the explanation.

A key point virtually overlooked by other treatments of issue linkage is the fact that linkage attempts are not costless. It is obvious that linking issues involves a cost to a party who gives something up in the way of a side payment, but this is part of the exchange that produces greater overall benefit. Less obvious are what I will term *appendant costs*, which are those costs that are incurred by the very act of linking issues. At a minimum, the inclusion of another issue will require that the governmental apparatus bring additional personnel into the deliberations, conduct further study and debate, and increase the bureaucracy required to implement any agreements. More important, trade-offs across issues may create domestic political costs in that various groups will prioritize issues differently. (Had the Austrians accepted the offer of cash for territory, those interests concerned with economic matters would have been elated at the expense of those concerned with maintaining the empire.) There can also be external costs in that issues used for linkage purposes often are of interest to additional states, which can induce them to become involved in the crisis, complicating the bargaining and existing relationships, perhaps creating the need for additional side payments and assurances, and possibly even increasing the probability of war. For example, German actions designed to force an issue linkage in the Agadir crisis led the British to become involved on the side of the French, which significantly increased the likelihood of war. Similarly, Kennedy's promise to remove the missiles in Turkey directly affected the Turks; and had the British been willing to support the United States in obtaining part of California during the Oregon Boundary Dispute, the additional issue would have been of prime concern to Mexico. The list of appendant costs involved in linkage attempts could continue (one very important factor, the fact that an issue brought into a crisis for linkage purposes can bring with it additional, perhaps intangible and nonseparable, issues, will be discussed in some detail below), but for the argument that follows, it is sufficient that we accept that such costs exist and that they are conceptually distinct from the direct costs involved in concession making.

In general, we may surmise that linkage failures occur when the benefits produced by the linkage are, for at least one actor, not sufficient to overcome the costs involved in bringing the additional issue into the bargaining. This, as a complete explanation, produces a tautology similar to that involved in Sebenius's (1983) explanation. To avoid this tautology, I develop arguments relating several variables to the likelihood of linkage success by showing how they affect the relationship of the appendant costs of a linkage attempt to the net direct benefits the linkage would create.[7] Resulting from these arguments are a number of hypotheses (that are in principle testable) associating a particular variable to the probability of linkage success. Keeping in mind that this model is not based on the assumption that a nonempty bargaining set is sufficient to ensure agreement, I also do not assume that linkage success is ensured when the net direct benefits created by the attempt outweigh the appendant costs. Rather, I assume that it is necessary for the benefits to be greater than these costs and that the probability of linkage success increases as does the difference between the benefits and costs.

The strategy that I follow is to assume that the variation in either the appendant costs or the benefits of linkage attempts is random with respect to the variable of interest while showing that the variable is associated with the other factor in a regularized fashion. We can then determine the effect that the variable has on the probability of linkage success. For example, if increases in the value of the variable lead to increases in the benefits expected from a linkage attempt, we know that higher values of the variable are associated with higher probabilities of linkage success.

First, the above discussion of the Deutsch/Pruitt explanation of linkage failure suggests one variable that may affect the probability of linkage success. Although the relationship between the parties' issue salience ratios provides only a minimal necessary condition for success, it may be that variations in this relationship affect the likelihood of success. If we assume that the appendant costs of a linkage attempt are largely independent of the benefits created by the attempt, then it follows that the greater the benefit created by a proposed linkage, the greater the likelihood that it will be accepted. Thus, how the relationship between the issue salience ratios affects the amount of benefit created by the linkage attempt determines how this relationship affects the probability of success.

For the purpose of simplifying this argument, we assume that the issues are separable (i.e., $a_{i12} = a_{j12} = 0.0$). Moreover, we can assume, with no loss of generality, that $a_{i11} = a_{j11} = 1.0$. This serves to normalize the salience ratios and permits us to focus only on the relationship between a_{i22} and a_{j22}. There is no loss in generality in that, for each actor, the relative salience of the issues can be expressed solely in terms of the parameter for issue 2—a_{22} will be less than 1.0 when issue 1 is more salient and greater than 1.0 when issue 1 is less salient. A final simplifying assumption is that the actors' ideal points, O_i and O_j, are located in the issue space at $(0,0)$ and $(1,1)$, respectively. This assumption also involves no loss in generality because the scale by which any issue is represented can be set so that any point is the origin and any interval the unit. Given these assumptions, it can be shown that for any pair of issues considered as possible linkage candidates, the issue providing the highest probability of linkage success will be that which maximizes

$$\left| \frac{1}{1 + \dfrac{a_{i22}}{a_{j22}}} - .5 \right| \tag{4.1}$$

Proof: Recall that $a_{i12} = a_{j12} = 0$, that $a_{i11} = a_{j11} = 1.0$, and that i and j's ideal points are at $(0,0)$ and $(1,1)$, respectively. Thus, the functions for the actors' indifference contours can be given by $f(x,y) = [(1 - x)^2 + a_{j22}(1 - y)^2] = P^2$ for j and $g(x,y) = [(x)^2 + a_{i22}(y)^2] = N^2$ for i. My aim is to show how changes in the actors' salience parameters affect the probability of linkage success by showing how these changes affect the curvature of the Pareto set. The first step is to specify the Pareto set in terms of a_{i22} and a_{j22}. Consider a function for j, $f(x,y)$. To find the Pareto optimal outcome for $f(x,y)$ and any given contour for i of length N^2, we must minimize $f(x,y)$ subject to the condition $g(x,y) - N^2 = 0$. First, we can determine the gradient for each function, $\nabla f(x,y)$ and $\nabla g(x,y)$. Following the method of Lagrange, we know that at the Pareto optimal point, the gradients will be colinear; thus, there exists a scalar, λ, such that $f(x,y) = \lambda g(x,y)$. The problem becomes finding the point (x,y) that satisfies the Lagrange condition $\nabla f(x,y) = \lambda \nabla g(x,y)$ subject to the side condition that $g(x,y) - N^2 = 0$. By using the partial derivatives, we can see that the gradients are $f(x,y) = 2(1 - x)i + 2a_{j22}(1 - y)j$ and $g(x,y) = 2xi + 2a_{i22}yj$. Setting $\nabla f(x,y) = \lambda \nabla g(x,y)$, our Lagrange conditions are $2(1 - x) = \lambda 2x$ and $2a_{j22}(1 - y) = \lambda 2a_{i22}y$; and our side condition can be written as $x^2 + a_{i22}y^2 - N^2 = 0$. Solving for λ in the first two equations gives us

$$\lambda = \frac{1 - x}{x}$$

and

$$\lambda = \frac{a_{j22}(1 - y)}{a_{i22}y},$$

so we know that

$$\frac{1 - x}{x} = \frac{a_{j22}(1 - y)}{a_{i22}y}.$$

Solving for y, we find

$$y = \frac{1}{1 + \dfrac{a_{i22}(1 - x)}{a_{j22}x}} \tag{4.2}$$

Inserting this equation into $g(x,y)$, we obtain

$$x^2 + a_{i22}\left(\frac{1}{1 + \dfrac{a_{i22}(1 - x)}{a_{j22}x}}\right)^2 = N^2.$$

Given specific values for a_{j22}, and a_{i22}, we can use this to determine the Pareto optimal outcome (point of tangency with $f(x,y)$) for an indifference contour of a given distance. We can also see that, given these salience parameters and any value of x, it is a fairly straightforward matter to determine the corresponding y coordinate for the Pareto outcome by using equation 4.2. By construction, we know that when there is no curvature in the Pareto set, the functional form of the set will be $y = x$. One means of comparing the degree of curvature in the Pareto set across several cases is to hold x constant at some value, use equation 4.2 to calculate y for each case, and determine the absolute value of the difference in x and y. The absolute value of this difference will increase, as does the degree of curvature in the Pareto set. For simplicity, let $x = .5$. Thus,

$$Y = \frac{1}{1 + \frac{a_{i22}}{a_{j22}}}$$

and, for any set of salience parameters, maximizing

$$\left| \frac{1}{1 + \frac{a_{i22}}{a_{j22}}} - .5 \right|$$

will maximize the curvature of the Pareto set and thus the probability of linkage success.

The generality of this result is obviously restricted to situations involving two separable issues. Extending the result to cases in which there are three or more issues or in which the issues are nonseparable is a fairly straightforward matter in terms of the logic of the argument. The method of Lagrange can be used to identify the Pareto set, in all dimensions, as a function of the x dimension coordinate and the salience parameters. Clearly, as issues and salience parameters are added, this calculation becomes quite complicated mathematically. Even the simplest extension, which is to remain in two dimensions and consider cases in which the issues are nonseparable, doubles the number of parameters in the equation. In the two-issue, general case, the determination of the Lagrange conditions is a fairly simple extension of the procedure followed above, but the additional parameters and the interaction terms makes the calculation of y in terms of x and the salience parameters an onerous task algebraically. Intuitively, we can see that the algebra should be complicated because the relationship it is capturing is quite complex: Some instances of issue nonseparability would increase the chances of agreement (e.g., if gains on one issue lead an actor to prefer less on the other issue, the range of acceptable outcomes is increased), while other cases would decrease the chances of agreement (if gains on one issue lead an actor to require even more on the other issue). Naturally, this is further complicated by the range of possible relationships across actors.

Note also that the conclusions regarding the Deutsch (1973)/Pruitt (1981) explanation for linkage failure discussed above can be formalized using equation 4.2. Recall that their argument holds that a necessary condition for linkage success is that "the parties have different priorities across the issues at hand" (Pruitt 1981, 153) and that the spatial model shows that the proper interpretation of this argument specifies only a minimal condition, requiring only that the actors have different relative saliences for the issues. That is, if both view the same issue as most important, linkage can still be beneficial as long as the ratio of salience parameters is different across actors. First, note that when the ratios of salience parameters are identical, there is no benefit in issue linkage. Since, by construction, $a_{i11} = a_{j11} = 1.0$, if the salience ratios are identical, $a_{i22} = a_{j22}$ and, by equation 4.1,

$$y = \frac{1}{1 + \dfrac{1 - x}{x}} = \frac{1}{\dfrac{1}{x}} = x.$$

Thus, when the salience ratios are identical, there is no curvature in the Pareto set and issue linkage will provide no additional benefit. At this point, it is easy to see that if $a_{i22} \neq a_{j22}$, even if both are greater than 1.0 or both are less than 1.0, $x \neq y$, indicating curvature in the Pareto set, and that linking issues can increase the amount of benefit available and thus increase the likelihood of a negotiated settlement.

In general, our task is to determine how the relationship between a_{i22} and a_{j22} affects the amount of additional benefit that would be created in a linkage attempt. Intuitively, it is plausible to suspect that this amount would be reflected by some form of either the difference between the parameters (i.e., $a_{i22} - a_{j22}$) or the ratio of the parameters (i.e., a_{i22}/a_{j22}). This would suggest that the greater the disparity in the salience ratios for the two parties, the greater the additional benefit created by the linkage and the greater the likelihood of linkage success. If, for example, issue 1 is much more salient than issue 2 for i and just slightly more salient than issue 2 for j, i would be willing to exchange many more units of 2 for a unit of 1 than would j, and the greater this difference, the greater the probability that a mutually beneficial exchange can occur. In fact, when a_{i22} and a_{j22} are either both greater than 1.0 or both less than 1.0, the amount of benefit created by the attempt is specified by a simple ratio: as the ratio increases, so does the amount of benefit. However, we must also be able to examine cases in which the actors do have opposite saliences for the issues, which is why our formula, though following the same general reasoning, must be more complex.

We know that one indication of the amount of additional benefit produced by linking two issues is the degree of curvature in the Pareto set (i.e., the more bowed the contract curve, the greater the benefit of the linkage). Equation 4.1 allows us to determine how various pairs of salience ratios affect the curvature of the Pareto set. The formula has been determined by specifying the general functional form of the Pareto set in terms of the salience parameters, which then enables us to take any pair of salience parameters and calculate for any x coordinate (i.e., point on the horizontal issue dimension) the y coordinate of the point in the Pareto set. By construction, we know that when the Pareto set is linear, at $x = .5$, y will also be at .5. Equation 4.1 is designed to calculate the y coordinate of the point in the Pareto set at $x = .5$ in terms of a_{i22} and a_{j22} and then determine the difference between this coordinate and .5. Thus, as equation 4.1 increases, so does the curvature of the Pareto set and the likelihood of linkage success.

Although this formulation is not as pleasingly simple as a simple ratio would be, it can be understood in very similar terms. The important point is that the relationship between the salience parameters can influence the likelihood of linkage success. This point can shed some light onto the problem of explaining linkage failures in that if a_{i22} and a_{j22} are nearly equal, the small benefit created by the linkage is less likely to outweigh the appendant costs of the attempt; thus, the likelihood of linkage success is low (even though it may not be logically prohibited). In the Cuban Missile Crisis, for example, the issue of the missiles in Cuba was probably more important than the issue of the U.S. promise not to invade for both the United States and the Soviet Union. At the risk of making interpersonal comparisons, however, I think it plausible that the issue of missiles was more important to the United States than to the Soviets (since the missiles altered the status quo in favor of the Soviets) and that the issue of the promise was more important to the Soviets than to the United States (since the United States had little intention of invading anyway and the promise provided the Soviets a face-saving way out of the crisis). Thus, even though both actors viewed the same issue as the more important, their salience ratios were vastly different. In the crisis leading up to the Winter War in 1939, on the other hand, it is likely that the salience parameters were more nearly identical. It is clear that both the Soviets and the Finns were much more concerned with the Finnish territory than with the Soviet territory offered in exchange, which suggests that the salience parameters were not too different. If that is correct, it is less likely that the appendant costs of the linkage attempt would have been overcome by the created benefits in the Russo-Finnish crisis than in the Cuban Missile Crisis. That would provide one explanation why the linkage attempt in the Cuban crisis provided a peaceful solution while the attempt in the earlier crisis failed.

The model can also be used to gain insight into the relationship between elements of the bargainers' relative power and the likelihood of linkage success.[8] In particular, we can see that the actors' relative war-fighting capabilities and resolve affect the amount of additional benefit that can be created by a given linkage attempt. Figure 21 will serve as the basis for this discus-

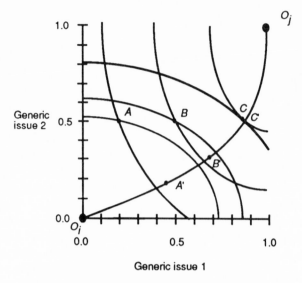

Fig. 21. Bargaining power and issue linkage

sion. It should be noted at the outset that there are some fairly important restrictions on the generalizability of the example. These restrictions are discussed below.

In this figure we again have two generically labeled issues, and issue 1 represents the initial issue with issue 2 representing the proposed additional issue. Of the two actors, j is more concerned with issue 1, and i is more concerned with issue 2, so $a_{j22} < a_{j11}$ and $a_{i22} > a_{i11}$. Our task is to determine how the amount of benefit created by the linkage changes as a result of differing capability and resolve relationships—assuming that the appendant costs are random with variations in these variables allows us to conclude that the greater the benefit created, the greater the likelihood of linkage success. For purposes of comparison, it is necessary to determine what the outcome would be in the absence of a linkage, which requires that the status quo on issue 2 be specified. I have set this, arbitrarily, at .5. Furthermore, it is necessary to demonstrate the effect on the nonlinkage outcome brought about by the power and resolve variables. Recall from chapter 3 that when one actor is advantaged in terms of having greater resolve, war-fighting capabilities, or both, it can expect to receive a more favorable negotiated outcome. To reflect this, there are three nonlinkage outcomes denoted in the figure: A, corresponding to an advantage for i; B, corresponding to a symmetrical situation; and C, corresponding to an advantage for j. The indifference contours that pass through these points are shown, as is the resulting Pareto set.

From figure 21 it is easy to see that, in this situation, the likelihood for success of a linkage attempt increases as does the power of actor i. An indication of the amount of benefit created by the linkage attempt is the distance along the Pareto set that separates the actors' indifference contours that pass through a particular nonlinkage settlement point. For point C there is very little additional benefit created by the linkage, suggesting that if j is the more powerful, linking the issues will make little difference in the outcome, so the additional benefit is unlikely to outweigh the appendant costs, and linkage is unlikely to be successful. As we move through point B to point A, we see that the amount of benefit created by the linkage steadily increases, indicating that the likelihood of linkage success also increases. One potential problem with this line of reasoning may be that even though the amount of benefit created by the linkage increases as does i's power, j's share of the additional benefit may decrease; and if this decrease is severe enough, the net benefits of linkage for j are likely to be less than the appendant costs of linking the issues. That does not seem to be a problem, however. If we assume that the additional benefit will be divided along the same ratio as a nonlinkage settlement (an assumption consistent with the model), we can see that the additional benefit for both i and j increases as i's power does. Note in particular points A' and B'—j's one-fourth of the benefit created at A' is greater than the one-half of the benefit created at B'.

There are two important limitations on the generality of this example; however, an understanding of these limitations leads us to some rather interesting conclusions. First, note the result depends on the salience parameters. If we reverse the relative saliences, so that $a_{j22} > a_{j11}$ and $a_{i22} < a_{i11}$ (making the Pareto set bow upward), our conclusion would be the exact opposite—the probability of linkage success would increase as does j's power. This result suggests an interesting interaction between the actors' power and their relative issue saliences: linkage success is more likely when the more powerful actor is (relatively) more concerned with the issue to be added.

We can also see that the conclusions depend on the status quo outcome on the potential additional issue. The reason that linkage success is more likely as i's power increases in figure 21 is that the farther the status quo outcome is from the Pareto set, the greater the benefit created by the linkage. Thus, when the status quo on issue 2 becomes very favorable to i, the relationship between the actors' power and linkage success can actually reverse itself. For example, if the status quo on issue 2 is at .05, A, B, and C would all be below the Pareto Set, and the amount of benefit created by the linkage would increase as does the power of j. This fairly complex relationship actually has a fairly straightforward explanation. Recall that issue 2 is the more salient issue for i; when the status quo on issue 2 is already very favorable to i and i, by virtue of being the more powerful, is likely to achieve a fair proportion of its aims on issue 1, i has little to gain by linking the issues. When j is the more powerful, however, the linkage may provide i enough on issue 1 to justify the losses on issue 2.

The general conclusion to be drawn is that the relative power of crisis participants (conceptualized as resolve and war-fighting capabilities) does affect the probability of linkage success, but this relationship is fairly complex and depends on the relative salience of the issues for the actors and on the status quo of the potential linkage issue. Although the relationship is complex and cannot be easily summarized in a single, pithy sentence, the model does capture the richness of the interactions and does suggest how the power of the participants effects the probability of linkage success in particular cases. One interesting point that can be made is that in a crisis between states of unequal power, linkage is more likely to work if the status quo on the issue to be linked favors the weaker party and the relative saliences are such that the stronger party is more concerned with the additional issue while the initial issue is more salient for the weaker.

This point may provide part of the explanation for the failure of the linkage attempt in the bargaining preceding the Winter War in 1939. The status quo on the linkage issue (a piece of Soviet territory offered to Finland) favored the Soviets, who were clearly the stronger party, and the initial issue of the Finnish territory was definitely the more important issue to the Finns. For an issue linkage to provide a peaceful solution to this crisis, it would have been necessary to find an issue that (1) had a status quo favoring Finland and (2) was more important to the Soviets than the issue of the territory they sought. It is highly unlikely that such an issue could have been found. Condition (2) probably could not have been met because the Soviets viewed the Finnish territory they sought as essential for their defense against Germany. This adds another factor to our explanation of linkage failure and, particularly for international crises, suggests that issue linkage might actually be quite hard to achieve for states of unequal power.

While many issues meeting condition (1) could have been found, one implication is that the Finns would have, in essence, been paying a ransom to get the Soviets to drop their demands for Finnish territory. Paying this ransom would have involved a serious cost to Finland's reputation, could have opened the door to future demands by the Soviets and others, and would thus have involved fairly severe appendant costs. That leads to the final factor affecting the likelihood of linkage success that will be discussed. Issues proposed as linkage candidates may be associated with varying degrees of appendant costs; and as these costs increase for a given amount of additional direct benefit, the likelihood of linkage success decreases.

Recall the conceptual distinction between the direct costs associated with concessions, which are reflected by the distances between proposals representing such concessions and the actors' ideal points, and appendant costs, which refer to the additional costs associated with the very act of linking issues. A number of sources of appendant costs were mentioned above, but perhaps the most important is the fact that many potential linkage issues are inextricably tied to still other, often intangible, issues such as prestige or reputation. If, for one of the actors, the relationship between the linkage issue and these additional issues is such that gains on the former are associated with severe losses on the latter, the apparent direct benefit created by the linkage attempt may be far outweighed by these appendant costs, making a settlement less likely. Although the spatial model can be used to represent and to examine the general nature of this association, the interrelationships among the issues and the impact of various configurations can be quite complex, so I will not attempt to discuss all contingencies. Rather I will present an example that illustrates how the appendant costs created by these additional issues can inhibit linkage success.

For the point to be made here, we need focus on only one actor, i. Consider three generically labeled issues: x, the original issue under contention; y, a linkage issue on which j has proposed concessions in exchange for concessions by i on x; and z, an intangible issue (such as prestige) that is of concern to i. We will set i's ideal point as $O_i = (x,y,z)$ and a proposal that i is to consider as $\pi = (x',y',z')$. Recall that i will evaluate proposals in terms of their weighted Euclidian distances from O_i, which is given by $\|\pi - O_i\|_{A_i}$ where

$$A_i = \begin{bmatrix} a_{11} & a_{12} & a_{13} \\ a_{12} & a_{22} & a_{23} \\ a_{13} & a_{23} & a_{33} \end{bmatrix}.$$

We will assume that x and y as well as x and z are separable, so $a_{12} = a_{13} = 0$; but, since y and z are not separable, $a_{23} \neq 0$. Thus, the distance between O_i and π is given by $[a_{11}(x' - x)^2 + a_{22}(y' - y)^2 + 2a_{23}(y' - y)(z' - z) + a_{33}(z' - z)^2]^{1/2}$. Keep in mind that the larger the sum of the terms, the longer the distance and the less preferred the proposal.

To evaluate the effect of the relationship between y and z, we will, for purposes of comparison, establish initial values for the terms. Suppose that $a_{22} = a_{33} = a_{23} = 2$, that $(y' - y) = (z' - z) = .5$, and that the relationship between y and z is such that an increase in one brings about a decrease in the other of equal magnitude, so $\Delta(y' - y) = -\Delta(z' - z)$. The values of a_{11} and $(x' - x)$ will be held constant and are immaterial for this discussion. It is easy to verify, and should be intuitively obvious, that under this condition, any offer of an improvement in y will be exactly offset by an equal decline in z. Thus, changes in y will bring no additional benefit for i and will not improve the chances of a negotiated settlement; in fact, if the improvements in y are offered in exchange for concessions on x, i's benefit would decrease and settlement would be less likely. This would be the case even if y is more salient than x for i (e.g., if $a_{11} = 1$), so a trade that, ignoring z, appears very beneficial to i could actually harm the chances of settlement by involving the additional issue, z.

This conclusion obviously depends on the specific values assigned. Other values do produce other results. For example, if $a_{22} > a_{33}$ or $\Delta y = -\epsilon \Delta z$, where $\epsilon < 1.0$, the proposed linkage of y to x could still provide additional benefit to i, though the amount of this benefit would be decreased by the interdependence of y and z. This linkage would increase the likelihood of a negotiated settlement, but to a lesser degree than would be expected by a j ignorant of z. On the other hand, if $a_{22} < a_{33}$ or $\epsilon > 1.0$, gains on y would be accompanied by even greater losses on z, and the likelihood of a settlement would decrease rapidly. Similarly, changes in a_{23} are inversely related to changes in the benefits of the linkage.[9]

It should also be noted that a function expressing the relationship between y and z may not always be linear, or even continuous, and that that can have a number of effects on a linkage attempt. It may be, for example, that i suffers heavy costs on z at very low levels of additional benefit on y but that the rate of increases in costs on z diminishes as the amount of gains on y increases. Or it may be that the costs associated with z are in the form of a step function—they are absent when y is omitted from the bargaining but present in a constant amount when y is included. If that is the case, small concessions by j on y may decrease the chances of linkage success while large concessions would increase these chances by providing i sufficient benefit on y to overcome the costs on z.[10]

At this point, the interpretation of this result appears so obvious that it is somewhat surprising that no general theoretical treatment of issue linkage has dealt with it extensively. We can see that the probability of linkage success is less when the potential linkage issue is interdependent with still other issues in such a way that, for at least one party, any benefit on the linkage issue is offset by losses on the others. This factor explains the failure of linkage in the bargaining that preceded the Seven Weeks War. Recall that Austria refused to consider cash payments from Prussia and Italy in exchange for the territories each sought. The reason for this refusal was the feeling, on the part of many Austrians, including Franz Joseph, that to do so would involve a serious blow to the prestige of the Empire and would be highly immoral (for selling people and their homes to foreigners). For this reason, the likelihood of a settlement may actually have been decreased by the attempt to link the issue of the money to the issue of the territory. That is particularly true with regard to Venice. Austria was willing to transfer the territory to Italy indirectly by first giving it to Napoleon, who would then cede it to Italy. This arrangement was unacceptable to the Italians, for they desired the increased prestige involved in dealing directly with Austria. Thus, the appendant costs involved in the linkage attempt were so great that linkage failed, even though the parties' preferences on the initial issue were relatively close. This explanation will appear obvious to those familiar with the history of the situation; the contribution here is that it is included in a broader, general theory of issue linkages in crisis bargaining.

Conclusion

A number of conclusions can be drawn from the analyses presented in this chapter. First, I have shown that the bargaining agenda matters. Bargaining outcomes can be affected by the order in which the issues are settled and by whether the issues are linked. This result is fairly intuitive, but were the model to lead to some other conclusion, the usefulness of the model would be suspect. Furthermore, this result is important in that it explains and provides a useful conceptualization for at least one fairly common phenomenon—that negotiations between nation-states are often preceded by long and arduous arguments over the bargaining agenda. Since each side knows that the agenda will affect the ultimate outcome, they negotiate as cautiously over the agenda as over the actual issues.

Furthermore, this chapter has served to develop further the theory of issue linkages as used in crisis bargaining. Arguments showing the beneficial aspects of linkages have been well developed in previous work, so I have focused on the conditions that can account for the failure of linkage attempts. In particular, I have focused on three factors that can influence the likelihood of linkage success: the relative salience of the issues for the actors; the relative power of the actors; and the possibility that the linkage issue raises other issues with which it is inversely related. The results, though supporting the notion that linkages can often serve as the basis for negotiated settlements, suggest that issue linkages in international crisis situations may be more difficult to realize than previous theoretical work on issue linkage would indicate.

Linkage is more likely to succeed when the ratios of issue salience for the actors are divergent. Since states are unlikely to become involved in crises over issues of little concern, both parties are likely to see the original issue as highly salient, so it may be difficult to find a linkage issue that creates a great deal of additional benefit. This requirement can be even more stringent if the actors are disparate in power. If that is the case, it is beneficial to find an issue on which the status quo favors the weaker party and on which the salience parameters are such that the stronger party is relatively more concerned with the linkage issue. Since crises between unequals are often initiated when the stronger demands something it values highly, it may be very difficult to find another issue about which it cares even more. Finally, states involved in crises are often gravely concerned about their reputations and prestige. If a linkage proposal involves an issue that threatens these values to a greater extent than does the original dispute, the attempt may reduce the probability of a settlement. Since states usually wish to avoid the impression that they have paid a ransom or accepted a bribe, crisis situations make it very difficult to propose a linkage that can be accepted.

Many may find these conclusions rather obvious. To the extent that I have accounted for some well-known relationships (e.g., that the greater the bribe, the more likely it is to be accepted), I would stress the importance of providing explanations for even the well known. More important, the exercise has integrated these conclusions into a general theory of issue linkage. The theory tells us when linkage should fail as well as succeed and explains the outcomes that occur. Historians may know that Austria refused the linkage offered before the Seven Weeks War because to accept would have involved a loss in prestige, but it is useful to incorporate this ad hoc explanation into a more general theory of crisis bargaining.

This research is also critically important for the crisis management literature. One of the primary conclusions of these studies is that successful crisis management frequently depends on the ability of the parties to find a face-saving formula. This formula usually involves concessions by one party on some additional issue that enables the other party to create the impression that it has not lost the crisis (see, e.g., Snyder and Diesing 1977). Kennedy's promise to Khrushchev that the United States would not invade Cuba is often seen in this vein—it allowed the Soviets to claim that their missiles had served their purpose, ensuring the safety of Cuba. The results presented here suggest that such face-saving formulas may be exceedingly difficult to devise. The party offering an issue for such a linkage must take exceptional care to ensure that the effect is not the opposite of that desired. The adversary may actually see concessions on linkage issues offered with the intent of protecting the adversary's reputation and prestige as damaging. This argument supports the notion that a face-saving formula can provide a peaceful solution to a crisis, but it suggests that great sensitivity is required in the search for an appropriate issue.

CHAPTER 5

Third Parties in International Crises

The analyses included in this book have, to this point, considered only two-party conflicts. This limitation is clearly fairly serious in that many international crises are characterized by the involvement, or attempted involvement, of parties other than the original disputants. Other states, international organizations, and private individuals often intrude in the hopes of aiding an ally, preserving the peace, or achieving their own aims on the issues at stake. The frequency of third-party involvement in international crises is suggested by a cursory examination of the cases included in the Appendix. Italy and France were prominent actors in the crisis preceding the Seven Weeks War, as was Britain in the Agadir Crisis. Third parties were also involved, though in less significant roles, in the Cuban Missile Crisis and in the crisis preceding the Russo-Finnish Winter War. Since these cases were selected in part because of their simplicity (one aspect of which is the relative unimportance of third parties), this is particularly impressive evidence of the frequency of third-party involvement in crisis bargaining. While the frequency with which third parties attempt to affect crisis outcomes does not guarantee that such behavior is consequential, it is safe to assume that crisis outcomes can be affected by the behavior of additional actors.

In spite of the ease with which one can identify third-party involvements in international disputes, many analysts of crisis bargaining have not extended their studies beyond a focus on two actors. This neglect has usually been the result of a desire to simplify the analyses by concentrating only on the most important actors involved in the process, but it is also the case that many of the analytical tools applied to the study of crisis bargaining prohibit analyzing the behavior of more than two participants. Snyder and Diesing (1977), for example, based their well-known study on the normal form representation of 2 × 2 games, which makes it virtually impossible for them to evaluate the impact of third parties. If third-party involvement is an important factor affecting crisis outcomes, this is a serious restriction on this type of research. Clearly, any theory designed to explain behavior and outcomes in international crisis cannot be complete without accounting for the impact of third parties.

The model developed in this book is extremely fertile in that it can be extended to incorporate additional explanatory variables and the spatial representation of conflict can handle any number of actors (see, e.g., Bueno de Mesquita 1990; Enelow and Hinich 1984; Morrow 1986). The purpose of this chapter is to extend the spatial model to examine the role of third parties in international crises. This chapter will be brief, and I will not attempt a thorough analysis of all aspects of third-party involvement in international crises. My more modest goal is to demonstrate that the spatial model can incorporate this important factor. I concentrate on using the model to identify various motivations for additional actors to become involved and on showing how this determines the form that their involvement takes; however, I do include a cursory discussion of the impact third parties can have on crisis outcomes.

Existing Research on Third Parties

Although students of international crises have often overlooked third parties, a fairly substantial literature concerning multilateral negotiations and mediation in more general types of conflict situations does exist. While a thorough review of this work is not necessary, a few comments are in order because I draw quite heavily from this literature in the discussion that follows. Most such studies fall into one of two categories.

First, there is a substantial amount of scholarship devoted to the examination of third parties as mediators or arbitrators. This track is aimed at determining what characteristics of mediators and what tactics used by them best facilitate the resolution of conflict by the principal actors (see, e.g., Carnevale and Wittmer 1987; Lall 1966, chap. 7; Pruitt 1981, chap. 7; Raymond and Kegley 1987; Rubin 1981; Rubin and Brown 1975; Touval and Zartman 1985; Young 1967 and 1972; Zartman and Touval 1985). In general, mediators are thought to serve a number of functions that increase the probability of a peaceful solution to conflicts. The most obvious function of a mediator is to facilitate communication between the dipsuting parties. Mediators can serve as indirect channels of communication and can often induce disputants to exchange information directly. Since negotiated settlements are difficult to achieve in the absence of communication, a mediator that serves only this function should reduce the likelihood that negotiations will break down. Mediators can also serve to increase the willingness of the parties to make concessions. Responding to a mediator's suggestion or conceding through a mediator can be much easier for a disputant because it results in less loss of face than would a concession made directly to the enemy.

Mediators can also increase the probability of a negotiated settlement by actively altering the context of negotiations. This alteration can occur in at least two ways. By bringing a fresh perspective to the dispute and by being less bound by commitments made during the early bargaining, a mediator is in a better position to search for creative solutions to the conflict. A mediator can separate or package issues to facilitate agreement, and because disputants are more willing to communicate openly with a mediator, it might be better able to identify possible opportunities for logrolling across issues. In addition, a mediator might be able to use its own resources to create additional issues that can be used for side payments. In short, mediators can help move disputants away from pure distributive bargaining and toward an effort at creative problem solving.

This body of literature also focuses on the characteristics thought to be associated with successful mediators. The conventional wisdom holds that mediators will have a greater chance of success if they have a substantial resource base and the respect and trust of the disputants—i.e., if they have the ability to influence the parties. Many have argued that this requires a mediator to be unbiased (e.g., Young 1967), but as we shall see, recent research suggests that this characteristic may not be necessary. In addition, it is often asserted that a mediator's chance of success will depend on the skill with which it can conduct its mission.

The second category of relevant research comprises those who have approached the analysis of multiple-party conflicts through the use of *n*-person game theory, which, in general, conceptualizes the problem as a coalition game (see, e.g., Luce and Raiffa 1957; Morrow 1986; Riker 1962; Sebenius 1983). The general focus of this body of work is on identifying what coalitions will form, what outcomes will be imposed, and how the members of the winning coalition will divide the spoils. Most such studies focus on voting problems and assume that once a majority coalition has formed, it can impose its agreed on position as the outcome. Thus, all actors are treated as being equally powerful, and the outcome is determined primarily by the actors' preferences on the issues at stake. That is not necessary, however (see, e.g., Morrow 1986), and one can assume the actors have differential weights and that the outcome can be a negotiated settlement. A number of useful insights have been derived from this work. In the first place, it is easy to show that many coalitions will be extremely unstable in that one coalition can often lure opposing coalition members with promises of a greater share of a more desirable outcome. Furthermore, we can see that while coalition members augment each others' capabilities, this augmentation can come at the expense of reducing their resolve. This reduction occurs because the position advanced by the coalition is usually a compromise of the members' preferred outcomes. Since the compromise might not be all that attractive to many, they would be less willing to stand firm and risk war. In short, we can see that including third parties into the bargaining process considerably complicates matters and has no clear-cut impact on dispute outcomes.

The distinction between these two traditions is somewhat artificial in that coalition analyses can allow for more than two coalitions (with one interested in a compromise between the others), and, as Touval (1975) has argued, we can view a mediator as a potential coalition partner for the initial disputants. Each tradition has some difficulty in dealing with some questions regarding additional parties in international crises, however. Much of coalition analysis centers on the free-for-all competition for membership in a decisive coalition. Such a conceptualization is limited for the study of crises primarily because possible coalitions are largely preestablished. That is because many potential third parties will be closely tied to one of the original disputants and because feasible coalitions will be restricted, at least to a degree, in that it is hard to imagine the original actors coalescing against a mediator. Any straightforward use of coalition analysis that recognized these constraints would somewhat trivialize the problem by tending to reduce the situation to a two-party dispute. Viewing third parties strictly as mediators, on the other hand, forces one to ignore other roles that the additional actors might play. Even if we consider biased mediators, we are still implying a level of impartiality that may not exist in many situations.

One of my aims in this chapter is to extend the spatial model of crisis bargaining in such a way as to provide, in the context of international crises, an analysis of third-party involvement that is a generalization of both of these traditions. The model permits the analysis of both coalition games and the effects of mediation and thus enables us to compare the impact on crisis outcomes of the different types of third-party involvement. Many of the conclusions to be drawn can undoubtedly be found elsewhere in the literature. The goal here is to incorporate these into the context of a well-integrated theory of crisis bargaining as well as to use the model to provide additional insights.

Third Parties in International Crises

The first question we must address is, Why do additional parties become involved in international crises? The answer to this question is important not only for its own sake but also because it may provide some indication of the impact of third-party involvement. The general answer to this question has been provided by Young (1972) and Touval (1975), among others, who have argued that third parties become involved when they perceive it is in their interest to do so; that is, they become involved when they are concerned with the outcome of the issues in dispute or with the issues that are created by the conflict. At this level of generality, the answer to our question is not particularly interesting, but it does suggest a potential avenue of inquiry. We can identify a number of ways in which issues draw third parties into international crises, and we can show that each of these has particular implications for the nature and impact of the involvement.

First, we can identify three ways in which a third party can be concerned with one or more of the issues over which the crisis began. Examples of these types of third-party involvement are depicted in figure 22. This construction represents a dispute over two issues, generically labeled issue 1 and issue 2, involving two original participants, i and j, and three potential third parties, labeled *l*, k, and m. We should expect the nature of each potential third party's involvement to depend on its issue positions relative to those of the other actors.

If the third party's preferences are nearly identical to one of the original participants, we would expect these actors to align. In our example, we would expect i and k, whose issue positions are very similar, to align against j. Under some conditions, actor k might try to remain aloof from the dispute (if i is expected to win, k can enjoy the benefits without bearing the costs), but if k is to become involved, it would be on the side of i since they are fighting for the same thing. The general effect of this type of alliance would be for the third party, k, to augment the capabilities of the initial disputant, i, relative to those of j, and we would expect the crisis, in most instances, to appear very similar to a two-party dispute. An interesting variation on this example exists, however, when the relative issue saliences are opposite for the allies. This would be the case, for example, if i is more concerned with issue 1 than with issue 2 while k is more concerned with issue 2. Here, a possible strategy for j would be to acquiesce on the issue about which it cares less (assuming j is much more concerned with one issue than with the other) in an attempt to break the alliance of i and k. Thus, we can see that additional parties can complicate the agenda-setting questions addressed in the last chapter. Actor

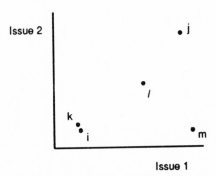

Fig. 22. Third parties concerned with original issues. Indifference contours are circular.

j's strategy would be similar to one in which it was trading concessions on the less important issue for benefits on the more important, but the benefits to j would actually accrue by separating the issues. Its concessions on one issue would serve to remove one opponent from the bargaining, improving j's bargaining position against the other opponent.

An example of such a third-party involvement was the alliance between Italy and Prussia in the crisis leading up to the Seven Weeks War. Their issue preferences were nearly identical, in that both preferred that Italy gain control over Venice and Prussia gain control over Schleswig-Holstein. As we would expect, they were allied in the crisis and in the war. The relative saliences of the issues were different for each actor, however, and in the obvious direction. This would suggest that Austria could have benefited from the tactic of surrendering one territory and concentrating its energies and forces on retaining the other. The historical record indicates that at least some in the Austrian government favored such a policy (some effort was made to transfer Venice to Italy by ceding it first to Napoleon). As we saw in the previous chapter, however, additional intangible issues forestalled this Austrian tactic.

Another type of third-party involvement occurs when its ideal point falls roughly between the original participants' ideal points. In this case, the potential third party is likely to behave much like a mediator; but rather than attempt to facilitate a fair or acceptable (to the original parties) outcome, it would attempt to persuade the others to accept a split-the-difference solution. An actor at l, for example, would attempt to persuade i and j to accept an intermediate outcome which, it just so happens, would be close to l's ideal point. Such a mediator might appeal to notions of fairness and reciprocity, but the motivation would be aimed at achieving an outcome favorable to the mediator. Thus, we would expect l to discourage the original participants from being too conciliatory if that would move the outcome too far from l's ideal point. We would also expect a mediator operating under these incentives to be unwilling to search for creative solutions. It may be that i and j have completely opposite saliences over the issues and that both would be satisfied with an outcome near point m. Since l would see this outcome as less desirable than a pure split-the-difference settlement, it would not attempt to facilitate such a trade-off. Thus, a potential mediator with motivations similar to l's might not be particularly effective. While still able to serve some of the traditional functions of a mediator (e.g., it might be easier for each original participant to make concessions in response to suggestions by the mediator), l's interests on the issues at stake would inhibit its ability to serve other useful functions.

Finally, if the additional actor is neither near one party nor between the parties (i.e., the actors' ideal points form a triangle in the issue space), we would expect a three-way bargaining game. Each would attempt to achieve an outcome close to its own ideal point, but much of the competition would involve efforts to form coalitions. With an actor at m, for example, we have a third party who is in agreement with each of the original participants on one issue. This would result in a classical coalition game in which each of the disputants would attempt to lure m into an alliance against the other. Such a game could also be affected by the shape of the actors' indifference contours since the possibility of logrolling (i.e., an agreement by two, or more, actors, each of whom considers a different issue to be most important, by which each receives its most preferred outcome on the issue with which it is most concerned) exists when the actors have different relative saliences for the issues at stake.[1] Actor m could achieve most of its aims on the issue of greater importance by cutting a deal with the actor for whom this issue is less important. Of course, all that assumes the parties are relatively equal in power. If one is overwhelmingly superior to the others combined, it could take what it wants. The illustration also shows that the analysis could become more interesting, and complicated, if there are more than one potential third parties. With actors at *l* and m, for example, we might see a coalition of third parties attempting to force an intermediate outcome that represents a compromise between the third-party positions.

A second general way in which third parties can become involved in a crisis is when the crisis generates additional issues with which they are primarily concerned. The third party may have preferences on the original issues, but these issues are much less salient to the actor than are the created issues. Furthermore, the original issues are most salient for the original parties—after all, these were the issues over which they became involved in the crisis. At this point, we can draw a further distinction between types of third-party involvement on the basis of whether the third party views these additional issues as being separable from the original issues.

In many cases, the third party enters the bargaining out of concern with additional issues that the third party sees as separable from the original issues. This would be the case when the motivation for involvement is concern for the effect the crisis is having on, for example, the cohesiveness of an alliance or the stability of a region. Here, the third party is worried more about how the conflict is resolved than about what form the solution takes. The concern is with the very occurrence of the crisis rather than with the outcome on the issues at stake. We would expect a third party with this motivation to assume the role of mediator. Furthermore, we would expect such a mediator to have the highest probability of facilitating a peaceful resolution since it would use its influence to push for any peaceul solution and could probably be expected to use its own resources to create additional issues that could be used as side payments.

This situation appears to be what we have seen in some recent cases such as the U.S. involvement in the Middle East peace process at Camp David and the U.S. efforts in the Falklands/Malvinas dispute. In both cases the United States sought to mediate because it was more concerned with maintaining peace and preserving its relationship with allies than with the outcome on the original issue. In the Camp David example, President Carter was willing to use U.S. resources for side payments and was successful in his mediation attempt. However, if the third party is unable to achieve its aims on the issue it deems important, it may take sides either to preserve the more important relationship (which is demonstrated by the Falklands case) or to achieve its preferences on other issues.

Finally, the most interesting case may be when a third party becomes involved when a crisis creates, for it, other substantive issues that are not separable from one or more of the original issues. That is, while the third party is relatively unconcerned about the original issues per se, it does perceive them as creating an important additional issue, and the outcome on the former issues will affect what is desired on the latter. In these cases, the created issue will usually pit the third party against one of the original protagonists, causing an alliance between the third party and the other original actor. This situation will not result in a coalition game, however, because the allies are, in a sense, forced together by their common enemy. Each is concerned with an issue about which the other cares little and has little control, and (most important) actions taken by their opponent affect each ally's interests in a similar way. Each ally may desire similar behavior from the opponent, but for different reasons;[2] thus, such situations will appear very much like separate, parallel crises except that the allies have similar goals (in terms of the behavior of the enemy) and should be expected to attempt to coordinate their actions to a degree.

A classic case of such a crisis was the 1911 Agadir crisis, depicted in figure 23. The French and the Germans were in conflict over the degree of French dominance in Morocco and the amount of compensation to be paid to Germany for this dominance. In an attempt to force the French hand, the Germans sent a warship to the port of Agadir, which created in the British the fear that Germany would attempt to establish a fortified port in Agadir. The British participation was aimed at protecting their interests on this additional issue. The British preferences on the original issues were actually somewhat closer to those of the Germans than to those of the French, but these issues were much less salient than the created issue. Even though the Germans had little intention of establishing a fortified port at Agadir, their actions created in the British the perception that this issue was closely linked to the degree of French control in Morocco (they believed that low French control would mean a strong German presence), which had the effect of shifting the

British ideal point on this issue toward the French. Thus, the British and French were aligned in seeking a German withdrawal from Agadir.

In figure 23, we can see that the Germans and French were not too far apart on the issue of French control in Morocco—the question mainly concerned the form of guarantees to German economic interests—but were far apart on the amount of compensation to be paid Germany. Britain was between the two principals on these issues but was somewhat closer to Germany. The three were actually fairly close on the issue of the fortified German port, in that Germany had little intention of seeking one though it was willing to use the prospect of such an action to gain bargaining leverage. The major differences were in the shapes of the indifference surfaces (which I have not attempted to draw). For Germany and France, the most salient issue was the amount of compensation; the issue of the German port was, in their mind, so unimportant that it was almost nonexistent; and the issues were separable. For the British, the original issues paled in importance to the issue of the port, and this issue was not separable from the issue of French control. That, in effect, shifted the British ideal point on issue 1 to a place very near the French.[3]

In this case, our expectations about the third-party behavior are largely borne out. The British did, to a great extent, behave as if they were in a separate crisis with the Germans. Though they did confer with the French,

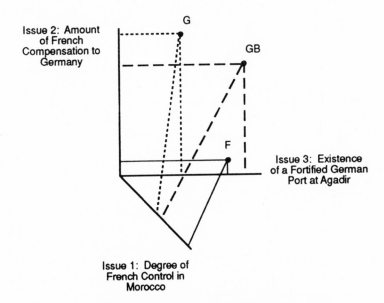

Fig. 23. A spatial representation of the Agadir crisis

they bargained with the Germans more or less independently, and the crisis was resolved for the British long before it was for the French. It is also interesting to note that the British came much closer to going to war than did the French. We would expect this result to occur only in a situation such as this in which the third party is, for the most part, involved in its own crisis.

From the above discussion, we can see that third parties in international conflicts can assume a variety of roles. They can become involved as mediators, they can align with one of the original disputants, or they can be opportunists who use the crisis to achieve their own aims. We can also see that all mediators (or all allies) are not alike. The interests of a potential third party dicatate what role it will assume and how it will play that role. Some mediators will do everything they can to resolve a crisis peacefully while others will push the disputants toward a particular solution. Some allies will be unshakably loyal and simply augment the capabilities of an initial disputant, others will adopt parallel policies but for their own ends, while still others will be quite fickle—even to the point of turning the crisis into an extremely unstable coalition game.

Third Parties and Crisis Outcomes

We can speculate from the above discussion that the effect third parties have on crisis outcomes depends, in part, on what form the third-party involvement takes and on what motivates the third-party involvement. In this section, I shall discuss the effect third parties have on crisis outcomes, primarily with regard to their impact on the probability of war. Within each type of involvement, I shall show, to a degree, how different characteristics of the crisis situation and participants affect the likely outcome.

Consider first situations in which the third party acts not as a mediator but as a potential ally for at least one of the disputants. If the third party has issue positions so close to one of the original parties that an alliance is dictated, the analysis of its impact on outcomes is a straightforward extension of the results presented in chapter 3. Since the allies can be expected to behave as one, the third party serves to augment the military capabilities of its ally, and its impact can be determined by the results relating the power relationship to outcomes. If the additional state adds insignificant capabilities to the alliance, the likely outcome will change none at all. On the other hand, if the third party adds to the alliance's capabilities vis-à-vis the opponent, the alliance can expect a negotiated settlement to be more favorable. Recall from chapter 3 that the derivations of the model suggest that crises are more likely to end in war when the parties are disparate in war-fighting capabilities; thus, if the enhanced capabilities create a situation of power parity, war is less likely, while if they create a situation of power disparity, war is more likely.

If the third party is located such that a three-way conflict results (as would be an actor at point m in figure 22), the effect is more complicated and more interesting. This situation is one for which traditional *n*-person game theory provides a great deal of insight. The analyses by Morrow (1986) are especially relevant for international relations scholars in this regard. Essentially, Morrow has shown that the game is one in which the actors compete for coalition partners and, in so doing, must decide whether the support of an ally is worth the concessions one must make to that ally. For example, if j and m in figure 22 were to align, the alliance position would presumably lie somewhere between their ideal points. Each must decide if it is preferable to advocate a less desirable solution in exchange for the increased capabilities an alliance provides. When such a coalition forms, the likely negotiated settlement, should one occur, will be altered. This is because the conflict line (which is analogous to a contract curve, or Pareto set) has as its end points the ideal points of the protagonists. When the initial position of one side is shifted by coalition formation, the set of likely outcomes will also shift. As to the probability of war, it is affected in the same way that the above situations were by the changes in the capability relationship. It is also affected in another way. Since the coalition members are defending a position somewhat removed from their ideal points, each may be less willing to go to war to achieve the coalition demands than it would have been to achieve its own ideal point. If that is the case, we would expect a coalition to be less likely to push a crisis to war than would be a single state, all else being equal (i.e., the reduced willingness to fight from this factor may not be sufficient to overcome any increased willingness from an increase in capabilities).

Finally, if the alliance is formed because the crisis created a nonseparable additional issue for the third party, we would expect the probability of war to be increased by the third-party involvement. Since the coalition members are adopting nearly an identical issue stance, the mitigating effect of defending a less than perfect solution would not exist. Furthermore, since the situation resembles, to an extent, two separate crises with the alliance partners acting somewhat independently, there is a greater chance of at least one choosing to go to war (e.g., if the probability of war between i and j is .25 and the probability of war between k and j is .2, the probability that at least one of i and k would go to war with j is .4). Naturally, this would be lessened somewhat to the extent the enemy is inhibited from fighting by the possibility of a more costly war against two foes.

It is also interesting to note that in this type of case the enemy of the coalition has an additional conflict strategy available. Since the basis for the coalition is the perception by the third party that the issue it deems important is nonseparable from another issue, the enemy can try to change this perception and convince the third party that it need not be involved. In the Agadir

crisis, Germany handled this very poorly, with almost disastrous consequences. The French, on the other hand, were able to capitalize on the
situation by manipulating the British perception of a linkage between the
issues. This case also illustrates the danger in such a strategy, since the British
almost caused the war the French hoped to avoid.

Turning to third parties who act as mediators, we can again see that the
reasons for adopting this role affect the impact the third party has on the
outcome. If the mediator assumes this role because of issue preferences that
lie between those of the protagonists, we can again usefully approach the
problem from the perspective of n-person game theory. This will probably be
a coalition game in which the original actors shift their positions toward one
another (and the mediator) in hopes of attracting the third party to their side.
While the general effect of the third party will be similar to that discussed
above, there should also be an additional lessening of the probability of war
since the actions of the parties competing for the mediators' favor would tend
to lessen the degree of conflict between them. This is clearly consistent with
the conventional view of mediation advanced by Touval (1975), Morrow
(1986), and others.

Mediators can also serve a number of functions that reduce the probability of war, as was noted above. It has been argued, for example, that
mediators can serve to improve the communications between the disputants
and that mediators make concessions more likely since they result in less loss
of face if made to a third party. We might expect mediators trying to achieve
their aims on the issues at stake to serve less well in this capacity than those
who work toward a peaceful resolution of the conflict out of concern for issues
threatened by the crisis; but their conflict-easing function should still be
important.

A mediator can also reduce the likelihood of war by bringing additional
issues into the bargaining. We saw in chapter 4 that when additional issues are
included, the probability of a settlement can be increased if the issues provide
an opportunity for logrolling. A mediator may be exceptionally able to bring
in such issues, especially if they are in the form of guarantees or side payments. An example of this is the Camp David agreement in which the United
States, acting as mediator, was able to bring Egypt and Israel to an agreement,
largely by using its economic resources to make the agreement acceptable to
the parties. This point also illustrates that the ability of a mediator to reduce
the probability of war will partially depend on its capabilities. The more
resources a mediator has relative to the disputants, the more likely it will be to
pull them toward a compromise.

The ability of a mediator to reduce the probability of war should not be
exaggerated, however. If there are outcomes that the disputants prefer to war,
a mediator can increase the chances of achieving one, but if none exist, the

mediation attempt will fail. Even if the bargaining zone is not empty, a mediator can still fail for a number of reasons. We can consider the mediator's task to be essentially one of bargaining with two disputants over the issue of whether they should engage in conflict. If the mediator is in a weak bargaining position, it may fail. Such weakness on the part of a mediator could arise, for example, from a lack of determination or from an unwillingness to expend resources for side payments. If the disputants are highly resolved to achieve their aims, even if it means a high risk of war, and the mediator is not determined to achieve its aims, the mediation is unlikely to affect the crisis outcome.

This model can also contribute to the debate regarding whether mediators must be unbiased to contribute effectively to the peaceful resolution of disputes. The conventional wisdom that mediators could not be biased and be effective has been challenged on empirical and theoretical grounds (Carnevale and Wittmar 1987; Rubin 1981; Touval 1975). It has been shown that many mediators have had preferences for one side's position and have still been effective. Touval's argument is essentially that a biased mediator can be effective if the party against whom the mediator is biased prefers the likely outcome with the mediator to the outcome that is likely without the mediator. One can easily imagine such a situation, particularly when one recalls some of the functions of mediators. Concessions made through a mediator can result in less loss of face than those made directly to the opponent. Thus, a bargainer who prefers conceding to the no-agreement outcome, but only if there exists a face-saving way of making the concessions, might seize an offer of mediation by even the most biased of mediators.

The spatial construction shows that there is a more basic reason why a biased mediator can function effectively. Figure 24 illustrates a situation in which i and j are in dispute over the division of territory x. We have two potential mediators, k and l, who are concerned with a separable second issue, say the stability of the region, that has been created by the conflict between i and j. Actor k's prefered outcome on issue 1 falls between the ideal points of i and j, while l prefers an outcome closer to i's ideal point. The important aspect of this construction is the shape of the indifference contours. Both k and l see the second issue as much more salient than the first and would move a great distance from their preferred points on issue 1 to achieve relatively little additional stability. Thus, even though l appears more biased than k on the initial issue in dispute, their positions are virtually indistinguishable in the context of the entire situation because l's bias is overwhelmed by the salience of the second issue. If there are characteristics of l that would make it an effective mediator (such as a great resource endowment or a history of close relations with both i and j) l, even though biased, could be preferable to k as a mediator.

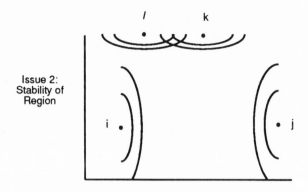

Issue 2:
Stability of
Region

Issue 1: Ownership of Territory X

Fig. 24. Biased and unbiased mediators

It is also instructive to compare actor *l* in figure 24 to our actor *l* in figure 22. Recall that the earlier actor *l* would appear to the initial disputants as completely unbiased on the issues at stake. Its ideal point was midway between those of the original protagonists, and its actions would be geared toward persuading both i and j to make concessions and agree on a split-the-difference outcome. Clearly, however, the earlier actor *l* is biased in a different sense—it is motivated by a desire to achieve a particular outcome on the issues at stake rather than by a desire to achieve some peaceful solution. While not biased toward either of the parties, it is biased toward particular settlements. Recall that this bias inhibited its ability to function as an effective mediator by eliminating the incentive to search for creative solutions to the dispute. Thus, it is possible that the biased *l* in figure 24 would be more effective as a mediator.

Touval's (1975) argument suggested that a biased mediator can be accepted by the disputants and can function effectively if its involvement is seen as leading to outcomes preferred to those expected in the absence of any mediator. The results presented here show that a biased mediator can, under some circumstances, actually be expected to do a better job than an unbiased mediator. This result can occur when the biased potential mediator is able to function more effectively than can the unbiased potential mediator. This ability can arise because of greater resources and skills or because of the underlying motivations for becoming involved.

Conclusion

The purpose of this chapter has been to develop further the spatial model of bargaining in international crises by evaluating the impact of third parties on crisis outcomes. A number of familiar arguments have been placed in the context of an integrated theory of crisis behavior, and a few additional insights have been provided. The main point has been that a third party will not have a straightforward impact on the outcome of a crisis. The impact will depend on the role the third party takes—whether mediator or ally—and the motivations for adopting this role. Though the impact will depend on each of the variables incorporated into the model, at least two general propositions can be stated: (1) When the third party becomes involved as a potential ally for one, or both, of the disputants, the probability of war will increase if the third party is acting out of concern for an issue created by the crisis that is nonseparable from one of the other issues or when the coalition creates a situation of power disparity. If the coalition creates a situation of power parity, or if the process of coalition formation leads to a significant softening of the actors' positions, then the result will be a decrease in the probability of war. (2) When the third party is involved as a mediator, the probability of war will generally decrease. The ability of a mediator to lessen the probability of war will depend on a number of factors, however. Mediators with greater capabilities should be more effective than those with few capabilities, and we expect a mediator to be more effective when motivated by an issue created by the crisis than when motivated by a desire to achieve a specific outcome on the original issues.

One conclusion that clearly emerges is that an analysis of the impact of third parties on crisis outcomes cannot be conducted without taking into consideration the variables addressed in the previous chapters. How a third party behaves and how the original disputants react to its participation depends to a great extent on the power and resolve of the third party relative to the other actors. A relatively determined and powerful intervening actor will be better able to pull an outcome toward its own preferred solution, whether in terms of the issues at stake or in terms of the means used to resolve the dispute. Furthermore, the impact a third party can have on crisis outcomes partially depends on how it can affect the bargaining agenda. Third-party interventions influence whether issues are considered sequentially or simultaneously as well as the order in which the issues are addressed. Mediators especially, though not exclusively, can bring additional issues into the bargaining for linkage purposes. This demonstrates that a useful theory of crisis bargaining cannot be based on simple notions of bivariate relationships. The effect on crisis behavior and outcomes of any single variable depends on the value of other important variables. Thus, our understanding must be based on a theoretical framework capable of incorporating a number of factors and capable of accounting for their interrelationships.

The results presented in this chapter also suggest that the underlying motivations for a third party's involvement will have an impact on the nature of the bargaining that occurs. If the third party is a potential coalition partner, much of the bargaining will be aimed at enticing the third party to join one of the coalitions. If the third party is an ally to one side because of an additional, nonseparable issue, much of the effort will be aimed at its perception that the issues are nonseparable. If the third party is a mediator, much of the bargaining will originate with the third party and will be aimed at cajoling the disputants to accept a compromise outcome, and the third party may use side payments to achieve this end.

In addition, I have shown that mediators need not be impartial to be effective. A mediator biased toward one of the parties can facilitate a resolution to the conflict. That a biased mediator can be preferable to no mediator has been widely accepted in the literature. The derivations from the spatial model go even further, indicating that a biased mediator, depending on its capabilities, resource endowments, and motivations, can hold a greater prospect for success than an unbiased mediator. This finding is not obvious, but the spatial construction shows that it is quite sensible.

Clearly this does not represent the final word on third parties in international crisis. Many more questions could be asked, more precise predictions of third-party impacts and behaviors could be made, and the propositions must be tested empirically. This chapter does show that the spatial model can be used to derive insight into multiple party conflict situations, however. This model constitutes a significant improvement over many other formal models of crisis bargaining and does allow us to fit a few more pieces into the puzzle.

CHAPTER 6

Conclusion

This study began with the argument that our understanding of the causes of war can be furthered by focusing on state behavior in international crises. I accepted both the position that crises are generally the situations from which wars evolve and the notion that by understanding the conditions and processes that make bargained agreements in crises more likely, we simultaneously increase our knowledge regarding the causes of war. A complete answer to the question, Why do some crises end in war while others are resolved by mutual agreement? has not been developed here. My purpose has been limited to proposing a formal model to be used in approaching this broad question and to using this model to solve a few of the more basic pieces of the puzzle. In this conclusion I shall evaluate what has, and has not, been accomplished and attempt to determine whether even my modest goal has been achieved. At least some of the major limitations of the approach adopted here will be acknowledged, but I shall try to argue that the relatively simple analyses performed in this book have provided insight into why some crises end in war and that many of the questions remaining unanswered can be addressed within the framework of the spatial model of crisis bargaining.

Throughout the course of this book, I have introduced the two components of the spatial model, the issue space and the utility space; I have shown how a number of variables, deemed by many to be important determinants of crisis outcomes, are incorporated into the model; and I have used the model to derive a number of hypotheses linking these variables to crisis outcomes. Many of the conclusions reached have been intuitive; that a state holding a preponderance of military capabilities can expect a favorable negotiated settlement, all else being equal, is but one such example. If the model produced contrary conclusions in many such instances, we would have good reason to doubt its sensibility; but a useful model must also tell us some things we do not already know. Counterintuitive conclusions have also been derived, however, suggesting that the model is shedding new light on the phenomenon. That a linkage attempt can successfully contribute to a peaceful crisis resolution even when both sides see the additional issue as less important than the original issue is one important example. Another is the finding that, under some conditions, a biased mediator may be able to be more effective than an unbiased mediator. Findings such as these are useful not simply because they provide new insight into the subject matter, which they do. These conclusions can also have immediate policy implications by giving decision makers a reason to try potentially peace-preserving strategies that they otherwise would have believed to be hopeless.

In my opinion, the single most important contribution of this model is that it incorporates a number of quite varied factors into a single explanatory framework. Rather than relying on a series of ad hoc hypotheses linking individual variables to outcomes, the model provides the basis for an integrated theory of crisis behavior. It permits the analysis of the interaction effects among the variables and leads to more precise hypotheses (i.e., we can conclude not only that the correlation between X and Y should be positive, but that it should be weak, or strong, and that the strength, and possibly direction, of the relationship should vary depending on the values of the other variables). We can also provide, under the single framework, analyses of different aspects of crisis behavior. For example, we can analyze issue linkages with the same model that we analyze the effects of disparities in war-fighting capabilities on the probability of war.

I have tried to structure this book so that each chapter builds, in a logical way, on those preceding. Chapter 3 examined very simple situations involving only two parties and zero-sum disputes and focused on variables characterizing crisis participants in terms of their power and resolve. Chapter 4 focused on the bargaining agenda, including the strategy of issue linkage, and extended the analysis to non-zero-sum situations in which more than one issue is under dispute. The results indicate that there are some fairly complex relationships in which the power and resolve of the participants affect the likelihood that a linkage attempt will be successful. This suggests quite strongly that we must consider the analysis of chapter 3 to understand completely the effect that the agenda and issue linkages have on crisis outcomes. Similarly, the results in chapter 5 can only be appreciated fully if the analyses in chapters 3 and 4 are taken into account. Chapter 5 extended the model to situations involving more than two parties. We considered several types of third-party involvement and discovered that the effect of a third party's involvement is heavily influenced by the power relationships, the issue positions of the parties, and the additional issues that the third party brings to the crisis.

Numerous advantages come from having an integrated model incorporating all these factors. Obviously, we have a more complete picture of why some crises end in war than is provided when few factors are considered or when many factors are considered in an ad hoc fashion. We are also afforded a means by which to have some confidence in the empirical validity of conclusions that cannot be directly tested. Empirical results supporting some of the derivations of the model serve as an indirect indication that other conclusions are also valid since all are derived from the same logical framework. The major benefit comes simply from the additional insight afforded by examining the interactions of the various factors. We have seen that the relationships between the variables considered here and crisis outcomes are actually quite complex. The precise impact of the actors' resolve and their ability to impose bargaining costs depends on the distribution of military capabilities; whether an attempt to resolve the crisis by linking issues can be successful depends on the power and resolve variables; and a third party can either increase or decrease the probability of war, depending on the values assumed by the other variables. These results demonstrate that many of the conclusions reached in previous studies based on simple bivariate analyses are either wrong or are only correct in a restricted set of circumstances. Integrating these factors into a single model thus provides a means for identifying complex relationships overlooked in other research.

This complexity comes at a cost, however. I cannot summarize the findings presented in this book in a simple and straightforward manner. I cannot state directly that mediation attempts will always reduce the probability that crises will escalate to war because in certain cases the attempt may make war more likely. I cannot state assuredly that a crisis participant will always benefit from a firm demonstration of its resolve because in some cases such a demonstration may do more harm than good. Furthermore, the added complexity will make any attempt at empirically testing hypotheses derived from the model more difficult. Simple, particularly bivariate, analyses can lead to quite misleading inferences if not interpreted with the utmost care. I believe the additional complexity is worth the price, however, and probably more. Any search for simplistic answers to why some crises end in war is doomed to fail.

While I firmly believe that the research presented in this book contributes to our understanding of international crises, I must admit that a number of deficiencies remain. All of the important questions have not been answered (or even asked), additional avenues remain to be explored, and, unfortunately, there are probably errors yet to be found. Some of the shortcomings can be corrected with further research, though others are inherent in the approach I have adopted. The limitations of the approach cannot be ignored, but I believe they are no more serious than those facing other approaches and that the insight already provided, as well as the potential insight, justifies the continued use of the spatial model.

One thing I clearly have not provided in this book is systematic empirical support for the hypotheses derived. I have tried to show that the results of a number of extant studies are consistent with the model and that the model provides a means for reconciling some apparently contradictory results. Case studies have also been used to provide an empirical referent for the model.

These studies show that the model can be used to represent real-world events and that the model can produce explanations for the outcomes of these historical crises. Though informative, these efforts do not constitute confirmation of the empirical expectations. Empirical support from direct tests is required before we have great confidence that explanations offered here are valid.

Perhaps the most serious obstacle to conducting such a test is that the variables included in the model have not been adequately operationalized. Until this problem is solved, a satisfactory empirical test is not possible. The problem regarding what *power* and *resolve* actually mean is one that has plagued international relations scholars for years, and I will not pretend to have a final solution at this time. The model does, however, provide a theoretical context in which to define these concepts, which can, at least, clarify matters somewhat. One task of future research will be to determine what factors constitute these variables and to devise suitable indicators for them.[1]

A great many theoretical questions have also been overlooked in this book. Perhaps the most important to our understanding of why wars occur is that I have not attempted to determine why crises occur in the first place. I begin the study at the point where two, or more, states are already in a situation in which war is believed to be a distinct possibility. I have not completely ignored variables characterizing the background of crises—the power relationships and the issues under dispute are prominent—but it is at least as important to know what brings states to the brink of war as to know what determines whether they go over the edge once there. This is the subject for another book; however, the analysis contained here could inform such an effort if we assume that decisions to enter crises are influenced by expectations regarding their outcomes.

Even the picture of crisis bargaining is incomplete in some respects. Numerous variables have been excluded. While any attempt to incorporate all possible variables into a single framework would produce a model so complex that it would be useless, it is clear that some of the omitted variables are potentially very important. The analyses performed here have not considered the impact of a number of domestic political, bureaucratic, social-psychological, and psychological variables deemed by many to be important in crisis behavior (see especially Allison 1971; George 1980; Janis 1972; Lebow 1981).

Crisis participants are not unitary actors, as has been assumed throughout this book. By and large, I think the costs of the unitary actor assumption are outweighed by the simplification it affords, but it is clear from the case studies that bureaucratic politics do occasionally play a role. The Fashoda Crisis, for example, would not have occurred and would have been handled differently had the French spoken and acted with a single voice. Similarly, domestic political factors, which can affect crisis behavior and outcomes, have been overlooked. Research has indicated that domestic political structure (e.g., whether a state is democratic or not), economic conditions, and diversionary pressures can all affect crisis behavior (see, e.g., Bueno de Mesquita and Lalman 1992; James 1988; Morgan and Bickers 1992; Morgan and Campbell 1991; Morgan and Schwebach 1992b; Russett 1990). Thus, a fully developed theory of international crises must include these sorts of factors.

The failure to incorporate psychological variables also renders some of the analyses incomplete. Note that I have nowhere assumed perfect information acquisition or processing on the part of crisis participants. The realization that crises occur in a noisy, uncertain environment is the primary reason that the model was constructed to express its predictions in terms of probability distributions rather than as determinate outcomes. Incorporating these types of factors directly could do much to fine tune the explanations, however. In the crisis preceding the Seven Weeks War, for example, the Austrians grossly overestimated their military capabilities compared to the Prussians. Accounting for this misperception within the model would provide a more complete explanation for the outcome of this particular crisis.

The model has been designed to be flexible in terms of the variables incorporated, and some of these considerations can be included. Since any number of actors can be considered, we are not restricted to viewing the participants as unitary nation-states. We could consider the actors to be subnational individuals or groups and analyze the interactions within as well as between national actors (see, e.g., Bueno de Mesquita, Newman, and Rabushka 1985). Such a task would be exceedingly complex, but in principle, it could be done. A more feasible task would be to examine the impact of some types of misperceptions on crisis outcomes. For example, Levy (1983a), among others, has argued that there are a number of types of misperceptions that can contribute to war. A number of these involve misperceptions regarding the balance of military capabilities between the disputants. In this book, I have only considered the effect of the objective balance of capabilities. One way of incorporating misperceptions into the analysis would be to allow the parties' perceived probabilities of winning a war to be independent of each other. We could then determine how the probability of war is affected when, for example, both sides believe they have a decided advantage in war-fighting abilities (see Carlson 1992 for a recent attempt at addressing this question).

Another factor omitted from this study is the risk orientation of the actors. I have assumed the actors to be risk neutral throughout. This assumption was not necessitated by any limitation of the model; it was done solely to simplify the derivation of the results. One interesting avenue of research would be to determine the impact of various combinations of risk-acceptant and risk-averse actors on crisis outcomes as well as how this variable interacts with the variables already considered. Such an analysis could possibly produce some rather surprising results. We might expect at an intuitive level, for example, that if one (or more) of the actors is risk averse, the probability of war would be less than with risk-neutral or risk-acceptant actors. It may be, however, that in some cases war is the least risky alternative, particularly if the risk-averse actor is vastly superior militarily. In this case, risk aversion may actually increase the probability of war (see Bueno de Mesquita and Lalman 1990 for a formal analysis of this question).

Even without extending the model to incorporate other factors, a great deal of research remains to be done. The predictions of crisis outcomes are made in terms of probability distributions over all possible outcomes, but I have made use of only a small amount of the information available concerning these distributions. This restriction was somewhat misleading in at least one instance—the conclusion that increasing the costs of disagreement for a party less likely to win a war makes that party more likely to get its way in a negotiated settlement. The problem is that the mode of the distribution did shift in that direction, but the overall shift in the distribution favored the party more likely to win a war. In some cases, aspects of the distribution other than the mode, such as the variance or skewness, may tell us a great deal about what behavior and outcomes we should expect. At the very least, analyses of how changes in the variables affect these aspects of the distribution would tell us how close to our prediction we should expect to find an actual outcome.

The omission of these factors raises important questions that have not been addressed in this book; but the fact that some consideration of these variables can be incorporated into the model speaks to its flexibility and its usefulness. The analyses presented here do not exhaust the insights that can be produced by the spatial model, and further research should be based on it. A number of deficiencies are inherent in the approach, however, and these cannot be ignored.

The model is based on the assumptions that crisis decision makers are rational, that their preference orderings can be represented by von Neumann–Morgenstern utility functions, and that the probability of acceptance functions are monotonically decreasing with respect to utility loss. Such assumptions, or others serving similar purposes, are necessary abstractions from reality. The important question is not whether these are abstractions but whether they deviate from reality to such an extent that the model is meaningless. Assuming that bodies fall in a vacuum causes little difference between prediction and observation when a shot put is dropped from a roof, but the friction of air causes the prediction to be completely wrong when the object dropped is a feather. At this point, I cannot say whether the simplifying assumptions adopted for this model cause the expectations to be more like those for the shot put or more like those for the feather.

Perhaps a more important limitation is that I have constructed what is essentially a static model. Crisis bargaining is an inherently dynamic process in that outcomes highly depend on the actors' strategies and moves in terms of concession rates, threats, and promises. Furthermore, actors' strategies are not selected in isolation. They constantly undergo revision and are influenced by the actions of the opponent. The model developed in this book cannot address these aspects of the bargaining process. A dynamic model, perhaps one based on a well-developed theory of moves, could produce a number of additional insights and could provide policy prescriptions regarding concessions and concession rates. Such a model might prove more useful to a crisis participant.

Part of the problem in this regard arises because, in constructing this model, I have adopted the perspective of the analyst rather than that of the bargainer. The model draws heavily from game theoretic models, but it is not intended as a contribution to game theory. My aim has been to use the model to derive testable hypotheses relating a number of variables to expected crisis outcomes. In adopting this perspective and this goal, I have sacrificed an ability to analyze the dynamic unfolding of crises and to address many strategic questions. Adopting the perspective of the bargainer would permit many additional insights; but at this point, it is not absolutely certain that such an approach would be more fruitful or more parsimonious. It should also be stressed that even a static model adopting the perspective of the analyst can be of use to crisis participants. Taking the vantage point of the observer can be suggestive to decision makers and using a rigorous, systematic model to organize their thinking about the situation has obvious benefits.

Without a doubt, other models could provide other insights and the future will probably bring a superior alternative. The proper question is whether this effort leaves us better off than we were before. I believe the spatial model does clarify much of our thinking about international crises and does improve our explanations for why some crises are resolved peacefully while others end in war. Obviously, we remain quite ignorant of why nations go to war. The results presented in this book address part of this ignorance, and the insights provided move us in the right direction. I believe, and I hope I have convinced others, that the spatial model of crisis bargaining has potential for providing further insights sufficient to warrant its use in future research. I suspect, and hope, that readers of this book will remain somewhat skeptical of what I have produced. Such skepticism is necessary for our knowledge to advance, and ultimately, the quality of that knowledge is what determines whether crisis participants can untie the knot of war.

Appendix

In this appendix, I shall use the spatial model to guide brief analyses of six historical cases of international crises. For each, I provide a synopsis of the crisis outlining the parties and issues involved, the bargaining moves taken, and the resolution of the conflict. I then characterize the crisis in terms of the model. This characterization involves three steps. First, the issue space characterization of the crisis is presented. The issues are identified, the parties are located in the space, and the parties' preference orderings over the possible outcomes are specified by placing the proposals made during the bargaining within the issue space. Second, a utility space is derived by specifying the actors' utilities for the possible outcomes identified in the issue space. I also characterize the crisis in terms of the resolve, war-fighting capabilities, and cost-imposing abilities of the parties. This characterization is not accomplished through a systematic coding of these variables; rather, I characterize each variable in quite general terms that seem most reasonable on the basis of what can be justified by the historical record. The final step is to use the probability of acceptance functions defined by the characterization to specify the expected negotiated outcome (in terms of both utilities and issue outcomes) and the probability of war. This result can then be compared to the actual crisis outcome to determine whether the model produces reasonable expectations.

It should be stressed at the outset that the material in this appendix is intended neither as a systematic empirical test of the model nor as an in-depth historical analysis of the cases. Since I consider only a few, nonrandomly selected cases and the variables have not been coded systematically, we cannot draw general empirical inferences. The information comes solely from secondary sources, the descriptions and analyses are by no means detailed, and, to some extent, the exercise is aimed at forcing the cases to fit the model. Thus, these case studies are not based on an objective rendering of historical fact. The aim is to present an abstract, stylized description of the facts surrounding each case in an effort to demonstrate that the model can serve as the basis for reasonable representations of real-world events. This appendix should provide some empirical referent for what is otherwise an extremely abstract model. My goal is simply to demonstrate that allowing our thinking to be structured by the model enables us to gain insight into historical events and improves our understanding of real-world processes. This purpose is served by showing that the relatively few variables included in the model provide reasonable characterizations of the crises as well as reasonable explanations for the outcomes, not by detailed descriptions.

The six crises analyzed are the Oregon Boundary Dispute between the United States and Great Britain, the crisis leading to the Seven Weeks War between Prussia and Austria, the Fashoda crisis between Britain and France, the Agadir crisis involving Germany, France, and Britain, the crisis preceding the Winter War between Finland and the Soviet Union, and the Cuban Missile Crisis between the Soviet Union and the United States. A number of criteria guided the selection of these particular cases. Individually, these crises were all relatively significant (and are thus reasonably familiar), a fair amount of source materials are available for each, and each was relatively simple in terms of the number and types of issues involved and in terms of the number of important participants. Furthermore, the historical record for each is fairly consistent. That is, there is a broad consensus regarding the facts—at least for those facts important for the spatial model. As a group, the set of cases provides a large amount of variation in the variables of interest. Some are characterized by a parity in war-fighting capabilities, others by a disparity; some involved high levels of bargaining costs, others low levels; some ended in war, others in capitulation, and still others in compromise settlements. Furthermore, the cases span a fairly long historical period, involve a number of different actors (and different types of states), and occurred on three different continents. There are also some in which additional issues were brought into the bargaining and some in which attempts at linkage failed. Finally, there is one case in which a third party played a significant role. In short, the desire was to select cases for which the analysis would be straightforward and to select a sufficiently varied set of cases to show that the model applies under a variety of circumstances.

Before turning to the case studies, one final note is in order. I have kept the citations in the presentations to an absolute minimum. The information I present is restricted to the most salient, the most familiar, and the most reported aspects of the crises. In addition, I have made an effort to structure the analyses only on that information about which there is a broad (though not necessarily total) consensus. For these reasons, I see no need to provide specific citations to justify the characterization of each variable. Rather, I provide, for each case, a selected list of the sources used. Most of these sources are in agreement regarding the characterization of the crisis.

The Oregon Boundary Dispute

Throughout most of the first half of the nineteenth century, Great Britain and the United States were at odds over the division of the Oregon territory.

Although the territory covered an area from the continental divide to the Pacific Ocean and from the forty-second parallel in the south to 54°40′ in the north, the actual area in dispute was much smaller. The Americans were always willing to concede the area north of 49° to the British while the British were willing to have the boundary follow the forty-ninth parallel until it met the Columbia River and then follow the river to the ocean. For much of the period, the parties agreed to disagree and were willing to abide by a joint occupation agreement signed in 1818 and renewed for an indefinite period in 1827.

A number of attempts to reach a negotiated settlement ended in failure. The United States generally refused to grant the British anything south of the forty-ninth parallel, which constituted the U.S.-Canadian border across most of the continent. Much of the American intransigence was due to a desire for a port on the Pacific, which could be met by acquiring the Puget Sound. At one point it was suggested that the United States would be willing to concede the Oregon issue if Britain would assist it in acquiring Northern California, including San Francisco Bay, from Mexico. However, neither party apparently took this suggestion very seriously. The American desire for a harbor on the Pacific did prompt the British to offer to grant the United States an enclave around Puget Sound. This offer was rejected on the grounds that the port facilities would be isolated from other American territory and would therefore depend on British good will for supply and communication (since the British navy could also control the sea).

On the other hand, the British were concerned with protecting the interests of the Hudson Bay Company in the Oregon territory. The base of the company's trapping and agricultural operations was in the area between the Columbia River and the forty-ninth parallel, so the British were unwilling to have this territory fall to the Americans. The need to control this area was lessened by the fact that much of the company's operations were moving northward, but the British perceived that they still needed to control the Columbia River to provide transportation access to the interior. Some proposals that would give control of the territory to the United States included a provision that would allow the British free access to the river. This proposal was resisted by the Americans, who did not wish to grant such access to an internal waterway.

The pressure for a permanent resolution began to build in the early 1840s when the number of American settlers in the area dramatically increased. The dispute reached crisis proportions with the election of President Polk in 1844. He was elected partly on the basis of an expansionist platform that, among other things, asserted that the U.S. claim to the whole Oregon territory was "clear and unquestionable." Polk was determined to settle the issue, and though he claimed to be wedded to "54-40 or fight," he was actually willing to accept the forty-ninth parallel as the boundary (he claimed, however, that this was only because he felt bound by previous American proposals). The need to settle the issue was forced when Polk requested that Congress resolve to provide Britain with a year's notice of the American intention of abrogating the joint occupation agreement. This action was intended, and perceived, to signal that in the absence of a settlement, the United States would use any means, including force, to establish control over the territory. Shortly after Congress had passed such a resolution, the issue was settled in a manner largely favorable to the American position. The border was set at the forty-ninth parallel to the water's edge and then along the Juan de Fuca Strait to the Pacific. This left the British in full possession of Vancouver Island. The United States also agreed to allow the British access to the Columbia River.

Applying the Model

The first step in applying the spatial model to an analysis of the Oregon Boundary dispute is to identify the parties involved and to specify the characteristics of the parties. We know that the only states involved in the dispute were Great Britain and the United States. It is necessary, however, to justify the specification of the actors' relative power and resolve.

At first blush it would seem that the British were greatly advantaged in terms of the parties' relative war-fighting abilities. Britain was widely regarded as the most powerful nation on earth, and the British navy ruled the seas. The United States had not yet risen to great power status and, in fact, had not even established its dominance in the Western hemisphere. The United States maintained a very small military in peacetime, and even at the height of the crisis, it did not dramatically increase military preparations. Furthermore, the United States was also faced with the possibility of a war with Mexico.

The United States did have a number of important advantages, however. It was generally accepted that the British position in Oregon was militarily indefensible. The American settlers greatly outnumbered the British, and given the distance from England, there was little the British navy could do to support the British in Oregon. Partly because of this threat to their holdings in Oregon, the Hudson Bay Company moved the majority of its stores and the base of its operations to Vancouver Island. On other fronts, while the British had the superior military, it would be faced with the problems associated with fighting far from home. The Americans were also blessed with a vast territory and plentiful resources while the British were faced with economic problems at home, particularly with regard to the potato famine, which necessitated the importation of food.

Most important, however, was that the British were concerned with how the French would react. It was believed that the French would either align with the Americans or use a British-American war as an opportunity to attack Britain. The French and Americans together would likely have been able to defeat the British, and even if France did not join in the war, it would have served to neutralize a sizable portion of the British military since many British forces would have to remain at home to guard against a French attack. In considering all these factors, it is likely that the Americans would have fared quite well in a war with Britain. In any case, both parties perceived the situation in this way. Thus, I will consider the Americans and the British to have had a roughly equal chance of prevailing in war.

In considering the ability of each side to impose bargaining costs on the other, we find that both sides had some tools at their disposal. Britain could have used its navy to disrupt American trade and, more important, could have completely denied the Americans access to the British markets. This action would have been particularly costly to American agricultural interests. On the other hand, the United States could have curtailed economic relations with the British. This action could have been particularly costly since the British were at that time somewhat dependent on imports of American grain. It should not be surprising that none of these tools were used during the crisis since actions taken by one party to impose costs on the other would have proved costly to the first. In addition, the value of a settlement would not decrease for either party the longer it was delayed. The necessity of resolving the issue was created by Polk's actions, not by some natural timetable. The bargaining costs for both sides were thus negligible, and I will not consider them as important.

In terms of the resolve of the parties, the United States had a significant edge. A large segment of the country favored standing firm on the issue, and Polk's strongest support came from the "54-40 or fight"-ers. Many Americans believed it to be the country's manifest destiny to span from ocean to ocean, and many others were disposed to help American settlers in Oregon avoid coming under British domination. By comparison, Great Britain was lacking in resolve. It was generally felt that the territory under dispute was worthless, especially since the Hudson Bay Company had moved the base of its operations north. Most in Britain were willing to grant the Americans all of the disputed territory—but only if it could be done in a way that would maintain the British prestige. On a number of occasions, the British offered to submit the dispute for arbitration with the intention that the arbitrator would draw the boundary at the forty-ninth parallel. At one point, they even explicitly told the Americans that they would help find an arbitrator predisposed toward the American claim. The Americans refused because the issue was perceived as too important to submit to arbitration.

Our next step is to specify the issues involved in the crisis and to characterize the bargaining process in terms of the model. Figure A-1 will serve as an illustration of the Oregon Boundary Dispute. Only one issue was involved

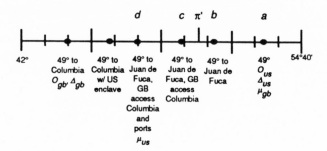

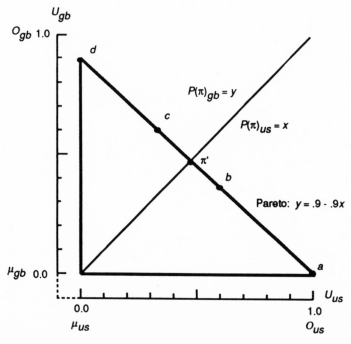

Fig. A-1. The Oregon boundary dispute, 1846: *a*) The issue space;
b) The utility space

in this particular crisis: how to divide the Oregon territory. We can thus represent the crisis with a single issue dimension, as in figure A-1a. The endpoints of the scale represent solutions in which the border would be at 42° (all of the territory to Britain) and 54°40′ (all of the territory to the United States). The preference orderings of the parties are such that each side prefers receiving more of the territory to less. Though each party had concerns other than the absolute amount of territory received (the British desired navigation rights on the Columbia, and the United States wanted harbors), these concerns were directly related to the amount of territory controlled, so the dispute can be reflected with a single dimension.

The various proposals advanced by the parties are also indicated in figure A-1a. The British opening proposal (O_{gb}) would have the boundary follow the forty-ninth parallel to the Columbia River, and the American opening proposal (O_{us}) would set the border at 49°. These points are also Δ_{gb} and Δ_{us}, which reflect the negligible bargaining costs involved. I have set μ_{gb} at O_{us} since the British did give some indication that they would be willing to accept such a settlement under the appropriate conditions. μ_{us} has been set at the point where the border would be drawn at 49° to the water's edge then follow the Juan de Fuca Strait to the Pacific and the British would be granted navigation rights to the Columbia and free access to the ports in the disputed area. It is unlikely that the United States would have accepted a border any farther south, but pressure from those wishing to avoid war would have brought about the additional concessions. Other points shown are the British offer of the 49°-Columbia border with a U.S. enclave at Puget sound, the U.S. offer of the 49°–Juan de Fuca Strait border, and the British offer of the 49°–Juan de Fuca Strait border with British navigation rights to the Columbia (the final settlement).

Given the existence of a single issue, questions regarding the agenda did not arise. The attempts to link other issues to the border question, while made, were not feasible. The suggestion that the United States concede the Oregon territory in exchange for British help in obtaining northern California from Mexico was not taken too seriously by either side and was never made during the crisis period. There were some suggestions in the British press that the British surrender Oregon in exchange for U.S. trade concessions, but there is no evidence that the negotiators ever considered this proposal. Therefore, we can ignore questions regarding the agenda in this particular case.

The pattern of bargaining proposals each actor made essentially followed the path of the issue dimension with the United States moving from right to left and the British from left to right. There were few cases in which proposals were retracted. When the final round of negotiations began, the British appeared to retract the enclave offer they had made in 1826, but this retraction was the result of a bureaucratic foul-up—the government and negotiator were not aware that the enclave offer had been made. The election of Polk seemed to portend that the United States would take a harder line and press for 54°40′, but this action did not actually occur. Polk did withdraw his offer of the 49°–Juan de Fuca Strait border when the British negotiator rejected it (against the instructions of his government), but he was willing to accept such a settlement when the British offered.

Both sides took very few actions intended to apply pressure. The most obvious was the U.S. notification that it intended to abrogate the joint occupation treaty with the implication that it would impose a settlement when the treaty lapsed. The tone of the Congressional resolution somewhat softened this position by expressing the hope for a negotiated settlement. The British did undertake some war preparations, but a great deal of this effort was intended to defend against the French.

Figure A-1b is the utility space representation of this dispute. I have characterized the situation as non–zero sum, and for each party I have specified the utility scale so that μ provides 0 utility and O provides 1.0 utility. Points a, b, c, and d are the utility points associated with the four proposals indicated in figure A-1a. Note that the precise location of these points is arbitrary, as is the construction of a linear Pareto set, though these representations are consistent with the details of the case. The particular values selected were chosen to simplify the presentation with as little distortion to the facts as possible. This simplification means that we cannot place too much weight on the precise solutions generated (e.g., that there was exactly a .1 probability of war); rather, these figures must be seen as very rough estimates. Recall that for each party, $\Delta = O$ and that I have classified the actors as equally likely to win a war. The probability of acceptance functions can thus be specified as $p_{us}(\pi) = x$ and $p_{gb}(\pi) = y$. The function characterizing the Pareto optimal frontier is given by $y = .9 - .9x$. In this case, π' will be the point that maximizes xy, subject to the condition that $y = .9 - .9x$. Inserting $.9 - .9x$ for y, we must maximize $.9x - .9x^2$. The derivative is $.9 - 1.8x$; and setting the derivative equal to 0, we find that $x = .5$. Solving for y in $y = .9 - .9x$, we find that $y = .45$. Thus, π' is at $(.5,.45)$, as indicated in figure A-1b.

Note that the predicted outcome is more favorable to the United States than the actual outcome, point c. A number of points are of interest. First, a solution at π' would probably have been one that was similar to point c, except that the British access to the Columbia River would have been restricted in some way (either by limiting the access to a specified number of years or to the Hudson Bay Company). The United States considered such a proposal before point c was accepted, and had it been made, it is very likely that the British would have accepted. Furthermore, it must be remembered that in the total context of the dispute, even point c must be considered as a highly favorable outcome for the United States. Second, probably the most objectionable of my coding decisions is the characterization of both parties being equally likely to win a war. If one were to accept that the British were actually more likely to win, π' would move toward point c. Finally, this construction does provide a fairly accurate description of the crisis in that point c would have a relatively high probability of being accepted.

We can also see that this characterization specifies that the probability of war was about .1. Each player's PDF would be a uniform distribution with all of the United States' and .9 of Britain's being within the bargaining set. This result does seem to reflect the true probability in that this crisis never was all that close to war. Lest one think that a .1 probability of war is extremely low, however, one should remember that less than 10 percent of all militarized disputes escalate to war (Gochman and Maoz 1984). Crises are among the most serious militarized disputes, so a .1 probability of war represents a significant likelihood of war, compared to other situations. There is one surprise in this representation: it seems to suggest that it was Britain, not the United States, that was more prepared to go to war. This proposition would appear to go against the common interpretation of the crisis, in which the United States is portrayed as being the side that forced the issue with the threat of war. One should remember, however, that the British did undertake war preparations (sending ships and materiel to Canada and the Oregon coast), whereas the United States did not. An entirely plausible explanation is that the United States was engaged in bluffing tactics and would have backed down (at least to the point of continuing the joint occupation) if faced with strong British opposition.

Selected Bibliography

Bailey, Thomas A. 1964. *A Diplomatic History of the American People*. 7th ed. New York: Appleton-Century-Crofts.

Billington, Ray Allan. 1967. *Westward Expansion*. New York: Macmillan Co.

Cramer, Richard S. 1963. "British Magazines and the Oregon Question." *Pacific Historical Review* 32, no. 4 (November): 369–82.

DeConde, Alexander. 1963. *A History of American Foreign Policy*. New York: Charles Scribner's Sons.

Dodds, Gordon B. 1977. *Oregon: A Bicentennial History*. New York: W. W. Norton & Co.

Galbraith, John S. 1953. "France as a Factor in the Oregon Negotiations." *Pacific Northwest Quarterly* 44, no. 2 (April): 69–73.

Graebner, Norman A. 1961. "Politics and the Oregon Compromise." *Pacific Northwest Quarterly* 52, no. 1 (January): 7–14.

Johnson, C. T. 1907. "Daniel Webster and Old Oregon." *Washington Historical Quarterly* 2 (October): 6–11.

Jones, Wilburn D., and J. Chal Vinson. 1953. "British Preparedness and the Oregon Settlement." *Pacific Historical Review* 22 (November): 353–64.

McCabe, James O. 1960. "Arbitration and the Oregon Question." *Canadian Historical Review* 41, no. 4 (December): 308–27.

Merk, Frederick. 1924. "The Oregon Pioneers and the Boundary." *American Historical Review* 29 (July): 681–99.

———. 1932. "British Party Politics and the Oregon Treaty." *American Historical Review* 37 (July): 653–77.

———. 1934. "British Government Propaganda and the Oregon Treaty." *American Historical Review* 40 (October): 38–62.

———. 1967. *The Oregon Question*. Cambridge: Belknap.

———. 1978. *History of the Westward Movement*. New York: Alfred A. Knopf.

Pletcher, David M. 1973. *The Diplomacy of Annexation: Texas, Oregon, and the Mexican War*. Columbia: Univ. of Missouri Press.

The Austro-Prussian Crisis, 1864–66

In 1864, Austria and Prussia defeated Denmark in war and jointly acquired the duchies of Schleswig and Holstein. Questions regarding the ultimate disposition of the territories proved to be a bone of contention between the erstwhile allies, and within two years, Austria and Prussia were fighting each other in a war precipitated by this issue. Many have interpreted the history of this period as suggesting that war between Prussia and Austria was inevitable. Bismarck was clearly concerned with the underlying issues of economic, political, and military dominance in greater Germany, and he saw the dispute, and war, with Austria as one step toward his goals. War was not necessary for his broader aims, however. A major diplomatic victory leading to the expansion of King William's domains would have served Bismarck's purposes well. Furthermore, seeing the war as an inevitable result of Bismarck's machinations overemphasizes the authority he exercised at that time. The decision for war was the king's, and he was influenced by a number of advisors, including the crown prince, who mistrusted and detested Bismarck. The king preferred a negotiated settlement to war, providing that his interests and prestige were protected. Thus, this was a true crisis in which both war and a negotiated settlement were distinct possibilities.

The primary issue under dispute was the disposition of Schleswig-Holstein. Prussia desired to annex the territories while Austria preferred to establish an independent state under the Duke of Augustenburg. Prussia also advocated the establishment of an independent state, but its choice of ruler was the Grand Duke of Oldenburg (who would probably have sold his rights to the territories to Prussia). Augustenburg had the better claim to the title, but Austria was motivated more by political considerations than by legal arguments. Franz Joseph generally favored granting the territories to Prussia provided that adequate compensation was paid. A number of forms of compensation were proposed. Prussia, on numerous occasions, offered a cash payment to Austria to relinquish its claims. Many within Austria favored such a resolution, particularly since the Empire was in dire financial straits. Franz Joseph insisted he could never accept such a trade-off, though as the crisis wore on, he hinted that he might accept cash for partial compensation. Most of the Austrian offers would grant Prussia title to Schleswig-Holstein in exchange for territorial compensation in Silesia, though it had other interests as well. The empire faced internal turmoil in Hungary and was challenged from Italy in the south. Italy, which sought to acquire Venetia, was the immediate foreign concern, but it was supported by Napoleon III, who also coveted German territories. Austria hoped to maintain, and strengthen, the alliance with Prussia as a counter to these threats. Some therefore suggested that Austria accept, as at least partial payment for the duchies, Prussian guarantees of Venetia and promises of territorial compensation from France after the anticipated Franco-German war. A number of formulas were proposed throughout the crisis, including some that were fairly creative, but none proved satisfactory to both parties.

A great deal of the diplomacy of the crisis involved third parties, but these parties had a relatively minor impact on the crisis bargaining. Austria and Prussia both sought diplomatic support, but most of the energy directed at other states was aimed at gaining allies, or promises of neutrality, for the war. Principal among the third parties were the smaller German states, most of whom supported Austria out of fear of Prussia; Italy, who aligned with Prussia to seize Venetia; and France, who remained neutral because Napoleon, expecting a long war favoring Austria, hoped to strike a better bargain later. That Prussia was able to secure an alliance with Italy is somewhat curious, but it illustrates the importance of prestige for the actors. Italy had offered Austria a cash payment for Venetia which, if accepted, would have kept Italy out of the war. Austria was willing to part with Venetia, as indicated by the agreement struck with France. Austria promised, in exchange for French neutrality, to cede Venetia to Napoleon after the war with the understanding that it would be turned over to Italy. Austria forwent the much needed cash and fought a two-front war, not to preserve the territory but because directly dealing with the Italians was seen as too great a blow to its prestige.

The bargaining between Austria and Prussia was not conducted in a straightforward manner with each side progressively moving closer to the other's position. Offers were retracted or altered with the changing circumstances surrounding the crisis. King William grew increasingly intransigent throughout the crisis as events served to convince him that Austria sought his humiliation. He was quite insulted, for example, by Augustenburg and his supporters in the duchies, whose democratic liberalism sought to undermine his royal authority. This situation made William less willing to accept Augustenburg as time wore on. The primary sticking point was whether compensation would be in the form of cash or territory. Significant elements in each country's government favored accepting the other side's terms, but these were never quite able to carry the day. Near the outbreak of war, both parties nearly agreed to one possible settlement. This settlement would have given the duchies to Augustenberg but tied them economically, politically, and militarily to Prussia. The issue of control over greater Germany was also brought into this agreement, with Austria and Prussia dividing the smaller states into two areas of hegemony. Neither of the powers would accept this settlement unless it were officially proposed by one of the smaller German states acting as mediator. Since no third party would propose a settlement that so clearly disregarded its own interests, this agreement was not reached. In the end, as is well known, Austria and Prussia went to war.

Applying the Model

In one respect, this is a very tough case for the model. A number of factors not incorporated into the model clearly contributed to the outbreak of war. Bureaucratic politics were important in that both governments were divided about what constituted an acceptable settlement. On a number of occasions, influential elements of one government advocated accepting the terms the other offered. It is entirely possible that minor changes in events could have led the internal bargaining on either side to produce a different outcome. At one important meeting, for example, the two most conciliatory Austrian ministers were absent due to illness. Had they been present, their position might have been adopted and the crisis would have been settled. Misperceptions also appear to have played a critical role in this crisis. In particular, Austria fully expected to win the war, and Napoleon's willingness to remain neutral was based on his assumption that Austria would prevail in a long war. Had Franz Joseph known how the war would turn out, he might have been much more likely to have accepted Prussia's terms. Admittedly, the model does not, at this time, incorporate bureaucratic politics and misperceptions, so the story of this case is somewhat incomplete. Keep in mind that the predictions derived from the model are presented in probabilistic terms specifically because the model does not incorporate every variable that might be important in every case. That the model can provide a reasonable representation of this case using the few variables included attests to its ability to provide general representations of international crises.

The first step toward representing this case in terms of the model is to identify the parties involved and to specify the characteristics of these parties.

While other states were clearly involved in the diplomacy of this case, I shall treat it as a two-party dispute between Austria and Prussia.

It is tempting to classify this case as one in which Prussia had a substantial advantage in war-fighting capabilities. Hindsight is, of course, perfect, and the Prussian army routed the Austrians. However, the outcome of the war was not widely expected at the time. The Austrians believed they would win, as did most other observers. Some have noted that the Prussians were very confidant of victory and that, with the information regarding weapons technology, force structure, and strategy available at the time, all of Europe should have expected the Prussian victory. I believe the confidence that each side had in victory is somewhat exaggerated. Prussia was not so confident that it was willing to fight without the alliance with Italy, and Austria made great efforts to form alliances with the smaller German states, whose armies were small and of questionable value. Both sides thus appear to have believed that the balance of capabilities was close enough that a small edge in alliances could determine victory. Napoleon III actually believed that the war would be long (had Prussia pressed on rather than settling for limited aims, it might have become so), suggesting a perception that the sides were evenly matched. Events may have proven this wrong, but it is reasonable to assert that the crisis decisions were based on such a belief. Prussia did derive some advantages by the alliance with Italy and by the fact that Austria's internal situation made it difficult to mobilize and to devote all its forces to the north. It is probably reasonable to classify this situation as one in which Prussia had a slight advantage in war-fighting capabilities. I shall, for the purposes of the calculations, treat the sides as equal. This facilitates the exposition without too much distortion.

Resolve was clearly high for both parties in this case. Neither side was willing to let the other achieve the majority of its aims. Each held this position even though allowing the other some advantage was fairly costless. For example, Austria did not seek possession of the duchies for itself, nor was it overly committed to the Augustenberg candidacy. Austrian preferences on the issue were driven by a desire to deprive Prussia of gain, not to avoid some costs. Particularly given Austria's desperate financial situation, it would have been far better off accepting a cash payment from Prussia than it was fighting the war. This condition probably would have held even if Austria had won the war. Similarly, Prussia was determined not to agree to any settlement that could be interpreted as an Austrian victory. Prussia had suffered a diplomatic humiliation in 1850 at the hands of Austria and was determined to avoid a repeat. Both sides were determined not to lose, and both were willing to forgo outcomes that were probably better than what could be expected from war simply to avoid the appearance of a defeat.

Bargaining costs were not excessive for either side, but they were felt. Military and economic pressure was not used until the mobilizations began late in the crisis. The costs involved significantly increased with the mobilizations, but this increase lasted for only a short period before the war began. The costs of the crisis were largely diplomatic. The crisis consumed a great deal of the time and energy of both governments and detracted attention from other problems. They were heavily engaged in a propaganda battle in the duchies, the financing of which was not insignificant. Furthermore, the almost continuous effort to woo third parties was not cheap. Thus, while the burden of the crisis was not excessive for either party, it was sufficient to provide some incentive for a speedy settlement.

Our next step is to specify the issues involved in the crisis and to characterize the bargaining process in terms of these issues. The issue space of the model is depicted in figure A-2a. I have characterized the Austro-Prussian dispute as a two-issue crisis. The first obviously concerns the disposition of the duchies. One extreme outcome is for the duchies to have been granted to Prussia; the other is for the establishment of an independent state under Augustenburg. Possible intermediate outcomes labeled in the figure are the option of an independent state under Oldenburg and the option of Augustenburg but closely tied to Prussia. Second is the issue of the type and amount of compensation to be paid Austria. Some distortion occurs by considering this as a single issue, but various possible outcomes can be meaningfully arrayed. Prussia's most preferred outcome would be for Austria to receive no compensation, while Austria preferred to acquire part of Silesia. Other possibilities were for a cash payment and for Prussia to align with Austria and guarantee its possessions (primarily Venetia).

Note that O_p is located so that Prussia obtains the territories and pays no compensation while O_a is located so that Augustenberg receives the duchies and Austria gains part of Silesia. The parties' indifference contours are drawn nearly circular, but the issue of the duchies is slightly more salient for both. The Δ contours indicate the moderate bargaining costs involved. Δ_a indicates that Austria would immediately have settled for Augustenburg and a continued alliance or for a seriously weakened Augustenburg for part of Silesia. Δ_p is drawn such that Prussia would quickly have settled for Oldenberg with no compensation or for the acquisition of the territories with monetary compensation for Austria. The reservation contours reflect the resolve of both parties. Austria required some fairly significant compensation for the territories, as indicated by μ_a, while Prussia was unwilling to allow the duchies to pass to an unconstrained Augustenburg or to part with any of Silesia in exchange for Schleswig-Holstein, as shown by μ_p.

Several of the proposals made during the crisis are represented by points in the figure. Prussia's offer of money for the territories is at point b; point c

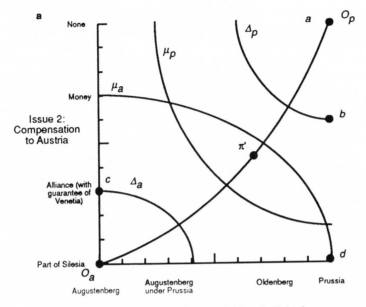

a

None

μ_p

Δ_p

a ● O_p

Money

μ_a

Issue 2:
Compensation
to Austria

b ●

π'

Alliance (with
guarantee of
Venetia)

c ●

Δ_a

Part of Silesia ●
O_a

d ●

Augustenberg

Augustenberg
under Prussia

Oldenberg

Prussia

Issue 1: Disposition of Schleswig-Holstein

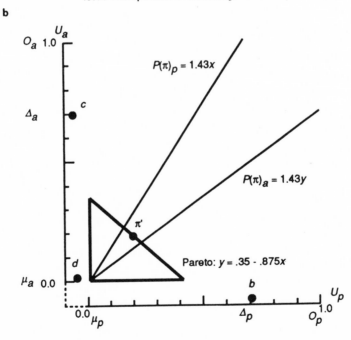

b

U_a

O_a 1.0

$P(\pi)_p = 1.43x$

Δ_a ● c

$P(\pi)_a = 1.43y$

π'

d ●

Pareto: $y = .35 - .875x$

μ_a 0.0

b ●

U_p

0.0
μ_p

Δ_p

O_p 1.0

Fig. A-2. The Austro-Prussian crisis, 1864–66: a) The issue space;
b) The utility space

represents the duchies to Augustenburg with Austria and Prussia forming an even tighter alliance; and finally, Austria's demand for part of Silesia is at point *d*. Note that the figure does not depict that the bargaining set is empty, but none of these proposals are within this range. The crisis might have been resolved peacefully had any of a number of potentially face-saving trade-offs been considered. (Oldenburg in exchange for a closer alliance and a monetary payment represented as a reimbursement for war expenses is one such example.) It is also interesting to note that during the bargaining, the parties did not move continually closer to one another's positions in the bargaining space, nor did their offers tend to converge toward the Pareto set. Rather, the offers tended to move around the bargaining range. It may be that the failure to find the bargaining set led to the war, but it may be that the parties knew where this set was and avoided it because they really did seek a war. The final point to note about the bargaining over the issues is that the two issues were always considered simultaneously. One proposal was made to fractionate the issues. It was suggested that Prussia accept Augustenburg and then work out the other arrangements later. Not surprisingly, Prussia did not receive this suggestion enthusiastically.

The utility space for this case is presented in figure A-2b. The scale for each party is set such that 0 and μ provide 1.0 utility and 0 utility, respectively. The Δs are located to reflect the bargaining costs involved, and because of the classification of the parties as equally likely to win a war, the probability of acceptance functions are linear. In particular, $P_p(\pi) = 1.43x$ and $P_a(\pi) = 1.43y$. The Pareto set is given by $y = .35 - .875x$. Thus, π' equals the maximum of $(1.43x)(1.43y)$, subject to the condition that $y = .35 - .875x$. This places π' at $(.2, .175)$. Each actor's PDF is a uniform distribution with .5 of Austria's and .57 of Prussia's within the bargaining range. The probability of war specified by the model is .71.

The model thus suggests that the probability of war was extremely high in this case. While it may have been possible to arrive at a peacefully negotiated settlement, the prospects were dim and would probably have required a fortuitous set of circumstances. While bureaucratic politics and misperceptions may have contributed to the war that ensued, the situation was such that practically everything had to go right to avoid war. In this regard, the model does seem to correspond with the history of the case.

Selected Bibliography

Albrecht-Carrié, René. 1973. *A Diplomatic History of Europe*. Rev. ed. New York: Harper & Row, chap. 4.

Clark, Chester Wells. 1934. *Franz Joseph and Bismarck*. Cambridge, Mass.: Harvard Univ. Press.

Friedjung, Heinrich. 1966. *The Struggle for Supremacy in Germany, 1859–1866*. New York: Russell & Russell.

Hayes, Carlton J. H., Marshall W. Baldwin, and Charles W. Cole. 1956. *History of Europe*. New York: Macmillan Co., chap. 48.

Holborn, Hajo. 1969. *A History of Modern Germany, 1840–1945*. Princeton, N.J.: Princeton Univ. Press.

Joll, James. 1960. "Prussia and the German Problem, 1830–66." In *The New Cambridge Modern History,* vol. 10, 493–521. Cambridge: Cambridge Univ. Press.

Kann, Robert A. 1974. *A History of the Habsburg Empire, 1526–1918*. Berkeley: Univ. of California Press.

Langer, William L. 1952. *An Encyclopedia of World History*. Boston: Houghton Mifflin, 678.

Macartney, C. A. 1960. "The Austrian Empire and Its Problems, 1848–67." In *The New Cambridge Modern History,* vol. 10, 522–51. Cambridge: Cambridge Univ. Press.

Pottinger, E. Ann. 1966. *Napoleon III and the German Crisis, 1865–1866*. Cambridge, Mass.: Harvard Univ. Press.

Smoke, Richard. 1977. *War*. Cambridge, Mass.: Harvard Univ. Press, chap. 5.

Taylor, A. J. P. 1954. *The Struggle for Mastery in Europe, 1848–1918*. Oxford: Clarendon.

———. 1962. *The Course of German History*. New York: Capricorn Books.

The Fashoda Crisis of 1898

In July, 1898, a French force under Marchand reached the abandoned fort at Fashoda along the upper Nile in the Sudan. The arrival of the expedition, which had taken nearly two years to reach its objective from the west coast of Africa, precipitated an international crisis that brought Britain and France to the brink of war. At issue was the control of the upper Nile region—which had broader implications for the colonial policies of both countries. If France could control the territory, it could link its possessions in west Africa and east Africa while denying the British the ability to control a corridor along the length of Africa from Cairo to Capetown. More importantly, it was believed that by controlling the upper Nile, the French could exert influence on Egypt and force a resettlement of the Egyptian question along terms more favorable to France. From the British perspective, having another power in control of the upper Nile was seen as an unbearable threat to its control in Egypt. For a number of years, the British had explicitly stated that the occupation of the upper Nile by another power would be interpreted as an act of hostility.

The initial French position was that the occupation of Fashoda by Marchand constituted an effective control of the area that gave them the right of possession. The British (who claimed to be protecting the interests of the Egyptians) argued that they should control the territory by right of conquest—

on the grounds that Kitchener's forces (which arrived at Fashoda in September) had defeated the Mahdist state that had seized control from the Egyptians.

During the ensuing negotiations, the British made virtually no concessions, insisting throughout that Marchand's forces must leave before negotiations on the territorial questions could even begin. The French foreign minister, Delcassé, seems to have recognized that France's position was untenable. Marchand was hopelessly outnumbered at Fashoda, the British navy was vastly superior to France's, France was diplomatically isolated from its allies, and while the British public was united on the issue, France was racked by internal strife (the Dreyfus affair). Delcassé seems to have delayed the settlement of the crisis only in hopes of gaining some face-saving concession that could be presented to the French public as a diplomatic victory. The French made a number of offers that successively reduced the amount of territory they would control, but Britain rejected each. Eventually, in the face of British war preparations, the French gave in and unconditionally withdrew Marchand (though the British did make a private promise to negotiate on the territory once Marchand was gone).

The withdrawal of Marchand in December, 1898, did not completely end the crisis, however. Negotiations over the territorial settlement continued for some months, as did the threat of war. When the dispute was finally settled in March, 1899, the French were completely denied access to the Nile and Bahr el Ghazal regions. The French did receive some gains, however. During the process of delimiting the boundaries of colonial control, the British did recognize French claims to some territory east of Lake Chad.

Applying the Model

The first step in applying the model is to identify the parties involved in the crisis and to specify the characteristics of the parties. We know that the only parties involved were Great Britain and France. As for the power and resolve variables, it is almost universally accepted that the British were advantaged in every instance.

In terms of the parties' relative war-fighting abilities, there was never a doubt on either side of the English Channel that the British would win a war. At Fashoda, Marchand's force numbered some 120 men, many of whom were ill, and though relatively well provisioned, they could not count on resupply or reinforcements. Kitchener's force, on the other hand, numbered in excess of 20,000 and could be supplied along the Nile. In the event of a broader war, the British navy had been in a rebuilding program for several years and, in addition to being more modern, was more than twice the size of the French navy. Even if France could count on support from its Russian ally, which it could not, the British navy was superior to both combined.

As for the costs involved in bargaining, the British felt virtually none. Marchand's presence at Fashoda was an irritant, but it was not sufficiently painful for the British to be willing to make concessions to remove him. The mobilization of the fleet also involved some expense, but this action came toward the end of the crisis and was of relatively short duration. The bargaining costs to the French were primarily the result of the domestic situation— the British took virtually no actions intended to impose costs on the French. At the same time as the Fashoda crisis, France was in the midst of domestic turmoil. The Dreyfus affair had come to a head, and a number of unions were engaged in strikes. These multiple crises had the effect of severely weakening the French government and seriously threatening the Third Republic (a military coup was a distinct possibility). The longer each crisis lasted, the more damage was wrought on the political system; thus, the French were under some pressure to solve the Fashoda problem quickly.

As to the resolve of the parties, it is relatively clear that the British were vastly more resolved. The British perceived control of the area to be in their vital interests because of the threat French control would pose to their position in Egypt. The French presence at Fashoda was a direct challenge to the Grey declaration (that such an action would be viewed as an unfriendly act), which had served as the statement of British policy toward the Sudan since 1895. The British public was almost unanimously behind a firm stance and would have supported a war. Lord Salisbury was willing to grant some minor concessions (perhaps leasing a commercial outlet) to avoid a war but was somewhat constrained by the more jingoistic members of his cabinet and the public.

French resolve, by comparison, was weak. This weakness was primarily due to the domestic turmoil that provided the government relatively little public support for anything, let alone a foreign adventure. More importantly, the government had always been divided over the wisdom of the Marchand mission. It was instigated and controlled by the Ministry of Colonies, which, for the most part, bypassed the Ministry of Foreign Affairs. The latter ministry had long seen such activities as damaging to France's overall foreign policy concerns, which were perceived to deal with issues on the continent (such as the dispute with Germany). Many in the government were thus more than willing to recall Marchand for nothing in return. This feeling was strengthened by the perception that the territory in question had very little value as far as France was concerned.

The next step is to specify the issues involved in the crisis and to characterize the bargaining process in terms of the model. Figure A-3 will serve to guide the discussion. The Fashoda crisis can be considered to have involved two issues. The primary issue concerned the control over the territory in the upper Nile region. A great deal of the bargaining was over the other issue—whether Marchand would abandon Fashoda before negotiations on the

a

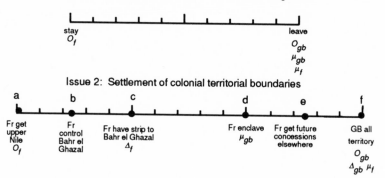

Issue 1: Marchand leave before other issue negotiated

stay
O_f

leave
O_{gb}
μ_{gb}
μ_f

Issue 2: Settlement of colonial territorial boundaries

a	b	c	d	e	f
Fr get upper Nile O_f	Fr control Bahr el Ghazal	Fr have strip to Bahr el Ghazal Δ_f	Fr enclave μ_{gb}	Fr get future concessions elsewhere	GB all territory O_{gb} Δ_{gb} μ_f

b

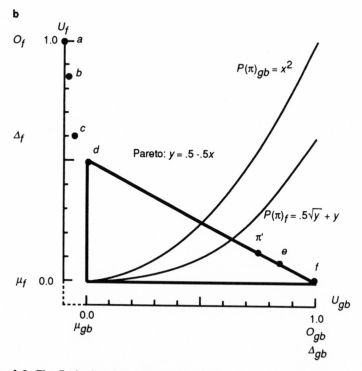

O_f 1.0 — a

b

Δ_f c

d

$P(\pi)_{gb} = x^2$

Pareto: $y = .5 - .5x$

$P(\pi)_f = .5\sqrt{y} + y$

π'

e

f

μ_f 0.0

U_{gb}

0.0
μ_{gb}

1.0
O_{gb}
Δ_{gb}

Fig. A-3. The Fashoda crisis, 1898: *a)* The issue space, two nonseparable issues, not linked; *b)* The utility space

territorial issues would proceed or would remain in place during negotiations. We could consider the dispute to have involved additional issues; for example, the territorial question could be viewed as several issues involving several parcels of territory, and intangible issues, such as the prestige of the participants, were certainly involved. The case will be represented by two issues for the sake of simplicity. The issues were not separable, as will be discussed below. They were negotiated sequentially, however, so I have used two single-dimension spaces to represent them in figure A-3.

The first issue, whether Marchand would leave before territorial questions would be discussed, is depicted in the first part of figure A-3a. The endpoints represent O_f, Marchand stays, and O_{gb}, Marchand goes. Bargaining over the agenda was crucial in this particular case. The French wanted to negotiate the two issues simultaneously and to have the agreements linked while Britain's preference was to consider the issues sequentially. France's territorial claims were based on the right of possession that Marchand's presence afforded. If Britain had allowed his force to remain, it would have constituted an acceptance of this right. Thus, the outcome on this issue largely determined the outcome on the territorial issue. Had Marchand remained, the outcome on the territorial issue would have been far below Britain's reservation point. The French were less resolved on the territory and thus less resolved on Marchand. Both reservation points on the first issue are located at O_{gb}.

For the second issue, the territory, the endpoints of the scale in figure A-3a are the two states' initial positions. Point a represents France's ideal point, that it control all the territory in dispute, and point f is Britain's ideal point, at which it would control all the territory. The preference ordering of each side is such that it prefers receiving more of the territory to less. Four additional proposals have been specified in the figure. At b, France would have withdrawn to the Bahr el Ghazal and maintained control over that region. Point c represents the proposal that France retain a strip of territory to the Bahr el Ghazal, which would provide it with an outlet to the Nile. I have set Δ_f at this point since it is likely that such a proposal would have met with immediate acceptance by France. Such an outcome would have allowed Delcassé to claim a victory and would have represented a better outcome than he probably hoped to achieve. The proposal that France be allowed to lease commercial enclaves along the Nile is represented by point d. I have set μ_{gb} at this point because it is possible that Britain would have settled for such an outcome rather than go to war. It is clear that Salisbury would have been willing to accept such an outcome, and had he perceived it as necessary, he may have been able to persuade the cabinet to go along. There is no question, however, that the probability of such an event was slim. The final solution, in which Britain retained control over the area in dispute in exchange for promises to discuss other French territorial claims, is denoted by point e. Finally, notice that I have set Δ_{gb} and μ_f at point f, Britain's ideal point. That reflects the negligible bargaining costs to Britain and the fact that French resolve was weak.

The pattern of the bargaining proposals basically followed the issue dimension. Britain, during the majority of the crisis, refused to move from its initial position while France made a succession of fairly significant concessions. During October, 1898, France successively moved from a to c to d. Marchand was recalled when Britain privately indicated that it would be willing to settle the territorial question once the French had evacuated Fashoda. The final settlement represented very little further movement on Britain's part and saw the French abandon all claims on the Nile. Virtually no actions intended to apply direct pressure to the other side were taken by either party during the crisis. The British did mobilize the fleet, which served to face the French with the distinct possibility of a hopeless naval war and probably helped to speed the resolution of the crisis.

Figure A-3b is the utility space representation of the conflict. I have characterized the dispute as non–zero sum, and for each party I have specified the utility scale such that μ provides 0 utility and O provides 1.0 utility. The proposals depicted in the issue space (a through f) are located in the figure, as are the actors' Δs. Since Britain was more likely to win a war, the probability of acceptance functions are $p_{gb}(\pi) = x^2$ and $p_f(\pi) = .5\sqrt{y} + y$. The Pareto optimal frontier is defined by $y = .5 - .5x$; thus, π' will be the point that maximizes $(x^2)(.5\sqrt{y} + y)$ subject to the condition that $y = .5 - .5x$. In this case, π' is located at $(.74, .13)$.

The predicted outcome is slightly more favorable to the French and slightly less favorable to the British than was the actual outcome. It is not entirely clear what a resolution at π' would have been in terms of the issue at stake; presumably, it would have involved somewhat more of the territory going to France. (It is also possible that, in terms of the utilities involved, point e should be more accurately located at π'.) However, since the ultimate division of territory was a prominent solution (the Nile-Congo watershed), it is unlikely that the parties would have adjusted this division to perfectly conform to an optimum solution. In any case, e is relatively close to π' and would have been a solution with a high probability of occurrence.

We can also see that this characterization specifies that the probability of war was about .27. This probability may seem somewhat surprising in that most historical accounts of the crisis suggest that war was extremely likely. First, note that this is a fairly high probability for war (wars are rare events, after all). Second, this result points out the static nature of the model. Given the specification of the conflict as involving the French government in October, 1898, the probability of war was relatively low. Delcassé in particular was unwilling to go to war for what was at stake. The perception of an extremely high probability of war was partially a product of the distinct possibility that the French government would be overthrown by the military. If that had happened, μ_f would have been located much closer to point d than to point f in figure A-3a, which would have the impact of significantly increasing the predicted probability of war.

Selected Bibliography

Albrecht-Carrié, René. 1973. *A Diplomatic History of Europe*. New York: Harper & Row, 223–26.

Brown, Roger G. 1969. *Fashoda Reconsidered*. Baltimore: Johns Hopkins Univ. Press.

Decle, Lionel. 1898. "The Fashoda Question." *Fortnightly Review* 70 (November): 665–76.

Diplomaticus. 1899. "Is It Peace? The Progress of Anglo-French Negotiations." *Fortnightly Review* 71 (March): 500–510.

Edwards, Frederick A. 1898. "The French on the Nile." *Fortnightly Review* 69 (March): 362–77.

Giffen, Morrison B. 1930. *Fashoda: The Incident and Its Diplomatic Setting*. Chicago: Univ. of Chicago Press.

Langer, William L. 1952. *An Encyclopedia of World History*. Boston: Houghton Mifflin, 748.

———. 1965. *The Diplomacy of Imperialism*. New York: Alfred A. Knopf.

Lebow, Richard N. 1981. *Between Peace and War*. Baltimore: Johns Hopkins Univ. Press, 317–26.

Riker, T. W. 1929. "A Survey of British Policy in the Fashoda Crisis." *Political Science Quarterly* 44 (March): 54–78.

Sanderson, G. N. 1962. "Contributions from African Sources to the History of European Competition in the Upper Valley of the Nile." *Journal of African History* 3: 69–90.

Snyder, Glenn, and Paul Diesing. 1977. *Conflict among Nations*. Princeton, N.J.: Princeton Univ. Press, 531–33.

Taylor, A. J. P. 1950. "Prelude to Fashoda: The Question of the Upper Nile." *English Historical Review* 65 (January): 52–80.

Wright, Patricia. 1972. *Conflict on the Nile*. London: Heinemann.

The Agadir Crisis

In the spring of 1911, the situation in Morocco was becoming critical as the Sultan was increasingly threatened by internal strife. The French took military action in support of the Sultan and ultimately found it necessary to march on Fez, the capital, ostensibly to protect the lives of European citizens. The French actions violated the Act of Algeciras, which had served as the agreement ending the earlier Moroccan crisis, and met with the resistance of the Spanish and Germans. The Spanish responded by committing troops to areas in which the French had recognized Spanish interests in a secret treaty. The Germans initially restrained themselves to diplomatic protests and took the position that no action would be necessary if the French were to restore order and withdraw from Fez fairly quickly. When the Germans finally took action on July 1, it was to send the warship *Panther* to the closed port of Agadir. The Germans claimed to have taken this action to safeguard German lives (though there were no Germans in the area), but in reality they intended to force the French to recognize German interests.

The French and German actions set in motion one of the pre–World War I European crises that nearly brought the powers to war. The German position was that they had colonial interests in Morocco and that while they were willing to recognize French dominance, the French would be expected to pay a price in terms of compensation elsewhere. The Germans initially demanded the whole of the French Congo in exchange for recognizing a French protectorate, but this demand was intended as a bargaining move from which further concessions could be made. The French were unwilling to allow the Germans any territory in Morocco but recognized that compensation elsewhere would have to be made. Thus, the principal parties to this crisis were never too far apart on the issues.

Though the Spanish played virtually no role in the Franco-German crisis, the British did influence events. The primary British concerns were that Morocco not be closed to their economic interests and that no power, especially Germany, obtain a fortified port at Agadir. Though the British supported France, at least in German eyes, during the crisis their position was actually much closer to that of the Germans. The British continually sought to urge concessions on the French and were even willing for the French to surrender part of Morocco to the Germans (provided that the Germans were prohibited from fortifying port facilities)—a position representing more than the Germans were actually demanding. This is clearly a case in which the British, though allies of France, became involved because the crisis created additional issues of concern to the British. This issue was not salient to the Germans, as they had no intention of establishing a fortified port at Agadir. The British bargaining actually affected the course of the Franco-German negotiations relatively little, and the situation was more like two parallel crises. French efforts to involve the British probably did little to aid them in achieving their aims, but it did serve to increase the chances of war. It is interesting that the British were actually the only party to undertake war preparations and that the probability of a British-German war was higher than that of a Franco-German war.

Throughout the summer of 1911, negotiations between Germany and

France continued. All parties recognized early on that the French would become dominant in Morocco; the question was what the price would be. The course of the bargaining concessions saw the Germans ask for less and less of the French Congo and the French offer more and more. Finally, in November, the Moroccan question was settled as the Germans recognized a French protectorate in Morocco in exchange for about one-fifth of the French Congo that included an outlet to the sea. The French also agreed that Morocco would remain open to German (and other) economic interests and recognized German interests in the Belgian Congo in the event that the Belgian territories required disposition. Finally, the Germans ceded to France a very small segment of their territory in the area of Lake Chad.

Applying the Model

The principal bargainers in the crisis were the French and Germans; however, the British clearly played a role. I shall present the formalization of this case in two stages to simplify the analysis. British involvement actually seems to have had little impact on the negotiations between France and Germany, and after the first month of the crisis, the British played virtually no role whatsoever. Thus, the first stage of the analysis focuses solely on the Franco-German dispute. The only way in which the British would have had a significant impact on the outcome of the crisis is if they had either given the French a blank check of support in the event of war, which would have made the French more obstinate, or if they had antagonized the Germans to the point of starting an Anglo-German war (which they nearly did). This situation will be captured in the second stage of the analysis, in which I depict all three parties in the issue space and focus on the Anglo-German dispute in the utility space. Separating the analysis in this fashion distorts the case to some degree, but as I argued above, the situation can be viewed as parallel disputes. In any case, separating the analysis reduces the number of dimensions required in the figures, making them more comprehensible.

In considering the relative war-fighting capabilities of the two sides, I have classified Germany and France as being equally likely to win a war between them. While it is generally accepted that Germany would have had an advantage in a bilateral war, it had to contend with the real probability that others, most importantly Britain, would have come to the aid of France. Germany was fairly certain that Austria would remain aloof and thus faced the possibility of finding itself alone against France, Britain, and Russia. The German leadership was not confident of its ability to prevail in war. The French, on the other hand, also were unsure of their chances of victory. They knew that they would find it difficult to stop the German army alone. They also knew that the Russians would not come to their aid. Although they felt they could rely on the British for assistance, this assistance was not assured; and they doubted that the British could do much good since the British army was relatively weak and the chief German threat was of a land war in France. Neither side could be confident of victory in war, but by the same token, neither had reason to view war as obviously hopeless. In the analysis that includes Britain, I characterize the case as one involving an asymmetry in war-fighting abilities favoring the British. In this case, it was clear that the Germans would face a French-British alliance. Britain was still the dominant world power, and Germany was not yet as strong as it would be in 1914. Thus, such a war would probably have gone against the Germans, though that was not absolutely certain.

Throughout the crisis, both sides had fairly significant cost-imposing abilities at their disposal. Each could have taken military actions against the other. The Germans, for example, could actually have seized part of Morocco. There were also a number of economic measures each could have taken against the other. Citizens of each country had investments in the other, trade between the two did exist, and each had economic interests in Morocco that the other could have disrupted. Finally, there were a number of other colonial disputes that provided an opportunity for one actor to gain leverage against the other. Given all of these available options, it is interesting that no significant cost-imposing actions were taken. The most important action that was taken was the presence of the *Panther* at Agadir and the corresponding threat that troops would be landed. This action involved something of an irritant to the French and British and was a minor affront to their prestige, but it likely affected the bargaining or outcome very little. I will thus consider the cost-imposing factor to have been negligible. The Δs do not coincide with the Os, however. While the bargaining costs were low, many of the bargaining positions advanced were not highly valued. France and Germany were both willing to make fairly significant concessions to end the crisis, and both moved far from their original positions fairly quickly.

The resolve of the parties was about equal and was weak. Each recognized and accepted the other's claims. The French reservation point was such that it would not allow Germany to obtain any of Morocco, but Germany's initial position did not demand any of Morocco. Similarly, Germany's reservation point required that it receive some compensation for recognizing French predominance in Morocco, but the French always recognized that some compensation would be required. Furthermore, the leadership of each country had decided that it would acquiesce to fairly extreme demands by the other rather than fight. The British were highly resolved on the issue of the fortified port at Agadir, however, and would definitely have fought to prevent such an occurrence.

Figure A-4 represents the two issues involved in the Franco-German

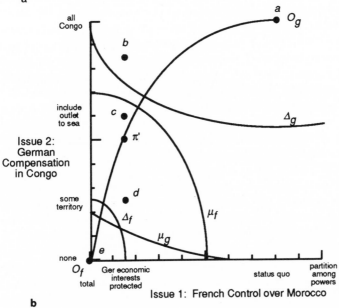

a

all
Congo

b

include
outlet
to sea

c

π'

Issue 2:
German
Compensation
in Congo

some
territory

d

Δ_f

μ_f

μ_g

none   *e*

O_f

Ger economic
interests
protected

status quo

partition
among
powers

total

Issue 1: French Control over Morocco

a O_g

Δ_g

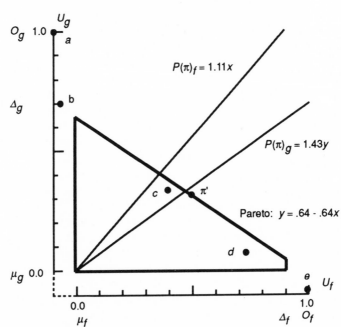

b

U_g

O_g 1.0   *a*

$P(\pi)_f = 1.11x$

Δ_g *b*

$P(\pi)_g = 1.43y$

c   π'

Pareto: $y = .64 - .64x$

d

μ_g 0.0

e U_f

μ_f

0.0

1.0

Δ_f O_f

Fig. A-4. The Agadir crisis, 1911—Germany and France: *a*) The issue
space; *b*) The utility space

dispute. The first involved control over Morocco. The main aspect of this issue was whether the French would be allowed to establish a protectorate or would continue to abide by the act of Algeciras. In addition, this issue involved the question whether the economic interests of Germany (and Britain, for that matter) in Morocco would be protected given the establishment of a French protectorate. The second issue concerned the territorial settlement involved in the German compensation. More specifically, this issue dealt with the division of the French Congo between France and Germany.

In figure A-4a, I have specified five points. Point a reflects Germany's ideal point on both issues, at which the French would not establish a protectorate over Morocco and would cede a large portion of the Congo to the Germans (perhaps in return for the Germans ceding portions of Togoland and the Cameroon to France). France's original position is represented by point e. At this outcome, France would establish a protectorate in Morocco, perhaps protecting the economic interests of other powers to some extent, and would compensate the Germans with only a small segment of territory. Points b, c, and d represent offers that were made during the crisis, with point c representing the ultimate solution. The French were able to establish a protectorate over Morocco though they had to ensure the economic interests of other powers. In return, Germany received a reasonably large section of the Congo, which included an outlet to the sea.

The bargaining costs were minor, but each party could make some movement at very low cost. Thus, the indifference contours representing Δ_g and Δ_f are set apart from the Os. France would have easily been willing to grant minor territorial concessions or give assurances that German economic interests would be protected. For all of the Congo, Germany would have immediately foregone any claims in Morocco. The Δs are drawn to reflect this. Furthermore, μ_g is not far from O_f, indicating Germany's low resolve but also indicating that some concessions were necessary. The contour for μ_f suggests that France was probably willing to cede a large portion of the Congo to Germany but that returning to the status quo ante on Morocco was out of the question. Note that if we consider only the issue of French control in Morocco, the bargaining set was empty. That indicates that the additional issue was necessary for the conflict to be resolved peacefully.

The preference orderings of the parties were relatively straightforward: each preferred gaining more on each issue to gaining less. The French wanted greater control over Morocco while the Germans preferred that the French have less, and each desired to own as much of the Congo as possible. In this crisis, the issues had different saliences for the two parties. The French were more concerned with gaining control of Morocco and were willing to pay to obtain it. The Germans, on the other hand, believed the French to be destined to control Morocco and were concerned primarily with extracting as high a price as possible in compensation. The indifference contours in figure A-4a reflect these saliences.

The question of the bargaining agenda did arise at several points in the negotiations. Once it was obvious that the crisis would be settled through negotiations, the French suggested that other outstanding colonial issues (e.g., concerning the Baghdad railway) be included. The Germans refused, and the matter was dropped. During the crisis, the two major issues were linked; as a matter of fact, it would have been difficult to have settled one without settling the other. In the final stages of the negotiations, however, we could view the issues as having been separated. The first issue was actually settled first since the Germans recognized fairly early on that the French would establish a protectorate in Morocco. However, the Germans withheld formal agreement on this until the second issue was also settled. I thus consider the issues to have been settled simultaneously with the recognition that convergence occurred on the first at an early stage of the bargaining. This is reflected in the figure by the fact that points b, c, and d are all on a vertical line.

The bargaining process was such that the first issue was essentially settled early in the crisis. By the end of July, the Germans had stated that they had no territorial ambitions in Morocco, and it was never expected that the French could gain total control of the territory. By the end of summer, the Germans acknowledged that they recognized the inevitability of French dominance. Thus, the differences between the parties on the first dimension narrowed fairly quickly. During the entire crisis, the parties' proposals closed the gap on the second issue. Successive German offers were to accept less and less of the Congo, while the French offered to surrender more and more.

The handling of the crisis bargaining did much to ensure that the crisis was resolved peacefully. The inclusion of the second issue created the possibility of a number of outcomes acceptable to both sides. In the absence of the second issue, the only outcomes would have been a French protectorate in Morocco (with no compensation to the Germans), which would have been unacceptable to Germany; the partition of Morocco among France, Germany, and Spain, which would have been unacceptable to France and Britain; or a return to the status quo ante, which had been made highly unlikely by the events preceding the crisis. In addition, the only action taken that was intended to put pressure on the opponent was the stationing of the *Panther* at Agadir. By presenting the French with the threat of a German landing, this action forced them to come to terms with the second issue. However, the action was mild enough not to threaten severely French prestige, thereby stiffening their resolve to the point that settlement was impossible.

Figure A-4b is the utility space representation of the Franco-German part of the crisis. The x and y axes represent the utility to France and Germany, respectively. I have set the utility scale of each actor so that O provides 1.0 unit of utility and μ provides 0.0 units. I have specified the parties as equally likely to win a war, and the Δs are somewhat beneath the Os; thus, $p_f(\pi) = 1.11x$ and $p_g(\pi) = 1.43y$. The function defining the set of Pareto optimal outcomes is given by $y = .64 - .64x$. From this function, we can determine that π' is at about (.5, .32). This point is very close to where I have located point c (the actual outcome) in the utility space. The predicted outcome, though fundamentally a compromise, would have favored the French slightly more than the Germans. In fact, that seems to be how the actual outcome was perceived. It was recognized that both sides had made fairly substantial concessions, but the outcome was viewed as something of a victory for France. This view was partially a function of the perception that the Germans had sought part of Morocco for themselves. While this was not exactly the case, the perception of a diplomatic victory is a diplomatic victory.

We can also see that this construction suggests that the probability of war was very low compared to that in most crises. All of France's probability of acceptance function is within the bargaining set, as is .92 of the PDF associated with Germany's. This suggests that the probability of war was .08. Given what we know about the unfolding of the crisis, this figure seems about right. Neither side undertook military preparations during the crisis, and the leaders of both sides were unwilling to fight over the issues at stake. The probability of war was not 0, however. Any one of a number of actions that were considered could have culminated in war. If, for example, the French had been successful in convincing the British to join them in sending ships to Agadir to challenge the Germans, a war may have resulted.

We now turn to the analysis that includes British involvement. The issue space in figure A-5a includes an additional issue—whether Germany would establish a fortified port at Agadir. Britain and France were clearly against this idea, and while Germany had little intention of establishing a fortified port, it was willing to use the threat for leverage. Note that Britain's preferences on the other issues are actually quite close to those of Germany. I have not included the indifference surfaces in the figure, but the third issue was not salient for Germany and France. Britain, on the other hand, was most concerned with this issue and was very resolved on this matter.

The utility space, depicted in figure A-5b, excludes France and focuses entirely on the Anglo-German relationship. As usual, the utility scales are set so that the Os are at 1.0 and the μs are at 0.0. The bargaining costs were negligible for both sides, so Δ_{gb} is located at O_{gb}. Though its bargaining costs were low, Germany cared little about the main issue of contention with Britain (the fortified port); thus, Δ_g is set somewhat below O_g. Given these parameters and the characterization of the relative war-fighting capabilities as asymmetrical, $P_{gb}(\pi) = x^2$ and $P_g(\pi) = .39\sqrt{y} + .96y$. The Pareto set has been

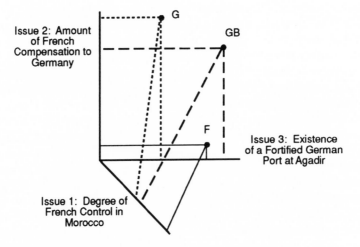

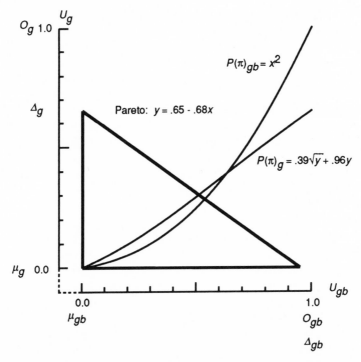

Fig. A-5. The Agadir crisis, 1911—Britain included: *a*) The issue space; *b*) The utility space, Britain and Germany defined for this case as $y = .65 - .68x$. We can now calculate that $\pi' = (.69, .18)$ and $p(\text{war}) = .25$.

The expected bargained solution is quite close to Britain's preferred outcome, which is what we observed in the actual crisis. My use of a linear Pareto set in this construction is a bit misleading, however. It suggests that the outcome was far from what Germany preferred, when in fact the outcome was not a disappointment for the Germans. Had I used a Pareto set that bowed upward, π' would have indicated an expected outcome much more favorable to Germany (and perhaps even a little better for Britain). In any case, the present construction does not distort the case too much, if we keep in mind that the utility scales have been normalized for each participant (i.e., we cannot make interpersonal comparisons of utility). The outcome was above Germany's reservation point, and in the grand scheme, this aspect of the crisis was not too salient for the Germans.

The most interesting aspect of this case is that the derived probability for war is much higher for Britain and Germany than it was for France and Germany. Since Germany actually had a low salience for the issue of concern to the British, this would seem counterintuitive. It does correspond with the details of the case, however, in that Britain came much closer to war with Germany than did France. This is a clear case in which the involvement of the third party was nearly disastrous. It changed a dispute in which there was a fairly low probability of war into a crisis in which war was a distinct possibility. This situation was driven primarily by two factors. First, Britain was motivated by additional issues the Franco-German crisis created for it. That led to a situation more like two parallel crises than a single multilateral conflict. Second, the British position forced it into an "alliance" with France, which shifted the crisis from one in which war-fighting capabilities were about even to one in which there was an asymmetry in power. Furthermore, since Britain and France each had different concerns, coordinating strategies was difficult.

Selected Bibliography

Albrecht-Carrié, René. 1973. *A Diplomatic History of Europe*. New York: Harper & Row, 272–75.

Barlow, Ima. 1940. *The Agadir Crisis*. Chapel Hill: North Carolina Univ. Press.

Edwards, E. W. 1963. "The Franco-German Agreement on Morocco, 1909." *English Historical Review* 78 (July): 483–513.

Fischer, Fritz. 1967. *Germany's Aims in the First World War*. New York: W.W. Norton & Co., 24–25.

———. 1975. *War of Illusions*. New York: W.W. Norton & Co.

Gooch, G. P. 1938. *Before the War Volume II*. New York: Russell & Russell.

Grey, Sir Edward. 1925. *Twenty-Five Years: 1892–1916*. New York: Frederick A. Stokes Co.

Holborn, Hajo. 1969. *A History of Modern Germany, 1840–1945*. Princeton, N.J.: Princeton Univ. Press, 337–40.

Langer, William L. 1952. *An Encyclopedia of World History*. Boston: Houghton Mifflin, 757–58.

Moon, Parker T. 1932. *Imperialism and World Politics*. New York: MacMillan Co.

Snyder, Glenn, and Paul Diesing. 1977. *Conflict among Nations*. Princeton, N.J.: Princeton Univ. Press, 541–45.

Staley, Eugene. 1932. "Mannesmann Mining Interests and the Franco-German Conflict over Morocco." *Journal of Political Economy* 40 (February): 52–72.

Taylor, A. J. P. 1954. *The Struggle for Mastery in Europe*. Oxford: Clarendon, 466–73.

Williamson, Samuel R. 1969. *The Politics of Grand Strategy*. Cambridge, Mass.: Harvard Univ. Press.

The Soviet-Finnish Dispute, 1939

In the late 1930s, with Europe on the brink of war, great power diplomacy focused on the minor states. Hitler was bent on bringing more and more territory under German control, Britain and France hoped to avoid war but also limit German expansion by guaranteeing the existence of smaller states, and the Soviet Union sought to provide itself with a buffer zone by controlling the small states that separated it from the rest of Europe. Stalin was not convinced that the Munich conference had sated Hitler's appetite and felt that a war with Germany was on the horizon. However, he did not trust the Western democracies (he believed that their strategy was to turn Germany against the Soviet Union so that both would be weakened) and was not willing to base Soviet security on an alliance with Britain and France. Stalin's goals were thus to buy time by aligning with Hitler and to provide a buffer zone between the Soviet Union and Germany by aligning with, or conquering, the small states in between.

By the fall of 1939, the Soviet Union had established its domination over the Baltic states and had extended its area of control into Poland. During the period of the "phony war," Stalin turned his attention to Finland. The Soviets had, for some months, been seeking closer ties with Finland that would include cooperation in military defenses. These overtures had been rejected by the Finns, who wished to maintain strict neutrality in the European conflict and who could see the price paid by the Baltic states for such cooperation. Having failed to achieve his ends by secret approaches, Stalin turned to more direct methods in October, 1939. In the first bargaining round, Stalin, who personally handled much of the negotiations, presented the Finns with a number of demands. The Soviets first suggested a mutual assistance treaty similar to the ones they had signed with the Baltic states. Finland rejected this suggestion outright but did agree to an extension of the Soviet-Finnish nonaggression pact to include a prohibition on the part of either for joining alliances hostile to the other. The main demands the Soviets made were territorial. First, they wished to lease from Finland the Hanko Peninsula for thirty years. They intended to construct a naval facility and made specific proposals regarding the number and types of forces that would staff the station. Second, they wanted Finland to cede some of the islands in the Gulf of Finland and to agree to move the common border on the Karelian Isthmus farther north. Third, the Soviets wanted Finland to cede its portion of the Rybachi Peninsula in the north. Finally, the Soviets offered the Finns compensation in the form of territory in Soviet Karelia that was twice as large as the combined territories the Finns were asked to surrender.

The Soviets were motivated by defensive concerns. The border on the Karelian Isthmus was only twenty miles from Leningrad, well within the range of artillery fire. The area in the north provided additional port facilities and some protection to the ice-free port at Murmansk. The shore batteries and air strip at Hanko could, along with similar facilities in Estonia, allow the Soviets to control the mouth of the Gulf of Finland, prohibiting a naval assault by Germany, or Britain. The Finnish negotiators argued that these adjustments were not necessary for Soviet defense. They stressed Finnish neutrality, promising that no power would be allowed to use Finnish territory as a base of operations against the Soviets. They also argued that, given modern weaponry and tactics, no power was likely to attack the Soviet Union through the Gulf of Finland. Stalin would not buy these arguments (which subsequent events proved correct) and pointed out that the Czars had found it necessary to control the same points and that the British had come through the Gulf of Finland during their intervention in the revolution. The first rounds of talks broke off with the Finnish negotiators returning to Helsinki for consultations with their government.

Over two more rounds of negotiations, the sides moved closer to a resolution of the dispute. The Finns gradually agreed to the Soviet demands on the Rybachi peninsula, and on the Karelian Isthmus, the Finns agreed to move the border somewhat north while Stalin softened his original demands. In addition, Finland was willing to cede some islands in the Gulf to the Soviet Union. The sticking point in the negotiations was Hanko. Stalin made two consecutive concessions on this issue, first offering to reduce the number of forces to be stationed in Hanko and then suggesting that he would settle for three islands off the coast. Finland refused to budge on this issue, however, claiming that it could not possibly surrender this territory to the Soviets or allow a foreign base on its soil.

Some in the Finnish government were opposed to this intransigence. The argument that they were unwilling to surrender territory had been undermined by previous concessions in Karelia and on the Rybachi Peninsula, though these territories were contiguous with Soviet lands whereas Hanko was not. Militarily, the Finns, though willing to fight, knew that without assistance they had no chance to defend themselves. Much of their diplomacy was directed at acquiring such assistance, but none was forthcoming. The Western democracies were more concerned about Germany, Germany only offered the advice that Finland should give in, and Sweden was unwilling to sacrifice its neutrality for the defense of Finland against a much more powerful adversary. Yet the Finnish government, believing that Stalin would ultimately back down, held firm.

Two aspects of the bargaining are of particular interest. First, although the Soviets had introduced a number of issues into the bargaining from the beginning, the Finns seemed to prefer to fractionate the issues. The Soviets had offered territorial compensation and, on at least one occasion during the bargaining, had sought to reintroduce this issue. The Finnish concessions were all contingent on compensation (and apparently monetary payments were also mentioned), but they insisted on settling the questions regarding which of their territories they would surrender before discussing the amount of compensation. Second, the Soviets were also willing to consider creative solutions by introducing potential additional issues. They informed the Finns that the agreement over Hanko could be put in any terms the Finns desired—lease (so they would not be ceding territory), sale (so foreign forces would not be on their soil), or cooperative defense. Furthermore, Stalin's offer to reduce the size of the military contingent on Hanko opened the door for discussions regarding the precise terms of the lease. Finland could have seized this opportunity to try and reduce the Soviet contingent even further and perhaps to impose technological restrictions that would serve to reduce the threat these forces would create for Finland (e.g., making it impossible for the shore batteries to point inland). By focusing their definition of the situation so narrowly, the Finns may have closed solutions that would have been acceptable to both parties. In the end, bargaining failed, the Soviets invaded, and though Finnish forces fought well and imposed a heavy cost on their enemies, the Soviets were able to impose a settlement that was worse for the Finns than a negotiated settlement would have been.

Applying the Model

The first step in applying the model is to identify the participants in the crisis and to characterize them in terms of the variables of interest. This is clearly a case in which there were only two parties, the Soviet Union and Finland, and in which these two parties were greatly disparate in war-fighting capabilities.

The Finns were able to put up a better fight than expected, and they held out longer than most believed possible; however, there was never any doubt how the war would turn out. Thus, the balance of military capabilities for this case is coded as a substantial advantage favoring the Soviets.

Resolve was high on the part of both actors, though it was much higher for the Finns than for the Soviets. Stalin believed that the Finnish territories were necessary for the defense of the Soviet Union and was unwilling to accede completely to the Finnish wishes. He did make some concessions on the Karelian border, and he was willing to come down from his original demands in Hanko—provided that some arrangements for a base were made. While resolved to gain something from the negotiations, Stalin did seem to believe that he was making a great effort to accommodate Finnish concerns and interests. The Finns, on the other hand, would not budge on the Hanko issue. They perceived this to be a disastrous change in the status quo on several fronts. It would be unpopular domestically because it would allow a foreign power on Finnish soil, it would create grave security risks by giving the Soviets a foothold from which to extend domination over Finland, and it would clearly end the Finnish foreign policy of neutrality. For all these reasons and because of the simple fact that the Finns were being asked to abandon territory and citizens, the Finns are coded as being very highly resolved.

Both sides suffered from some bargaining costs during the crisis, but these were greater for the Soviets. The Finish costs were primarily tied to military expenditures brought about by their mobilization, which had begun early in the crisis. They were fortifying the border region and purchasing additional equipment and supplies, which involved some strain on their budget. For the Soviets, the main cost was the time involved, and this cost was perceived to be substantial. They believed that war, with Germany or the Western democracies, was inevitable and that the Finnish territories were essential for their defense. Time to prepare these defenses was believed to be short, so the Soviets saw every day as critical. More than once during the bargaining, the Soviets pressured the Finns to speed up their decision-making processes. In fact, the time factor probably explains much of the Soviet willingness to make concessions. Behavior that the Finns interpreted as a lack of resolve and a willingness to back down on Stalin's part was probably motivated by a desire to reach a settlement as quickly as possible. Though the Soviets were willing to settle for less than they desired to end the bargaining quickly, they still saw obtaining some base near Hanko as critical for their defense. This case is thus coded as involving moderately high bargaining costs for the Finns and very high bargaining costs for the Soviets.

A number of issues were involved in this dispute. Each of the three areas in which the Soviets demanded territory is properly considered a separate

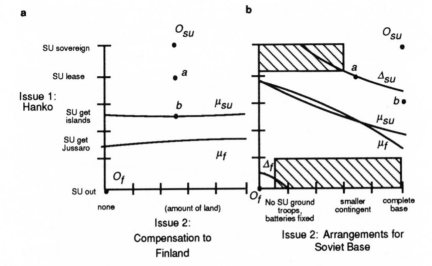

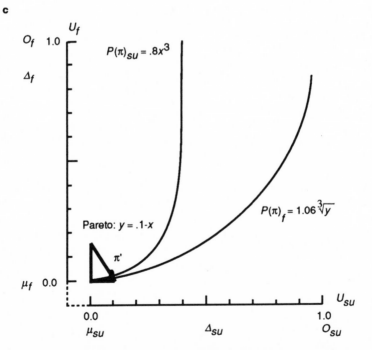

Fig. A-6. The Soviet-Finnish dispute, 1939: *a*) The issue space, Hanko and compensation; *b*) Hanko and specific arrangements; *c*) The utility space

issue, as are the Soviet offer of compensation and the discussion revolving around the alliance or nonaggression pact. In the issue space representation of this crisis, depicted in figure A-6 a and b, I have simplified the situation by ignoring most of these issues. This simplification will cause little distortion, because most of the issues (the nonaggression pact, the Karelian border, and the Rybachi border) were, for the most part, settled sequentially and relatively quickly. In the figure, I focus primarily on the difficult issue, Hanko, and in figures A-6a and b, respectively, I include two alternative second issues. This figure allows us to see, quite simply, where the possible area of agreement was missed

In A-6a and b, issue 1 concerns the location of the Soviet base in or near Hanko and the issue of sovereignty over this territory. The initial Soviet position provides it with all of the area around Hanko and essentially grants it sovereignty over the territory. Finland's initial position is the status quo: no Soviet presence. Intermediate points on this dimension represent changes in the amount of territory the Soviets would control, moving them to the islands off Hanko they requested or to Jussaro, as many in Finland wanted to offer. Figure A-6a contains the second issue that was included in the negotiations, the amount of territorial compensation the Finns would receive. Recall that this issue was never actually discussed, since the Finns chose to save that issue until last. Therefore, the two additional points located in this space are on a vertical line, indicating no changes in the offer on that issue were made. Point a corresponds to the Soviet offer to call the deal a lease of the land, while point b is Stalin's offer to accept the offshore islands. Finland's only offer was at O_f (no change in the status quo), though we would imagine that if some arrangement were reached regarding Hanko, the Finns would have preferred greater compensation to less. Note that the contours for μ_f and μ_{su} are nearly straight through the issue space presented. That is because the first issue, Hanko, was much more salient for both parties than was the second issue (i.e., the indifference ellipses are extremely elongated). These are also drawn, though it is difficult to see because of the elongation, so that the issues are not completely separable—the amount of territorial compensation would depend, in part, on the settlement of issue 1. The important facet of this figure is that the bargaining set is empty. There are no possible outcomes that could satisfy both parties' minimal needs, suggesting that war was a certainty.

Figure A-6b provides a slightly different view of the crisis, however. In this figure, issue 2 focuses on the specific arrangements regarding the Soviet base to be located in the Hanko area. Recall that the Soviets opened the door to this issue, but the Finns never were willing to consider it. Several possible arrangements are labeled in the figure, beginning with complete Soviet control, going to a Soviet lease with a smaller military contingent, and to even more restrictions on the number and types of forces the Soviets could emplace. Note that certain outcomes are shaded out because they are infeasible (e.g., the Soviets have no base in Hanko but it is completely staffed). In this figure, O_{su} is located so that the Soviet Union receives all the requested territory around Hanko and is completely sovereign within this domain. O_f is again at the status quo. Two suggested outcomes are noted in A-6b. Point *a* represents the Soviet offer to lease Hanko and to reduce the military contingent while point *b* represents the offer to accept only the islands but to have total control over the military base. It is interesting to note that during the bargaining, Stalin apparently felt that he was making substantial concessions on these issues while the Finns were incredulous that he would think that. They seemed to feel that his successive offers reflected virtually no movement in the Soviet position. The figure shows how the parties could harbor these contradictory beliefs. While the successive Soviet offers were less and less preferable from their standpoint, they remained a fairly constant distance from the Finnish reservation contour.

The Δ contours are included in this figure and show that to settle the dispute quickly, Finland was willing to make minor concessions and the Soviets were willing to make fairly substantial concessions. The reservation contours are drawn so that a nonempty bargaining set does exist. The type of possible settlement included in this set would have been one in which the Soviets settled for less territory than they initially requested (perhaps the islands Stalin mentioned) and for some fairly severe restrictions on the type of base to be established (perhaps very few ground troops and the batteries fixed to point only to sea). While it is not certain that the parties would have agreed to such an outcome, this figure suggests that it might have provided a way to end the dispute peacefully.

The utility space, depicted in figure A-6c, is based on the second issue space presented. As usual, the parties' Os and μs are scaled so that they provide utility of 1.0 and 0.0, respectively. The Δs are located to represent the moderate bargaining costs to Finland and the high costs to the Soviet Union. To represent the great disparity in war-fighting capabilities, cube functions are used, so $p_{su}(\pi) = 8x^3$ and $p_f(\pi) = 1.06\sqrt[3]{y}$. The Pareto set is defined by $y = .1 - x$, reflecting the exceedingly small bargaining range. Maximizing $(8x^3)(1.06\sqrt[3]{y})$ subject to $y = .1 - x$ provides $\pi'\ddot{a} \approx (.1, 0)$. Thus, the predicted negotiated settlement is very near both states' reservation level and is virtually on Finland's. Calculating the probability of war based on this representation shows that $p(\text{war}) = .99$. That is, the model suggests that, even in the best light provided by figure A-6b, war was a virtual certainty in this case. The model is suggesting that war could only have been avoided by extremely adept and creative bargainers, and possibly not even then. While it is easy with hindsight to say that war was unavoidable in a case in which war occurred, the characterization provided by the model does seem to correspond with the history of the case.

Selected Bibliography

Chew, Allen F. 1971. *The White Death*. East Lansing: Michigan State Univ. Press.

Coates, W. P., and Zelda K. Coates. 1941. *The Soviet-Finnish Campaign*. London: Eldon.

Dallin, David J. 1942. *Soviet Russia's Foreign Policy, 1939–1942*. New Haven, Conn.: Yale Univ. Press.

Engle, Eloise, and Lauri Paananen. 1973. *The Winter War*. New York: Charles Scribner's Sons.

Finland, Ministry of Foreign Affairs. 1940. *The Finnish Blue Book*. New York: J. B. Lippencott.

Jakobson, Max. 1961. *The Diplomacy of the Winter War*. Cambridge: Harvard Univ. Press.

Krosby, H. Peter. 1968. *Finland, Germany, and the Soviet Union, 1940–1941*. Madison: Univ. of Wisconsin Press.

Langer, William L. 1952. *An Encyclopedia of World History*. Boston: Houghton Mifflin, 1145–46.

Nevakivi, Jukka. 1976. *The Appeal That Was Never Made*. London: C. Hurst & Co.

Tanner, Vaino. 1957. *The Winter War*. Stanford: Stanford Univ. Press.

The Cuban Missile Crisis

The story of the Cuban Missile Crisis is a familiar one. In October, 1962, the U. S. government discovered that the Soviet Union was constructing medium- and intermediate-range nuclear missile sites in Cuba. President Kennedy found this development to be an unacceptable change in the status quo and resolved to have the missiles removed either voluntarily by the Soviet Union or by destroying them. The United States then used a blockade of Cuba, the threat of air strikes, and international pressure to convince the Soviets to remove the missiles. Most accounts of this crisis focus on the decision-making processes followed by the ExCom (the ad hoc body of advisors Kennedy assembled for dealing with the crisis), almost to the exclusion of the bargaining situation between the powers. While the processes by which the blockade option was selected make for an interesting study, my purpose is to focus on the general characteristics of the international crisis situation (which are actually quite simple). The specific decisions both governments reached clearly affected the outcome of the crisis; but I shall show that a broad view of the situation, guided by the spatial model, provides a parsimonious, general explanation of the outcome.

The crisis began when President Kennedy publicly announced that the Soviets had placed offensive missiles in Cuba and that the United States was imposing a naval quarantine of the island to prevent further deliveries of missile components. Kennedy also demanded the removal of the missiles already in place, and he left open the possibility that the United States would resort to stronger military measures if this demand was not met. For nearly a week, the superpowers stood on the brink of nuclear war. Neither wished to suffer the humiliation of a capitulation, and Kennedy's position seemed to leave little room for bargaining. Most of the early diplomacy was conducted by the United States and was geared toward rallying international support for its position. The United States was able to secure formal approval from the Organization of American States (OAS) for its actions as well as the general approval of its allies in the North Atlantic Treaty Organization (NATO). The case was also carried to the UN Security Council, in which the issue was hotly debated. None of this had much of an impact on the crisis bargaining, however. OAS approval provided a legal basis for the blockade, but the United States probably would have acted in the same manner without such approval. The UN provided a forum for the United States to challenge publicly the Soviet Union, and U Thant did use his position as acting secretary general to plead for restraint, but no effective UN actions were taken. The Soviets felt some obligation to consider the wishes of Castro, but Cuban positions were largely disregarded when they did not conform to Soviet interests. This was most definitely a two-party dispute between the United States and the Soviet Union.

The main issue was the presence of the Soviet nuclear forces in Cuba. The U.S. position was straightforward: these forces should be removed. Kennedy, at least in the early stages of the crisis, engaged in little bargaining. His diplomacy was based on demanding the removal of the Soviet forces and on threatening more forceful action if his demands were not met. The Americans brought in no additional issues. Kennedy was highly resolved and appears to have been motivated largely by the desire to maintain prestige. Many in the government believed that the missiles altered the strategic balance little, though they feared that they could be used for political advantage. Kennedy also appears to have taken the crisis quite personally. He felt the missiles were a direct challenge to his leadership, and he felt moral outrage at having been lied to by the Soviets in their repeated assurances that no offensive weapons would be placed in Cuba. (For the Soviet's part, they seemed genuinely surprised that these weapons were considered offensive by the Americans, who had stressed that similar American missiles in Turkey were purely defensive.) In general, Kennedy was determined not to be pushed around by Khrushchev.

Soviet bargaining was primarily devoted to finding a peaceful yet face-saving way out of the crisis. The Soviets were determined not to be humiliated, and their status as a great power would have suffered considerably had they simply capitulated to Kennedy's demands. Thus, to avoid the appearance of utter defeat, they needed to gain something from the crisis. Initial Soviet approaches were through unofficial channels though ultimately their proposals were made in personal letters from Khrushchev to Kennedy. In a first, hastily written letter, the Soviets offered, somewhat vaguely, to remove the missiles provided the United States would issue a promise not to invade Cuba. The second letter upped the ante and demanded that U.S. missiles in Turkey be removed as well. Thus, Soviet bargaining strategy was essentially to bring additional issues into the crisis for linkage purposes. Though the Soviets were resolved not to capitulate entirely, they were willing to accept relatively little for backing down. This is usually attributed to the fact that the United States was in a vastly superior military position, particularly in the Cuban theater.

Kennedy was willing to promise not to invade Cuba, but he preferred to avoid explicitly linking the missiles in Turkey with those in Cuba, even though he had previously ordered the removal of these obsolete missiles. This preference was largely because he believed that such a trade-off would signal to the NATO allies that the United States would sacrifice their security for its own. The United States thus responded to Khrushchev's first letter and agreed to issue such a pledge if the objectionable Soviet forces were removed. Kennedy also used a back channel to privately assure the Soviets that the Turkish missiles would be removed in the near future. (Recent accounts suggest that Kennedy would have explicitly traded the Turkish missiles had it become necessary for a peaceful resolution.) The Soviet linkage strategy worked. The United States would attain the removal of the missiles, and the Soviets could claim they had achieved their objective of ensuring Cuban security. While the crisis officially ended within a week after Kennedy's televised address announcing the blockade, the bargaining actually continued for some time after. The parties still had to work out the precise mechanisms by which the Soviet forces would be withdrawn and the measures that would be taken to prove to the Americans that the task had been carried out. However, the stickiest question was over exactly what were included in the list of offensive weapons. The Americans eventually succeeded in having the Soviet IL-28 bombers, as well as the missiles, included among the weapons to be removed. With this concession, the crisis that brought the world to the brink of nuclear war was ended.

Applying the Model

Representing this crisis with the spatial model is a straightforward exercise. Only two parties were involved, and the issues in dispute were fairly simple. The first task is to characterize the participants in terms of our key variables.

The balance of war-fighting capabilities clearly favored the United States. In the event of a conventional war in Cuba, the United States enjoyed an overwhelming superiority, and Soviet strategic capabilities were far behind those of the United States. The American advantage was not as great as was the Soviet advantage over Finland in the Winter War, and there is no doubt that the Soviets could have imposed great costs on the Americans; yet both parties believed the disparity in war-fighting capabilities to be substantial.

Both sides were faced with fairly significant bargaining costs during the crisis. These costs were not tangible (e.g., in terms of materials consumed) but instead came from the dangerously high probability of a catastrophic war and from the perception that time was short. The Americans felt pressured to resolve the crisis before the Soviet missiles became operational, which led them to impose very tight deadlines on the Soviets. The Soviets, having been told that the military pressure would be increased (presumably by an attack) roughly a week after the imposition of the blockade, must surely have felt the time pressures. Both sides were willing to make some concessions relatively quickly just to end the threat of nuclear war.

Resolve on the part of the Americans was very high. Kennedy believed the prestige of the United States to be at stake and was quite concerned about his own political future. The crisis occurred shortly before congressional elections, and Kennedy was certain that a perceived capitulation would seriously hinder the efforts of the Democratic party. He was unwilling to tolerate any missiles remaining in Cuba and was willing to go to war to prevent such an occurrence, even though the expected costs of the war were enormous. Khrushchev was moderately resolved, though not nearly at the level of Kennedy. He could not permit the Soviet Union to be humiliated and was willing to risk war if the United States was unwilling to make any concessions.

Figure A-7 represents the Cuban Missile Crisis in terms of the spatial model. In the issue space, which is presented in A-7a, I have included two issues. The first is the main issue—the presence of Soviet forces in Cuba. This issue ranges from no Soviet presence (the U.S. preference) to all forces being allowed to remain (the Soviet ideal point). Two intermediate outcomes have been noted: one representing the ultimate outcome in which only defensive forces would remain and the other representing an outcome in which the Soviet bombers would also remain. Two additional issues were suggested for linkage purposes in this crisis: the U.S. promise not to invade Cuba and the American missiles in Turkey. I have found it possible to represent both of these issues on a single dimension, which has been labeled issue 2. The possible outcomes on this issue that are listed begin with no U.S. concessions (the American ideal point) and range through a U.S. promise not to invade and a point that adds to this promise the private assurance that the missiles in Turkey would be removed (the final outcome) and end at a point representing the U.S. promise not to invade and the explicit linkage of the Turkish missiles

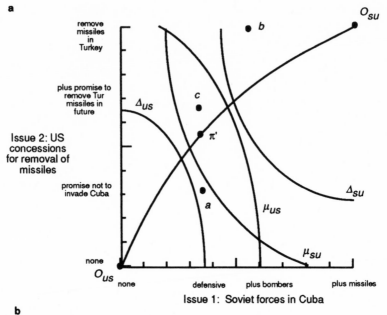

a

Issue 2: US
concessions
for removal of
missiles

remove
missiles
in
Turkey

plus promise to
remove Tur
missiles in
future

promise not to
invade Cuba

O_{us}

Δ_{us}

c

π'

a

b

μ_{us}

O_{su}

Δ_{su}

μ_{su}

none   defensive   plus bombers   plus missiles

Issue 1: Soviet forces in Cuba

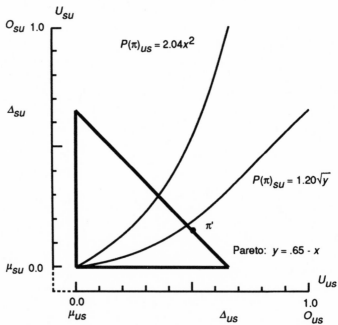

b

U_{su}

O_{su} 1.0

Δ_{su}

μ_{su} 0.0

μ_{us} 0.0

$P(\pi)_{us} = 2.04x^2$

$P(\pi)_{su} = 1.20\sqrt{y}$

π'

Pareto: $y = .65 - x$

U_{us}

1.0

Δ_{us} O_{us}

Fig. A-7. The Cuban Missile Crisis, 1962: *a)* The issue space; *b)* The utility space

with the Cuban missiles. Points representing three actual offers are identified in the space. The offer contained in Khrushchev's first letter is denoted by point *a*, at which the Soviet forces would be withdrawn in exchange for a promise that Cuba would not be invaded. Point *b* corresponds to the Soviet offer in the second letter, which demanded the removal of the U.S. missiles in Turkey. Finally, point *c* represents the final outcome.

The indifference contours in the figure are drawn in a way that indicates that the issue of the Soviet forces in Cuba was the most salient for both parties. The issues were more nearly of equal salience for the Soviets, however, so the Pareto set does have some upward curvature. The Δ contours reflect the relatively high bargaining costs for the actors. Δ_{us} indicates that Kennedy would immediately have settled for a withdrawal of Soviet offensive forces or for a withdrawal of all Soviet forces in exchange for the American concession ultimately made. The Soviets would immediately have accepted an outcome that allowed their missiles to remain in Cuba or one that would have traded these missiles for the American missiles in Turkey, as indicated by Δ_{su}. The parties' levels of resolve are reflected in the μ contours. These indicate that the Soviets were unwilling to remove their missiles without compensation and that the U.S. was unwilling to allow the missiles to remain in Cuba.

The utility space is depicted in figure A-7b. Again, the utility scales are set such that the μs provide 0 utility and the Os provide 1.0 utility. The Δs indicate the bargaining costs suffered by the actors. Since I have coded this case as involving a superiority in war-fighting capabilities on the part of the United States, square probability of acceptance functions are used; specifically, $p_{us}(\pi) = 2.04x^2$ and $p_{su}(\pi) = 1.20\sqrt{y}$. The Pareto set is given by $y = .65 - x$. Maximizing $(2.04x^2)(1.20\sqrt{y})$ subject to $y = .65 - x$ gives $\pi' = (.52, .13)$. Note that this point is quite close to both Δ_{us} and μ_{su}, indicating that the model would predict an outcome that was essentially a victory for the United States but that did involve some concessions. That is clearly how most historians have interpreted the actual outcome. Note also that when π' is translated back into the issue space, it is quite close to point *c*, the actual outcome. In this case, the probability of war given by the model is .28, which is fairly close to Kennedy's own estimate that the probability of war was between one-third and one-half. The model thus appears to provide a fairly accurate characterization of this case and can provide a general and parsimonious explanation for the observed outcome.

Selected Bibliography

Abel, Ellie. 1966. *The Missile Crisis.* New York: Bantam Books.
Allison, Graham. 1971. *Essence of Decision.* Boston: Little Brown & Co.

Detzer, David. 1979. *The Brink*. New York: Thomas Y. Crowell.

Dinerstein, Herbert S. 1976. *The Making of a Missile Crisis*. Baltimore: Johns Hopkins Univ. Press.

Divine, Robert A., ed. 1971. *The Cuban Missile Crisis*. Chicago: Quadrangle Books.

Garthoff, Raymond L. 1989. *Reflections on the Missile Crisis*. Washington: Brookings Institution.

Kennedy, Robert F. 1969. *Thirteen Days*. New York: W. W. Norton.

LaFaber, Walter. 1989. *The American Age*. New York: W. W. Norton.

Medland, William J. 1988. *The Cuban Missile Crisis of 1962*. New York: Praeger.

Snyder, Glenn H., and Paul Diesing. 1977. *Conflict among Nations*. Princeton, N.J.: Princeton Univ. Press, 567–70.

Notes

Chapter 1

1. Other studies using the model developed in this book do report on empirical tests of the derived hypotheses. See Morgan and Ray 1989 and Morgan and Schwebach 1992a.

2. In his application of bargaining theory to the study of war termination, Pillar (1983) notes a similar problem—several models are each useful for addressing different aspects of his research question. His solution was, for each aspect, to draw on the appropriate model for what insight it could provide (1983, 140). The problem with such an approach is that it does not provide an integrated theory for addressing the topic at hand. Our knowledge would remain fragmentary, empirical evidence supporting one hypothesis would have no bearing on others, and in some cases the different models could produce contradictory conclusions. It is much preferable to draw the useful aspects from a number of studies and incorporate them into an integrated model. In this way, we can ensure that the analysis is internally consistent and logically connected.

Chapter 2

1. The categorization employed here is similar to that used by Snyder and Diesing (1977). Other typologies could be used, such as distinguishing the studies on the basis of whether they focus more on bargaining outcomes or on bargaining processes. Since the concern here is to determine how best to approach the problem of examining behavior in international crises, it is appropriate to distinguish the models on the basis of the general approach they employ. Of course, there are a number of similarities among models in different categories (such as in terms of which independent variables are considered most important).

2. Other general treatments can be found in Kremenyuk 1991, Raiffa 1982, Fisher and Ury 1981, and Warschaw 1980. A review of this work that links these authors' prescriptions to extant empirical work can be found in Weiss-Wik 1983.

3. For recent attempts at developing formal models that treat nation-states as aggregates of competing groups, see McGinnis and Williams 1992 and Putnam 1988.

4. Schelling (1960) and Iklé (1964) focus on international bargaining more generally while making many similar points.

5. The literature on bargaining from the field of social psychology is exceedingly vast. An excellent review of this body of literature can be found in Rubin and Brown

1975. For the purposes of this discussion, I will focus on those studies emphasizing bargaining in an international context and, at this point, on those stressing theoretical arguments rather than empirical tests.

6. These assumptions can and have been relaxed by some scholars, however. Snyder and Diesing (1977), for example, examine the effects on bargaining of possible misperceptions of preference orderings.

7. This treatment can be compared to the depiction of the Agadir crisis following from the use of the model developed in this book. See the Appendix.

8. Since a noncooperative choice enables a player in a Prisoner's Dilemma to avoid its worst outcome and simultaneously have a chance of obtaining its best, we generally expect to see little cooperation in such situations (Brams 1975, 30–31). The reason that Snyder and Diesing find that mutual cooperation is the norm in Prisoner's Dilemmas is that their cases do not fully correspond to the standard rules of the game, which require a lack of communication, an inability to enforce agreements, or both. Clearly, communication is possible, and although there exists no authority or mechanism by which to enforce agreements, the parties can enforce them. This situation arises from the fact that the game does not consist of a single, binding choice by each player. If, for example, France were to go back on its word, Germany would still be able to go to war. Thus, these situations more closely resemble an iterated Prisoner's Dilemma, in which mutual cooperation is much more common (Axelrod 1980; Rapoport and Chammah 1965).

9. A number of axiomatic systems have been shown to lead to von Neumann–Morgenstern utility functions (Friedman and Savage 1948; Hausner 1954; Herstein and Milnor 1953; Luce and Raiffa 1957, chap. 2). Fairly simple explanations can be found in Marschak 1974, chap. 3, and Abrams 1980, 76–84. Basically, it is assumed that individuals have transitive preference orderings over various outcomes *and* over lotteries involving these outcomes. If one assigns utility numbers of 0 and 1 to the least and most preferred outcomes, respectively, one can construct a set of lotteries in which the individual receives the most preferred outcome with probability p and the least preferred with probability $1 - p$. Outcomes valued between the most and least preferred can be assigned utility numbers on the basis of comparisons with these lotteries. If, for example, an individual is indifferent between an outcome, x, and a lottery between the most and least preferred outcomes in which $p = .6$, his or her utility for x = .6. A utility function thus produced is invariant up to a positive linear transformation; that is, it provides an interval level measure by which to represent an actor's preference orderings.

10. Generally, this zero utility point is assumed to represent the utility for both players of no agreement. That points out one conceptual difficulty of applying such models to cases of international crises. These models have been developed by scholars more concerned with problems of economic exchange, in which it is reasonable to assume that the parties can refuse to associate or reach an agreement. Given the types of conflict usually involved in international crises, this option is rarely available. When the Austrians and Prussians were attempting to agree on the disposition of Schleswig-Holstein in 1866, it was not possible to avoid some solution or for one party to take its business elsewhere. Thus, in international crises, the origin, or "no agreement" point,

must be interpreted as the expected value of settling the dispute by some means other than bargaining—war.

11. In a subsequent paper, Nash (1953) argues that this is actually an incorrect interpretation of the symmetry axiom. He argues that assuming equal bargaining skills implies the possibility that one player can gain an advantage by duping its opponent (if skills were unequal). Since both players are assumed to be fully informed and rational, that is not possible. Essentially, the argument is that he is assuming no bargaining skills rather than equal skills. The important point to note, however, is that the symmetry axiom, under either interpretation, implies that neither player is afforded an advantage either by the situation or by superior bargaining skills.

12. That the symmetry axiom is seldom met should be fairly obvious—seldom are bargainers equal in bargaining skill and resources. That the independence axiom is unreasonable is less clear. By assuming that reducing the bargaining space will not alter the outcome (provided that the original outcome is contained in the reduced space), this axiom implies that the course of bargaining is not a determining factor in the outcome. We would expect, however, that removing potential intermediate proposals from the bargaining space would affect the outcome.

13. Some authors are careful to demonstrate how the utility space is derived from an issue space (see Hopmann 1978; Raiffa 1982, chaps. 10–11).

14. Ultimately, this arrangement will also enable us to show how the actors' utility functions over outcomes are affected by their preference orderings over issues and combinations of issues.

15. At this time, we are dealing with simple Euclidean distance, since a weighting scheme has no meaning when only a single issue is involved.

16. That is clearly the case in crises such as the Oregon Boundary Dispute and the crisis leading up to the Soviet-Finnish war in which the issue at stake was the division of some territory, and it is fairly obvious in cases such as the Agadir and Fashoda crises in which the issue was how control over some colonial territory was to be divided among great powers. Other issues, while less obvious, can also be defined as involving questions of division. We can consider, for example, the main issue of the Cuban Missile Crisis to have been *how many* Soviet missiles were to remain in Cuba.

17. In fact, we should keep in mind that the actors' initial offers may not be identical to their true ideal points. Since some outcomes outside the set of feasible outcomes may be preferred to the constrained ideal point, it is likely that preferences will not be symmetrical, or even monotonically decreasing, about this point.

18. I will discuss cases in which $a_{12} \neq 0$ below. This specification suggests that the actors' preferences on the two issues are not separable.

19. In fact, the Pareto optimality assumption that is so common suggests that such logrolling must and does occur by requiring that for a point to be a solution it not be the case that there exists some other point that can provide one party with greater utility and the other party with greater or equal utility.

20. The clearest example of this occurs when members of a committee are voting on a budget. Suppose there are two budget items, x and y. Member A may most prefer to allocate $60 to x and $60 to y. There may be a budgetary constraint that total spending cannot exceed $100, however. This constraint implies that some members

may prefer to spend less than $100 on both issues (and reflect this preference in their votes), but members, such as A, whose most preferred outcome leads to a total expenditure greater than $100 will have to make some sacrifices on at least one issue. Thus, A's votes on each issue will depend on what has happened, or what he or she expects to happen, on the other issue, and A's most preferred outcome will have to change as a result of the budgetary constraint.

21. In this light, it is possible for the solution point to represent an outcome that is actually impossible to achieve. If, for example, an issue is of a type that the possible outcomes do not form a continuum, it is possible for the solution to fall between two discrete points.

22. One method would be to argue that outcomes should be normally distributed around the prediction. The problem with this method is that we would then be making our predictions inductively since the accepted prediction would be the mean of the observed outcomes, not a theoretically deduced solution. As will be seen below, the goal here is to determine, on theoretical grounds, what the distribution of outcomes should be.

23. In my opinion, that is one of the major shortcomings with a number of attempts to provide operational measures for *power*. Many scholars seem to believe that "the most powerful wins" is a fundamental law of politics. If, according to some indicator, the least powerful won in even one case, it is assumed that the indicator is faulty and is in need of refinement. It will be much more fruitful to define and operationalize *power* independently from any outcome we are attempting to explain. If we assume that the most powerful has a higher probability of winning, we can determine what other factors affect determining a victor.

24. Note that the model generally applies to noninternational crisis bargaining situations. Applications to other types of bargaining situations would require different concepts of power; however, the type of bargaining power discussed here is analogous to that in other situations. Just as the likely outcome of a war would affect crisis bargainers, the likely outcome of a strike will affect labor-management bargainers, and the likely outcome of a trial will affect the bargaining that occurs between attorneys for litigants.

25. Here, *capabilities* are broadly defined to include all material factors that may affect the outcome of a war, such as, but not limited to, a party's military materiel, its ability to project its forces to the site of battle, and its ability to sustain a campaign economically.

26. There are also analogs to this type of power in other types of bargaining situations. In contract negotiations, for example, the parties can impose costs on one another in a variety of ways—through bad publicity, through layoffs or work slowdowns, etc. We can also separate the costs of a strike to each party from the expected outcome. One party may expect to win a strike in terms of getting most of what it wants, but the economic costs may be sufficiently high to warrant significant concessions.

27. We have probably all experienced this in our day-to-day bargaining with friends and relatives. We occasionally become exceptionally stubborn when trying to decide how some value (usually time) will be spent. We hold out indefinitely for our

option, not because we find our opponents' horrible but because we just want to get our way.

28. Naturally, these outcomes refer to utility payoffs. Once these payoffs are determined, we can return to the issue space to specify an outcome in terms of the issues involved or, more precisely, the probability that each solution, in terms of the issues at stake, will result.

29. Some would hold that assuming that war could result when the bargaining set is nonempty requires that the bargainers be nonrational. In fact, it has been shown that such outcomes can occur even when perfectly rational bargainers know the bargaining set is nonempty (Crawford 1982; Morgan and Dawson 1992).

30. There may, in fact, be cases in which a player would reject its initial demand. This would probably be the case in what Lebow (1981) has termed "justification of hostility crises," in which the initiator is actually interested in going to war rather than in settling some issue. This model can represent such a situation, but it is applied more usefully to cases with a nonzero probability of a negotiated settlement. In these cases, we may assume that a player would accept its initial offer.

31. That does not necessarily mean the player would begin the war the moment such an offer was made. It may make a counteroffer or simply reject the proposal and wait for another. That merely suggests that the player would definitely go to war rather than settle for such an offer.

32. It is possible for the bargaining set to be empty. This would occur if there were no proposals that all parties could accept and would indicate that war was certain. This model could represent such situations but would not be a particularly useful means of analyzing them.

33. Technically, in a continuous distribution the probability that any given point will be the solution is 0.0. We are actually looking at the probability that the solution will fall within an increasingly small range of points.

34. Note that the complete game is not purely zero sum because the act of going to war would presumably involve costs to both sides. The important point is that the possible outcomes on the issues in dispute constitute a zero-sum game.

35. This construction is somewhat confusing in that we must use a single scale to represent the utility to both players when, in fact, the utility to i decreases as one moves from left to right while the utility to j increases. We must keep in mind that the numbers specified represent the utility to player j and that the utility to i can be determined directly from this since $U_i(\pi) = 0.0 - U_j(\pi)$.

36. We can see what is involved in a relatively simple non-zero-sum case by referring to figure 10. Assume that $\mu_j = 0$ and that $\Delta_j = 1.0$ (one can make this assumption without any loss of generality since von Neumann–Morgenstern utility functions are invariant up to a positive linear transformation). The PDF for j would then be a horizontal line at $p_j(\pi) = 1.0$, and by definition, the area under this line in the interval $[\mu_j, \Delta_j]$ would equal 1.0. The probability that j would accept some π at least minimally acceptable to i would be equal to the proportion of this area (under $p_{j'}(\pi)$ within $[\mu_j, \Delta_j]$) that is within the triangle constituting the bargaining set. To determine this proportion of area we must first define two more points: the point on the vertical axis through which a horizontal line would intersect the intersection of $p_{j'}(\pi)$

and the hypotenuse of the bargaining set $\mu_j + \beta$ and the point on the horizontal axis through which a vertical line would intersect the intersection of the hypotenuse of the bargaining set and a vertical line through Δ_j, $\mu_i + \partial$. The proportion of the area within the bargaining set would then equal $\beta + \partial + 1/2 \{[1 - (\mu_i + \partial)(1 - (\mu_j + \beta))]\}$. This process could then be duplicated for player i, and the product of the two results would be the probability of avoiding war. Note that this becomes even more complex if $p_j{}'(\pi)$, $p_i{}'(\pi)$, and the efficient frontier are not linear.

37. Recall that the independence assumption suggests that if we take a subset of the bargaining set that includes the solution to the original set, that point will also be the solution to the smaller set. Since the bargaining set must be convex and compact, we cannot remove any points from the middle of the set. If we form a smaller bargaining set by removing a continuous set of points that includes one party's reservation point from the feasible set (which would serve to shift that party's reservation point), we must also cause the opponent's reservation point to shift an equivalent amount to maintain symmetry. Thus, the original solution point would stand, and independence is assured.

Chapter 3

1. Keep in mind that I am referring only to the segments of the probability of acceptance functions for which $1.0 > p(\pi) > 0.0$.

2. This results in no loss of generality since the nature of von Neumann–Morgenstern utility functions allows us to select any point on the utility dimension as the origin and specify any interval as constituting the unit. These points can be selected so that a_j is at 0 and $b_j = 1$.

3. Note that this construction is not arbitrary. The ratios represent the proportion of a distribution that falls within a particular range. The denominator is thus the unit of this distribution and can be set equal to 1.0.

Note also that in the case of

$$\frac{\int_{\mu_j}^{\mu_i} p_i(\pi)}{\int_{\Delta_i}^{\mu_i} p_i(\pi)},$$

$p_i{}'(\pi)$ will be negative. This is equivalent to multiplying $|p_{i'}(\pi)|$ by -1, and the -1 can be factored through the integral sign in both the numerator and the denominator. Therefore, we may treat this term as though both numerator and denominator are positive. That will simplify the presentation, but it must be remembered to avoid confusion below. When I refer to increases in b_i, these increases must be understood as increases in the magnitude of b_i.

4. Note that if $\mu_j = \mu_i = \Delta_j$, the term we are considering would be undefined since the denominator would equal 0. At this point, however, the problem would cease

to be interesting from the perspective of this model since war would be a certainty. Thus, we may also specify that $\mu_j < \Delta_j$. While this is not technically required, it does ensure that the problem is of interest.

5. The only way in which that could not be the case is if the sum of the terms increased at a sufficient rate to raise the product. Since the parameters are identical in both terms, however, this cannot happen. The more rapidly the proportion of i's PDF within the bargaining set increases, the more rapidly the proportion of j's PDF within the bargaining set decreases.

6. If the players' resolve increases an equal amount, the solution point will not be changed. If the increases are unequal, the shift will favor the party whose resolve increased the most.

7. Note that the same effect could be achieved by increasing the opponent's ability to impose costs.

8. I can demonstrate the complexity of the general solution by illustrating what is involved in its determination. If we consider only the square probability of acceptance functions, the solution point is given by the cubic equation $-4\pi^3 + 3(b_i - b_j)\pi^2 + 2(a_i + b_j b_i - a_j)\pi + (a_j b_i + a_i b_j) = 0$, which, by dividing through by -4, can be rewritten as

$$\pi^3 - \frac{3(b_i - b_j)\pi^2}{4} - \frac{(a_i b_j b_i - a_j)\pi}{2} - \frac{a_j b_i + a_i b_j}{4} = 0.$$

This can be reduced to the form $x^3 + cx + d = 0$ by substituting

$$x - \frac{(b_i - b_j)}{4}$$

for π and letting

$$c = \frac{1}{3}\left[3\left(\frac{a_i + b_j b_i - a_j}{2}\right) - 3\left(\frac{b_i - b_j}{4}\right)^2\right]$$

and

$$d = \left(\frac{1}{27}\right) \cdot \left(\frac{3(b_i - b_j)}{2} - \frac{27(b_i - b_j)(a_i + b_j b_i - a_j)}{8} + \frac{27(a_j b_i + a_i b_j)}{4}\right).$$

If we let

$$A = \sqrt[3]{-\frac{d}{2} + \sqrt{\frac{d^2}{4} + \frac{c^3}{27}}}$$

and

$$B = \sqrt[3]{-\frac{d}{2} - \sqrt{\frac{d^2}{4} + \frac{c^3}{27}}},$$

then the three values of x will be given by

$$A + B, \ -\frac{A + B}{2} + \frac{A - B}{2} \cdot \sqrt{-3}, \text{ and } -\frac{A + B}{2} - \frac{A - B}{2} \cdot \sqrt{-3}.$$

Of the three possible values for π' given by

$$\pi = x - \frac{b_i - b_j}{4},$$

only one would fall within the bargaining set and would thus be our solution point. We could then determine the effect on the solution point brought about by changes in the variables by determining how the value for π' changes as do a_i, b_i, a_j, and b_j. It should be apparent that even determining the solution for a single case in this manner would be a monumental task. Furthermore, this provides the general solution only for those cases in which square functions are used for the probability of acceptance functions—if cube (or greater) functions are used, there is no formula for the general solution. Clearly, it is much simpler (and perhaps preferable) to allow a computer to perform the calculations for functions of any power through an iterative process.

9. Naturally, at this point I am referring to gains in terms of a negotiated settlement. Assuming that the stronger party would, ceteris paribus, prefer avoiding war, it can improve its chances by increasing the costs it can impose on the opponent.

10. Keep in mind that this discussion says nothing about the likelihood of these various situations arising. Although the variables under consideration are analytically distinct, it is likely that the ability of one side to impose bargaining costs and its ability to win in war will covary. These results merely suggest that if one party can impose significant costs on an opponent even though the opponent has a high probability of winning a war, then the chances of war are slim.

11. This case indicates that misperceptions can often play an important role in crisis outcomes. If both parties believe that they are advantaged in terms of war-fighting capabilities, as was the case here, relatively little of either party's probability of acceptance function will be within the bargaining range, and the probability of war will be quite high. Thus, focusing only on the three variables addressed in this chapter probably leads the model to underestimate the probability of war.

12. This conclusion is consistent with some recent empirical work conducted by Stoll (1988), which suggests that, given the number of militarized disputes between the Soviet Union and the United States in the post–World War II era, that no wars have occurred between these states is a little unusual compared to the rates of great power dispute escalation in the prenuclear era (though such a result could have occurred by chance if the rates of escalation are identical). If we consider these disputes to have occurred between relative military equals and the possession of nuclear weapons by both parties to have raised the specter of very high costs in the absence of a peaceful settlement (or at least the continuing chance that the crisis could escalate to represent a significant bargaining cost in itself), the model would suggest that the probability of escalation to war is generally lower than was the probability in the average pre-nuclear-era crisis. (See also Morgan and Ray 1989 on this question.)

13. Some empirical work testing various aspects of these hypotheses has been conducted. See Morgan and Ray 1989 and Morgan and Schwebach 1992a.

Chapter 4

1. For the purposes of the illustration, I have set $a_{j11} = 2$, $a_{j22} = 1$, $a_{i11} = 1$, and $a_{i22} = 2$.

2. The coordinates of these points represent the least amount of territory the actors would accept when the issues were settled singly. For the multi-issue cases, we actually have reservation contours, which pass through these points.

3. A discussion of actors' expectations in the context of voting can be found in Enelow and Hinich 1984 (see especially chap 8).

4. There have also been some arguments against issue linkages. These arguments will be discussed more fully below.

5. Many scholars have argued that the stressful nature of crises increases the importance of psychological variables. My argument is not suggesting otherwise— only that the particular factors included in Fisher's argument are considerably reduced in importance in crisis situations.

6. The argument is somewhat ambiguous and could be interpreted in another way. Part of my purpose here is to show that the alternative interpretation is a correct deduction from spatial theory but that this necessary condition for linkage success is virtually trivial—hardly any issue candidates would be excluded.

7. Note that I am assuming that Sebenius's argument that was outlined above does describe a condition necessary for linkage success; that is, for linkage to succeed, it must bring about a net increase in direct benefits. My efforts here are focused on demonstrating how linkage attempts can fail when this condition is met.

8. A number of authors have suggested that relative strength is an important determinant of linkage success (see, e.g., Haas 1980, 372).

9. Note that it is conceivable that y and z could be positively related. In this case, a linkage providing the actor benefits on y would also provide benefits on z, and the probability of success would increase.

10. An example is that many more of us would accept a $5 million bribe to raise a student's grade than would accept a $50 bribe. We would all prefer having the $50 to not, but $50 is not enough to overcome the costs involved in an ethical violation. These costs do not decrease in the face of the $5 million, but the additional benefit would be sufficient to overcome these costs for many.

Chapter 5

1. This situation clearly can be seen as a generalization of all others though I am treating it as a residual category. Any analysis conducted at the general level (such as Morrow 1986) is worthwhile in that it provides insight into all such situations. I find it more useful to categorize the cases more finely. In this way, our understanding can incorporate more than the general conclusions.

2. Note that these situations are very similar to what Lebow (1981) has termed

"spinoff crises." The difference, of course, is that spinoff crises are those that result from the behavior of a party already involved in a war.

3. These differences are reflected in the salience matrices that determine the shape of the indifference surfaces. There are an infinite number of such matrices consistent with the construction of this example at the present level of generality, but for purposes of illustration, the relative saliences of the issues and their degree of nonseparability can be represented with the following matrices:

$$A_F = \begin{bmatrix} 1.0 & 0.0 & 0.0 \\ 0.0 & 3.0 & 0.0 \\ 0.0 & 0.0 & 0.1 \end{bmatrix}$$

$$A_G = \begin{bmatrix} 1.0 & 0.0 & 0.0 \\ 0.0 & 4.0 & 0.0 \\ 0.0 & 0.0 & 0.2 \end{bmatrix}$$

$$A_{GB} = \begin{bmatrix} 1.0 & 0.0 & 0.5 \\ 0.0 & 0.1 & 0.0 \\ 0.5 & 0.0 & 0.4 \end{bmatrix}$$

Chapter 6

1. In an ongoing research project, this model is being applied to the analysis of whether economic sanctions are useful policy instruments for crisis participants (Morgan and Schwebach 1992a). Much of the motivation for this project is grounded in the belief that examining economic sanctions provides a means of tapping the cost variable incorporated in the model, which in turn provides a means for conducting empirical analyses on a large number of cases.

Bibliography

Abrams, Robert. 1980. *Foundations of Political Analysis*. New York: Columbia Univ. Press.

Allan, Pierre. 1983. *Crisis Bargaining and the Arms Race*. Cambridge: Ballinger.

Allison, Graham T. 1971. *Essence of Decision*. Boston: Little, Brown.

Axelrod, Robert. 1980. "Effective Choice in the Prisoner's Dilemma." *Journal of Conflict Resolution* 24 (March): 3–26.

Bartos, Otomar J. 1977. "A Simple Model of Negotiation." *Journal of Conflict Resolution* 21 (December): 565–79.

Beer, Francis. 1981 *Peace against War*. San Francisco: W. H. Freeman.

Bernard, L. L. 1944. *War and Its Causes*. New York: Henry Holt.

Binmore, K. G. 1984. "Bargaining Conventions." *International Journal of Game Theory* 13:193–200.

Bishop, Robert L. 1964. "A Zeuthen-Hicks Theory of Bargaining." *Econometrica* 32 (July): 410–17.

Blechman, Barry M., and Stephen S. Kaplan. 1978. *Force without War*. Washington: Brookings Institution.

Brams, Steven J. 1975. *Game Theory and Politics*. New York: Free Press.

Brecher, Michael. 1980. *Decisions in Crisis*. Berkeley: Univ. of California Press.

Brecher, Michael, and Jonathan Wilkenfeld. 1982. "Crises in World Politics." *World Politics* 34 (April): 380–417.

———. 1989. *Crisis, Conflict and Instability*. New York: Pergamon.

Brown, Winthrop G. 1968. "The Art of Negotiation." *Foreign Service Journal* 45 (July): 14–17.

Bueno de Mesquita, Bruce. 1981. *The War Trap*. New Haven, Conn.: Yale Univ. Press.

———. 1990. "Multilateral Negotiations: A Spatial Analysis of the Arab-Israeli Dispute." *International Organization* 44 (Summer): 317–40.

Bueno de Mesquita, Bruce, and David Lalman. 1990. "Domestic Opposition and Foreign War." *American Political Science Review* 84 (September): 747–66.

———. 1992. *War and Reason*. New Haven, Conn.: Yale Univ. Press.

Bueno de Mesquita, Bruce, David Newman, and Alvin Rabushka. 1985. *Forecasting Political Events*. New Haven, Conn.: Yale Univ. Press.

Carlson, Lisa J. 1992. "A Formal Model of Misperceptions in Crisis Bargaining." Rice University, mimeograph.

Carnevale, Peter, and Jerry M. Wittmer. 1987. "Biased Mediators in International Mediation." Paper presented at the annual meeting of the International Studies Association, Washington, D.C., April 14–18.

Craig, Gordon A., and Alexander George. 1983. *Force and Statecraft*. New York: Oxford Univ. Press.

Crawford, Vincent P. 1982. "A Theory of Disagreement in Bargaining." *Econometrica* 50 (May): 607–37.

Cross, John G. 1969. *The Economics of Bargaining*. New York: Basic Books.

———. 1977. "Negotiation as a Learning Process." *Journal of Conflict Resolution* 21 (December): 581–606.

Cusack, Thomas R., and W. D. Eberwein. 1982. "Prelude to War: Incidence, Escalation and Intervention in International Disputes, 1900–1976." *International Interactions* 9:9–28.

Deutsch, Morton. 1973. *The Resolution of Conflict*. New Haven, Conn.: Yale Univ. Press.

Druckman, Daniel. 1973. *Human Factors in International Negotiations*. Sage Professional Paper in Internation Studies. Beverly Hills: Sage.

Enelow, James M. 1984. "A New Theory of Congressional Compromise." *American Political Science Review* 78 (September): 708–18.

Enelow, James M., and Melvin J. Hinich. 1981. "A New Approach to Voter Uncertainty in the Downsian Spatial Model." *American Journal of Political Science* 25 (August): 484–93.

———. 1984. *The Spatial Theory of Voting*. Cambridge: Cambridge Univ. Press.

Fisher, Roger. 1964. *International Conflict and Behavioral Science*. New York: Basic Books.

Fisher, Roger, and William Ury. 1981. *Getting to Yes*. Boston: Houghton Mifflin Co.

Foldes, Lucien. 1964. "A Determinate Model of Bilateral Monopoly." *Economica* 122:117–31.

Friedman, Milton. 1968. "The Methodology of Positive Economics." In M. Brodbeck, ed., *Readings in the Philosophy of the Social Sciences*. New York: Macmillan, 508–27.

Friedman, Milton, and L. J. Savage. 1948. "The Utility Analysis of Choices Involving Risk." *Journal of Political Economy* 56 (August): 279–304.

Garnham, David. 1976. "Power Parity and Lethal International Violence, 1969–1973." *Journal of Conflict Resolution* 20 (September): 379–94.

George, Alexander L. 1980. *Presidential Decisionmaking in Foreign Policy*. Boulder: Westview.

George, Alexander L., David K. Hall, and William E. Simons. 1971. *The Limits of Coercive Diplomacy*. Boston: Little Brown & Co.

George, Alexander L., and Richard Smoke. 1974. *Deterrence in American Foreign Policy*. New York: Columbia Univ. Press.

Gochman, Charles S., and Zeev Maoz. 1984. "Serious Interstate Disputes, 1816–1976: Empirical Patterns and Theoretical Insights." *Journal of Conflict Resolution* 28 (December): 585–616.

Gulick, Edward V. 1955. *Europe's Classical Balance of Power*. New York: Norton.

Haas, Ernst B. 1980. "Why Collaborate? Issue Linkage and International Regimes." *World Politics* 32 (April): 357–405.

Harsanyi, John C. 1956. "Approaches to the Bargaining Problem Before and After the Theory of Games." *Econometrica* 24 (April): 144–57.

Hausner, Melvin. 1954. "Multidimensional Utilities." In R. M. Thrall, C. H. Coombs, and R. L. Davis, eds., *Decision Processes*, 167–80. New York: John Wiley & Sons.

Hermann, Charles F., ed. 1972. *International Crises*. New York: Free Press.

Herstein, I. N., and John Milnor. 1953. "An Axiomatic Approach to Measurable Utility." *Econometrica* 21 (April): 291–97.

Hessel, Marek. 1981. "Bargaining Costs and Rational Behavior." *Journal of Conflict Resolution* 25 (September): 535–58.

Hinich, Melvin J., John O. Ledyard, and Peter C. Ordeshook. 1973. "A Theory of Electoral Equilibrium: A Spatial Analysis Based on the Theory of Games." *Journal of Politics* 35:154–93.

Hinich, Melvin J., and Walker Pollard. 1981. "A New Approach to the Spatial Theory of Electoral Competition." *American Journal of Political Science* 25 (May): 323–41.

Hopmann, P. Terrence. 1972. "Internal and External Influences on Bargaining in Arms Control Negotiations." In B. Russett, ed., *Peace, War and Numbers*, 213–38. Beverly Hills: Sage.

———. 1974. "Bargaining in Arms Control Negotiations: The Seabeds Denuclearization Treaty." *International Organization* 28 (Summer): 314–33.

———. 1978. "Asymmetrical Bargaining in the Conference on Security and Cooperation in Europe." *International Organization* 32 (Winter): 141–77.

Huth, Paul. 1988. *Extended Deterrence and the Prevention of War*. New Haven, Conn.: Yale Univ. Press.

Huth, Paul, and Bruce Russett. 1984. "What Makes Deterrence Work?" *World Politics* 36:496–526.

———. 1988. "Deterrence Failure and Crisis Escalation." *International Studies Quarterly* 32:29–45.

Iklé, Fred C. 1964. *How Nations Negotiate*. New York: Harper & Row.

James, Patrick. 1988. *Crisis and War*. Montreal: McGill-Queen's Univ. Press.

Janis, Irving L. 1972. *Victims of Groupthink*. Boston: Houghton Mifflin Co..

Jervis, Robert. 1972. "Bargaining and Bargaining Tactics." In J. R. Pennock and J. W. Chapman, eds., *Coercion*, 272–88. Chicago: Aldine Atherton.

———. 1976. *Perception and Misperception in International Politics*. Princeton, N.J.: Princeton Univ. Press.

———. 1978. "Cooperation under the Security Dilemma." *World Politics* 30 (January): 167–214.

———. 1979. "Deterrence Theory Revisited." *World Politics* 31:289–324.

Kahn, Herman. 1965. *On Escalation*. New York: Frederick A. Praeger.

Kalai, Ehud. 1977. "Nonsymmetric Nash Solutions and Replication of 2-Person Bargaining." *International Journal of Game Theory* 6:129–33.

Kalai, Ehud, and Meir Smorodinsky. 1975. "Other Solutions to Nash's Bargaining Problem." *Econometrica* 43:513–18.

Kecskemeti, Paul. 1958. *Strategic Surrender*. Stanford: Stanford Univ. Press.

Keohane, Robert O., and Joseph S. Nye. 1977. *Power and Interdependence*. Boston: Little Brown & Co.

Kissinger, Henry A. 1957. *Nuclear Weapons and Foreign Policy*. New York: Harper & Brothers.

———. 1979. *The White House Years*. Boston: Little Brown & Co.

Kremenyuk, Victor A. 1991. *International Negotiation*. San Francisco: Jossey-Bass.

Kreps, David M., and Robert Wilson. 1982. "Sequential Equilibria." *Econometrica* 50 (July): 863–94.

Lall, Arthur. 1966. *Modern International Negotiation*. New York: Columbia Univ. Press.

Lebow, Richard N. 1981. *Between Peace and War*. Baltimore: Johns Hopkins Univ. Press.

Leng, Russell J. 1983. "When Will They Ever Learn?: Coercive Bargaining in Recurrent Crises." *Journal of Conflict Resolution* 27 (September): 379–419.

Levine, Michael E., and Charles R. Plott. 1977. "Agenda Influence and Its Implications." *Virginia Law Review* 63:561–604.

Levy, Jack S. 1983a. "Misperception and the Causes of War." *World Politics* 36 (October): 76–99.

———. 1983b. *War in the Modern Great Power System, 1495–1975*. Lexington: Univ. Press of Kentucky.

Luce, R. Duncan, and Howard Raiffa. 1957. *Games and Decisions*. New York: John Wiley & Sons.

Malinowski, Bronislaw. 1968. "An Anthropological Analysis of War." In Leon Bramson and George Goethals, eds., *War*, 245–68. New York: Basic Books.

Mansbach, Richard W., and John A. Vasquez. 1981. *In Search of Theory*. New York: Columbia Univ. Press.

Maoz, Zeev. 1982. *Paths to Conflict*. Boulder, Colo.: Westview.

———. 1983. "Resolve, Capabilities, and the Outcomes of Interstate Disputes, 1816–1976." *Journal of Conflict Resolution* 27 (June): 195–229.

Marschak, Jacob. 1974. *Economic Information, Decision, and Prediction*. Boston: D. Reidel.

McGinnis, Michael D. 1986. "Issue Linkage and the Evolution of International Cooperation." *Journal of Conflict Resolution* 30:141–70.

McGinnis, Michael D., and John T. Williams. 1992. "A Model of Domestic Coalitions and International Rivalry." Indiana University, mimeograph.

McKelvey, Richard D. 1979. "General Conditions for Global Intransitivities in Formal Voting Models." *Econometrica* 47 (September): 1085–1112.

Morgan, T. Clifton. 1984. "A Spatial Model of Crisis Bargaining." *International Studies Quarterly* 28:407–26.

———. 1988. "A Spatial Theory of Deterrence." Paper presented at the annual meeting of the American Political Science Association, Washington, D.C., Sept. 1–4.

———. 1990. "The Concept of War." *Peace and Change* 15 (October): 413–41.

Morgan, T. Clifton, and Kenneth N. Bickers. 1992. "Domestic Discontent and the External Use of Force." *Journal of Conflict Resolution* 36 (March): 25–52.

Morgan, T. Clifton, and Sally H. Campbell. 1991. "Domestic Structure, Decisional Constraints and War." *Journal of Conflict Resolution* 35 (June): 187–211.

Morgan, T. Clifton, and Peter M. Dawson. 1992. "Bargaining Tough: Commitment Strategy in International Conflict." Rice University, mimeograph.

Morgan, T. Clifton, and James Lee Ray. 1989. "The Impact of Nuclear Weapons on Crisis Bargaining." In Richard J. Stoll and Michael D. Ward, eds., *Power in World Politics*, 193–208. Boulder, Colo.: Lynne Reiner.

Morgan, T. Clifton, and Valerie L. Schwebach. 1992a. "Fools Suffer Gladly: Economic Sanctions and Bargaining in International Crises." Rice University, mimeograph.

———. 1992b. "Take Two Democracies and Call Me in the Morning: A Prescription for Peace?" *International Interactions* 17:305–20.

Morrow, James D. 1986. "A Spatial Model of International Conflict." *American Political Science Review* 80:1131–50.

———. 1988. "Social Choice and System Structure in World Politics." *World Politics* 41 (October): 75–97.

———. 1992. "Signaling Difficulties with Linkage in Crisis Bargaining." *International Studies Quarterly* 36 (June): 153–72.

Most, Benjamin, and Harvey Starr. 1982. "Case Selection, Conceptualizations and Basic Logic in the Study of War." *American Journal of Political Science* 26 (November): 834–56.

———. 1983. "Conceptualizing War." *Journal of Conflict Resolution* 27 (March): 137–59.

———. 1984. "International Relations Theory, Foreign Policy Substitutability, and 'Nice' Laws." *World Politics* 36 (April): 383–406.

———. 1989. *Inquiry, Logic and International Politics*. Columbia: Univ. of South Carolina Press.

Moulin, H. 1984. "Implementing the Kalai-Smorodinsky Bargaining Solution." *Journal of Economic Theory* 33:32–45.

Nash, John F. 1950. "The Bargaining Problem." *Econometrica* 18 (April): 155–62.

———. 1953. "Two Person Cooperative Games." *Econometrica* 21:128–40.

North, Robert C., and Nazli Choucri. 1983. "Economic and Political Factors in International Conflict and Integration." *International Studies Quarterly* 27 (December): 443–62.

Ordeshook, Peter C. 1976. "The Spatial Theory of Elections: A Review and Critique." In I. Budge, I. Crewe, and D. Farlie, eds., *Party Identification and Beyond*, 285–313. New York: John Wiley & Sons.

Organski, A. F. K., and Jacek Kugler. 1980. *The War Ledger*. Chicago: Univ. of Chicago Press.

Oye, Kenneth A. 1979. "The Domain of Choice: International Constraints and Carter Administration Foreign Policy." In K. A. Oye, Donald Rothchild, and Robert J. Lieber, eds., *Eagle Entangled*. New York: Longman Press.

Paige, Glenn D. 1969. "The Korean Decision." In J. N. Rosenau, ed., *International Politics and Foreign Policy*, 461–72. New York: Free Press.

Pen, Jan. 1952. "A General Theory of Bargaining." *The American Economic Review* 27:24–42.

Perry, Motty. 1986. "An Example of Price Formation in Bilateral Situations: A Bargaining Model with Incomplete Information." *Econometrica* 54 (March): 313–21.

Pillar, Paul R. 1983. *Negotiating Peace*. Princeton, N.J.: Princeton Univ. Press.

Plott, Charles R. 1967. "A Notion of Equilibrium and Its Possibility under Majority Rule." *American Economic Review* 57 (September): 787–806.

Plott, Charles R., and Michael E. Levine. 1978. "A Model of Agenda Influence on Committee Decisions." *American Economic Review* 68 (March): 146–60.

Pruitt, Dean G. 1981. *Negotiation Behavior*. New York: Academic Press.

Putnam, R. 1988. "Diplomacy and Domestic Politics: The Logic of Two-Level Games." *International Organization* 42:427–60.

Quattrone, George A., and Amos Tversky. 1988. "Contrasting Rational and Psychological Analyses of Political Choice." *American Political Science Review* 82 (September): 719–36.

Raiffa, Howard. 1982. *The Art and Science of Negotiation*. Cambridge, Mass.: Harvard Univ. Press.

Rapoport, Anatol, and Albert M. Chammah. 1965. *Prisoner's Dilemma*. Ann Arbor: Univ. of Michigan Press.

Raymond, Gregory A., and Charles W. Kegley, Jr. 1987. "Third Party Mediation and International Norms: A Test of Two Models." *Conflict Management and Peace Science* 10 (Spring): 33–49.

Richardson, Lewis F. 1960. *Statistics of Deadly Quarrels*. Pittsburgh: Boxwood.

Riker, William H. 1962. *The Theory of Political Coalitions*. New Haven, Conn.: Yale Univ. Press.

Roth, Alvin E. 1979. *Axiomatic Models of Bargaining*. New York: Springer-Verlag.

Roth, Alvin E., and Uriel G. Rothblum. 1982. "Risk Aversion and Nash's Solution for Bargaining Games with Risky Outcomes." *Econometrica* 50 (May): 639–47.

Rubin, Jeffrey Z., ed. 1981. *Dynamics of Third Party Intervention*. New York: Praeger.

Rubin, Jeffrey Z., and Bert R. Brown. 1975. *The Social Psychology of Bargaining and Negotiation*. New York: Academic Press.

Rubinstein, Ariel. 1982. "Perfect Equilibrium in a Bargaining Model." *Econometrica* 50:97–109.

———. 1985. "A Bargaining Model with Incomplete Information about Time Preferences." *Econometrica* 53 (September): 1151–72.

Russett, Bruce. 1990. *Controlling the Sword*. Cambridge, Mass.: Harvard Univ. Press.

Russett, Bruce, and Harvey Starr. 1985. *World Politics*. New York: W. H. Freeman & Co.

Sawyer, Jack, and Harold Guetzkow. 1965. "Bargaining and Negotiation in International Relations." In H. C. Kelman, ed., *International Behavior*, 466–520. New York: Holt, Rinehart & Winston.

Schelling, Thomas C. 1960. *The Strategy of Conflict*. Cambridge, Mass.: Harvard Univ. Press.

———. 1966. *Arms and Influence*. New Haven, Conn.: Yale Univ. Press.

Sebenius, James K. 1983. "Negotiation Arithmetic: Adding and Subtracting Issues and Parties." *International Organization* 37 (Spring): 281–316.

Selten, R. 1975. "Reexamination of the Perfectness Concept for Equilibrium Points in Extensive Games." *International Journal of Game Theory* 4:25–55.

Shaked, Avner, and John Sutton. 1984. "Involuntary Unemployment as a Perfect Equilibrium in a Bargaining Model." *Econometrica* 52 (November): 1351–64.

Singer, J. David, and Melvin Small. 1972. *The Wages of War, 1816–1965*. New York: John Wiley & Sons.

Siverson, Randolph M., and Michael R. Tennefoss. 1984. "Power, Alliance, and the Escalation of International Conflict, 1815–1969." *American Political Science Review* 78 (December): 1057–69.

Small, Melvin, and J. David Singer. 1982. *Resort to Arms*. Beverly Hills, Calif.: Sage.

Snyder, Glenn H. 1972. "Crisis Bargaining." In C. F. Hermann, ed., *International Crises*, 217–58. New York: Free Press.

Snyder, Glenn H., and Paul Diesing. 1977. *Conflict among Nations*. Princeton, N.J.: Princeton Univ. Press.

Spector, Bertram I. 1977. "Negotiation as a Psychological Process." *Journal of Conflict Resolution* 21 (December): 607–18.

Stoll, Richard. 1982. "Major Power Interstate Conflict in the Post–World War II Era: An Increase, a Decrease, or No Change?" *Western Political Quarterly* 35:587–605.

———. 1988. "The Use of Force in the Post World War II Era." Rice University, mimeograph.

Sutton, John. 1986. "Non-cooperative Bargaining Theory: An Introduction." *Review of Economic Studies* 53:709–24.

Tollison, R. D., and T. D. Willett. 1979. "An Economic Theory of Mutually Advantageous Issue Linkages in International Negotiations." *International Organization* 33 (Autumn): 425–49.

Touval, Saadia. 1975. "Biased Intermediaries: Theoretical and Historical Considerations." *Jerusalem Journal of International Relations* 1 (Fall): 51–69.

Touval, Saadia, and I. William Zargman, eds. 1985. *International Mediation in Theory and Practice*. Boulder, Colo.: Westview.

Wagner, R. Harrison. 1983a. "The Bishop-Foldes Bargaining Solution and the Study of International Relations." Paper presented at the 24th annual meeting of the Internation Studies Association, Mexico City, April 5–9.

———. 1983b. "The Theory of Games and the Problem of International Cooperation." *American Political Science Review* 77 (June): 330–46.

Wallace, W. 1976. "Issue Linkage among Atlantic Governments." *International Affairs* 52 (April): 163–79.

Warschaw, Tessa Albert. 1980. *Winning by Negotiation*. New York: McGraw-Hill.

Weede, Erich. 1976. "Overwhelming Preponderence as a Pacifying Condition among Contiguous Asian Dyads, 1950–1969." *Journal of Conflict Resolution* 20 (September): 395–411.

Weiss-Wik, Stephen. 1983. "Enhancing Negotiators' Successfulness." *Journal of Conflict Resolution* 27 (December): 706–39.

Winham, Gilbert R. 1979. "Practitioner's Views of International Negotiation." *World Politics* 32 (October): 111–35.

Wright, Quincy. 1965. *A Study of War*. Chicago: Univ. of Chicago Press.

Young, Oran R. 1967. *The Intermediaries*. Princeton, N.J.: Princeton Univ. Press.

———. 1968. *The Politics of Force*. Princeton, N.J.: Princeton Univ. Press.

———. 1972. "Intermediaries: Additional Thoughts on Third Parties." *Journal of Conflict Resolution* 16 (March): 51–65.

———. 1975. *Bargaining*. Urbana: Univ. of Illinois Press.

Zagare, Frank C. 1977. "A Game-Theoretic Analysis of the Vietnam Negotiations." *Journal of Conflict Resolution* 21 (December): 663–84.

———. 1981 "Nonmyopic Equilibria and the Middle East Crisis of 1967." *Conflict Management and Peace Science* 5 (Spring): 139–62.

Zartman, I. William, and M. R. Berman. 1982. *The Practical Negotiator*. New Haven, Conn.: Yale Univ. Press.

Zartman, I. William, and Saadia Touval. 1985. "International Mediation: Conflict Resolution and Power Politics." *Journal of Social Issues* 41:27–46.

Zeuthen, Frederick. 1968. *Problems of Monopoly and Economic Warfare*. New York: Augustus M. Kelley.

Index